# Analysing Health Policy

*Edited by*
ALISON HANN
*De Montfort University, Leicester*

## Ashgate

Aldershot • Burlington USA • Singapore • Sydney

Published by
Ashgate Publishing Ltd
Gower House
Croft Road
Aldershot
Hants GU11 3HR
England

Ashgate Publishing Company
131 Main Street
Burlington
Vermont 05401
USA

Ashgate website: http://www.ashgate.com

**British Library Cataloguing in Publication Data**
Analysing health policy
   1.Medical policy - Great Britain
   I.Hann, Alison
   362.1'0941

10030245 8 x

**Library of Congress Catalog Card Number:** 99-76648

ISBN 0 7546 1153 1

Printed in Great Britain by Antony Rowe Ltd.

For Saffy, Libby and Kevin

# ANALYSING HEALTH POLICY

# Contents

# Acknowledgements

Bruce Wood (Dean of Faculty and senior lecturer at Manchester University) and Mick Moran (Professor of Politics at Manchester University) are clearly the two individuals who deserve the credit for the formation of the Health Politics specialist group, and without their inspiration and hard work the group would not have got off to such a good start, and this volume might never have come into being. Thanks are also clearly due to the PSA who have supported the group throughout its existence. I would also like to thank Rob Baggott (Reader in Public Policy at De Montfort University) for his sustained encouragement and support, and for his tactful and constructive criticism. I would also like to take the opportunity to thank those stalwart members of the Health Politics Group who have supported the group by presenting papers, turning up to our own conferences and by attending the PSA health panels at the annual conferences. The commitment of the members plus an enthusiasm for the subject has lead to the group becoming a highly effective research network, which is exactly what Bruce Wood and Mick Moran hoped it would become when they started the ball rolling. Last but not least, thanks are due to all those colleagues who contributed to this volume, who produced their chapters (mostly) on time, in (mostly) the right format, and who spent time obtaining permissions (where necessary).

# List of Contributors

**Rob Baggott** is Reader in Public Policy at De Montfort University at Leicester. His main research interests include health policy, particularly public health, user empowerment and pressure group politics. His main publications are *Health and Health Care in Britain* (1998 second edition) and *Pressure Groups Today* (1995).

**Helen Doyle** is currently working on her doctoral thesis for De Montfort University Leicester, she is currently taking a break from her studies, and from paid employment, to be a full time Mum to six-month-old twin boys.

**Mark Exworthy** is a Research Fellow in Health, at The London School of Economics; previously he was at the Institute for Health Policy Studies at the University of Southampton. His research interests include health policy development, central local relations, professional managerial relations and primary care. His current research includes an ESRC funded project examining the formation and implementation of policy on health inequalities.

**Alison Hann** is a Senior Research Fellow at De Montfort University Leicester. Her main research interests are the politics of preventive medicine and feminist theory. She is the author of *The Politics of Breast Cancer Screening* (1996).

**Steve Harrison** is Professor of Health Policy and Politics at the Nuffield Institute for Health, University of Leeds. He currently co-directs the Joint Programme of Research into Clinical Governance between the Universities of Leeds and Durham. His research interests include both the macro-politics of health policy and the micro-politics of medical/managerial and user/managerial relationships. He has also published widely in this area.

**Chris Nottingham** is Senior Lecturer in Politics at Glasgow Caledonian University, where he spends much of his time teaching politics to nurses and other health care professionals. He publishes in contemporary history as well as health politics. His most recent work is *The Pursuit of Serenity. Havelock Ellis and the New Politics* (Amsterdam UP, 1999).

**Fiona O'Neill** is currently completing her doctoral thesis on the politics of nursing for the University of Birmingham. She teaches politics to nurses on a part time basis for the University of Leeds. Before studying politics she trained and worked as a nurse. Her recent publications include a chapter on policy transfer in health in David Dolowitz (Ed), *Learning From American Experience?* (Open UP, 1999).

**Calum Paton** is professor of health policy at the Centre for Health Planning and Management, Keele University, and is the acting head of the Centre. Professor Paton has published a number of books on the UK National Health Service and writes regularly for the British Medical Journal and the Health Service Journal.

**Martin Powell** is a lecturer in Social Policy in the Department of Social and Policy Studies, University of Bath. He is the author of *Evaluating the National Health Service* (Open University Press, 1997) and many articles on health policy in the U.K. He is currently undertaking (with Dr Mark Exworthy, London School of Economics) a project entitled 'Understanding Health Variations and Policy Variation', which is part of the ESRC Health Variations programme.

**Damien Riley** is Senior Research Associate in the Local Government Studies Directorate at the Audit Commission, where he is working on the implementation of Best Value in local government. He is currently completing a PhD in Government at The London School of Economics. His research interests include the application of rational choice theory to social policy implementation and public policy and management.

**Rod Sheaff** is a Senior Research Fellow at the National Primary Care Research and Development Centre, Manchester University. His current research concerns policy and organisational innovations in English primary healthcare, focusing on Primary Health Groups and the Personal Medical Services Pilot Projects. He is author of *The Need for Health Care and Marketing for Health Services.*

**Kerri Smith** is a Research Associate at the National Primary Care Research and Development Centre at the University of Manchester. A Masters Degree in research methodology (at the University of Wales) led to her specialising in Ethnography. Currently continuing her work with Primary Care Groups for the next few years at least, Kerri's particular interests are inter-professional relationships and roles and lay participation and negotiation.

**Bruce Wood** is Senior Lecturer and Dean of the Faculty of Economic and Social Studies at the University of Manchester. His research interests include the politics of health care in international comparison, UK health policy, and urban and local government. He is co-author of *States Regulation and the Medical Profession* (with M. Moran), *Public Policy in Britain* (with M. Burch) and the forthcoming *Patient Power? Patients Associations in Britain and America.*

# 1 Health Policy Analysis in Perspective

ALISON HANN

The Political Studies Association conference at Durham in 1990 turned out to be rather a special one. It was my first PSA conference and I met many people that year who were destined to play a very large part in my career, including Bruce Wood and Mick Moran. The forming of the Health Politics Specialist Group was the brainchild of Mick Moran, and the first convenor of the group was Bruce Wood. The inaugural meeting in Durham that year was attended by ten potential members, and by December of the same year the membership had risen to a more encouraging thirty six (from twenty nine different institutions). The very first health politics group conference was held in September of 1990 at Connaught House in London, (which was to become a regular venue for the group until 1997). The very first paper given at a Health Politics conference was given by Rob Baggott (then at Leicester Poly), with other papers from Mick Moran (Manchester), Paul Spicker (Dundee) and Mike Connolly and Leslie Carswell (Ulster). The conference was attended by seventeen delegates. By the end of 1992, due mostly to a recruiting drive, the membership had risen to 53, and the membership has continued to grow steadily ever since. The group currently has ninety-seven members from both national and international institutions. In 1995, Bruce Wood handed the convenorship of the group over to Alison Hann, at De Montfort University, Leicester, who has introduced a number of changes. In 1998, the group had its first two-day conference at Mansfield College, Oxford. This was something of an experiment, as it entailed a much bigger commitment from group members, both financially and academically, as the number of papers rose from an average of four (at the day conferences) to ten, over the course of the two days. In addition to the papers offered by group members, the conference was opened by a keynote speaker, who is (or was) a practitioner in the 'real' world of health policy. The conference in 1998 was opened by Roy Cunningham, who although retired from the Department of Health is still very active as a consultant, and in 1999 we were lucky enough to have David Player, formerly Director General of the Health Education Council and Chairman of the Health Education Board in Scotland. Both of these keynote speakers were able to offer a view of policy making 'from the inside' which put the academic papers into context. The conferences have been a great success. The very high standard of papers together with the longer time span, the conference dinner, (and the college bar) gave delegates plenty of opportunity to mingle and discuss health policy research in a relaxed and informal atmosphere. The second two day conference, in 1999, again attracted very high quality papers, including one from the groups former leader, Bruce Wood!

From its inception, the group has always had clear objectives. Firstly, and most obviously, to encourage a health politics research community. This is clearly both an invaluable resource *and* an important support network. Members have used contacts from within the group on countless occasions to discuss work or to form collaborative partnerships, in the form of joint papers or research bids. The group's conferences, as well as its panels at the main annual PSA conference have also offered a platform for researchers both new and established from which to explore and share new work in a constructive and supportive atmosphere. Secondly, the group also has an ongoing commitment to support the work of its graduate student membership, and the groups specialist conference offers a particularly good opportunity for graduate students to 'try out' their research on colleagues, in a constructive and supportive environment.

The group's panels at the PSA as well as its specialist conference have benefited from consistently high quality papers, from some of the most highly respected researchers in the area, and many of the offerings, have found their way into reputable journals. We have had paper givers from as far afield as the United States and Hong Kong, on topics as varied as the Politics of Health Insurance in Taiwan to Health Reform in Poland. And it is from this rich vein of research papers that this book is drawn. The papers included in this volume are a selection from papers that have been offered in the past two years at either the PSA panels at the main annual conference or at the specialist group conferences in Oxford.

The growth in the membership of the group is perhaps a reflection of the growth in academic interest in the area of health policy. Since the 1989 White Paper *Working For Patients* (DOH, 1989) which is regarded by many as being something of a watershed as it introduced two major and highly controversial reforms - these were firstly the purchaser and provider split and secondly general practitioners were given the option of becoming fund holders, and following the publication of *Working For Patients,* both political and academic debate about the nature, structure and philosophy of the NHS increased considerably. In the academic arena, the analysis and debate has been wide ranging, but has tended to focus on the processes of change, especially with regard to stated party political strategies, to the

2

implications of change for patients, professionals and institutions, and to the creation of new structures within the National Health Service. This range of interests is clearly reflected in this volume of papers. All of the papers address the effectiveness of some aspect of Labour Party health policy, although each of the authors takes slightly differing approaches to their subject matter. The development of health policy and the changing mechanics of the process of change within and before the Blair government has been specifically tackled by Paton (chapter two) and Wood and Harrison (chapter three). Each of these chapters observes that while New Labour might be claiming a 'new' or 'modern' approach, the important differences may turn out to be not so much in terms of content, but rather in terms of the *nature* of the policy making process. Even the most recent policy proposals have to be considered in the context of the history of the NHS. Health care reform was something of an international epidemic throughout late 1980s and the 1990s. In the U.K., as in other Western countries there were increasing pressures on the health service from an ageing population, rising citizen expectations and an explosion in medical technologies, which coincided with a changing ideological attitude to welfare state provision. While each country had a slightly differing approach to solving the problems, there was also a good deal of consensus over the need for increased efficiency through the use of some sort of market system, the need to strengthen primary care and to move towards the public health paradigm of health policy. Broadly speaking these are precisely the themes addressed in this volume.

When the Conservatives embarked on their sweeping programme of changes, many observed that it lacked a clear vision. Even the Health Minister, David Mellor declared at the time that he had 'no idea what the NHS would look like in five or ten years time' (Butler, 1992). Since then, the NHS seems to have been in a constant state of upheaval. An institution which is 'constantly reinventing itself [like] a car that is being re-engineered even while it is roaring around on the test track' (Klein, 1995). The publication of *The Health of the Nation* (DOH, 1992) White Paper in 1992 marked an important shift in public policy. It stemmed from the premise that the general health of the population was based on a whole variety of factors, which included such things as the environment and life style. The White Paper also implied the inclusion of other agencies within the wider strategy of health promotion. Notably, local authorities, voluntary agencies and the media were all called upon to play a role in creating healthier homes and workplaces. The fall and rise of the public health agenda is charted by Baggott (1994) who suggests that some of the factors behind its revival are 'the growing awareness of public health and environmental issues during the 1980s, the governing party's support for certain prevention policies; [and] international pressures to conform' (p259). Klein (1995) explains the apparent political 'conversion' to two things: AIDS and money. The pressure to respond to public anxiety over the number of deaths from AIDS in the late 1980s, fuelled by intense media interest in the disease, prompted the Thatcher government to commit itself to a massive programme of public health education. This strengthened the hand of Sir Donald Acheson (Chief Medical Officer), whose report published in 1988 led to a more sharply focused approach to public health. The other reason for the new found enthusiasm was the ever-present concern over money. Demand seemed to be on a collision course with supply, and a way of dealing with this is to find a method of manipulating the demand side of the equation. One approach is to prevent illness. The White Paper also signifies a change in policy style, marked by the fall of Thatcher and the succession of John Major to the premier-ship. It also demonstrated an acknowledgement by the government that it had a responsibility towards health that went well beyond the provision of health services. But there were gaps in the policy. Conspicuously absent was any mention of income distribution or unemployment. To some extent the lack of attention to health inequalities is congruent with Conservative's dislike of interfering in the way people run their lives, and an inclination to roll back the state in the area of health policy, as with everything else. However, in May 1997 a new Labour government was returned to office, with some signs at least, that they want to use the mechanisms of reform to create a more equitable health service. Public health concerns are to be tackled more vigorously by the newly created Minister for Public Health, and in July 1997 Donald Acheson was commissioned to produce a second Black Report. Whether or not New Labour can indeed 'reduce the health gap between rich and poor' remains to be seen, and is examined in some depth by Exworthy and Powell in chapter four of this volume.

In recent years, the almost frantic rate of 'reinvention', that characterised the late eighties and early nineties has slowed, and given way to perhaps a more cautious approach to possible ways forward. This approach is reflected in the 1997 White Paper *Primary Care the Future: Choice and Opportunity*, (DOH, 1997). Unlike *Working For Patients*, the 1997 White Paper was based on prolonged consultations, and all its proposals were supposed to be piloted and evaluated before implementation. Even before the election, there were clear indications that the previous preoccupation with markets and competition was giving way to a preference for 'primary care led service' and 'evidence based medicine'. While the adoption by the NHS of a policy of evidence based medicine seems to be simple common sense, the problems associated with its application and logic are addressed specifically by Harrison (chapter seven), who points out that the assumptions upon which it is based are questionable, for instance there is an assumption concerning what 'counts' as sound evidence, or what is 'good' evidence, and this is not something over which there is complete consensus. In addition, there is debate concerning the use of clinical guidelines as a method of disseminating research evidence and guiding clinical practice. Restructuring health services and persuading clinicians to change their behaviour, even when the evidence is (mostly) clear-cut is something of an uphill task. What is clear is that there are no quick fixes, and the benefits may not be forthcoming quickly enough to satisfy politicians facing short term financial or media pressures. Moreover, the media attention to some of the less appealing consequences of changes was to prove something of a thorn in the side of policy makers. The scale and intensity of media attention to health matters in general and the NHS in particular was unprecedented, and in addition, had a wide influence since it could portray in very human terms, the 'failings' of the NHS by using concrete images, and by using real life accounts of people on waiting lists, or people who had been refused treatment, they were able to engage the emotions (and attention) of the viewing and reading public in a very direct way. Perhaps because the media has a tendency towards the dramatic, such stories almost inevitably painted a picture of an NHS 'in trouble', with a decline in services and a lack of ministerial commitment to the continued survival of the NHS. Throughout the nineties there were a succession of stories concerning hospitals having to close wards due to either a shortage of staff or a lack of funds. There was also a procession of surgeons and doctors who claimed that they were unable to carry out life saving procedures because of lack of money. Failures in service provision, such as the 'failures' of the various screening programmes (particularly breast and cervical cancer) became regular features in most broad sheet and tabloid newspapers, putting pressure on the government to 'do something about it'. Such stories invariably provoke questions or a statement from the House of Commons, and in the cases of breast and cervical cancer screening have led to independent inquiries. The pressure that can be exerted by the media on policy makers should not be underestimated. In chapter ten Doyle examines the effect that such stories have had in the area of food scares and 'new killer diseases'. She suggests that Ministers were put on the defensive by the 'panic' caused by the stories, and were more or less forced to issue statements and make policy to protect themselves from accusations of doing too little too late. More recently, the media have been highly influential in framing public opinion with regard to such things as genetically modified foods, Viagra, (the anti-impotence drug) and rationing and have arguably been key actors in changes in government policy in these areas.

But, as Klein observes (1995) the changes in the structure of the NHS have so far defied both the optimists and the pessimists, in that the changes have delivered less in the way of improved services than the architects of change had predicted, but on the other hand the changes have not brought with them disasters on the scale that the pessimists had warned. What the changes have undoubtedly done is to challenge the consensus that had existed in the previous forty years of the NHS. Furthermore the changes reflected a sea change in the political attitude towards the delivery of health care, the relationship between professionals and the state, rationing, funding and public health. Like David Mellor, when pondering on the ways health policy may develop in the future, academics can only postulate on what the NHS will look like in five or ten years. One suggested approach taken in this volume, is to analyse developments within the NHS in terms of two competing models of health care: i.e. as either a church or a garage, which is drawn from the work of Klein (1993). The model of health care as a kind of secular church is typical of the philosophy of Aneurin Bevan, which was that the creation of the NHS was an act of 'social communion' where all patients were equal in the sight of the doctor, who was also the ultimate authority. It was the doctor who would determine what treatment was received by whom, and the doctor/patient relationship embodies several power relationships. Firstly, the patient needs the doctor more than the doctor needs the patient, although of course the doctor needs some patient or other, he/she does not need any particular patient. It is the patient who comes to the doctor in the role of supplicant, not the doctor who supplicates the patient. Secondly, the doctor is the expert. This notion of expertise has several strands. The doctor can diagnose the ailment, through the use of various instrument, can see inside the patients body and identify *occult* disease: furthermore, in doing all this, the doctor resorts to a language which is the language of an elite which is incomprehensible to the patient unless the doctor provides a translation. Thirdly, the doctor is 'active' and the patient is 'passive'. The patient presents him/her self as a physical body to be 'managed' by the doctor. Lastly, the different roles are backed up by legal sanctions. It is given to the doctor alone to authorise most forms of treatment, whether this consists of signing a prescription form, declaring the patient fit for work, referring him/her to a hospital consultant or treating the patient's body in ways that would be regarded as criminal assault if done by anyone else. It is a criminal offence to impersonate a doctor or for a lay person to carry out medical procedures. In addition, the 'doctor-experts' would be instrumental in framing and implementing health policy on a national level. Both the structure and ethos of the health service, within this model are highly paternalistic. The 'garage' model on the other hand, suggests that the major decisions should be taken by 'the consumer' rather than the experts. The patients takes his or her 'body' to the garage and has the final say in what is done to it, and reflects a more general willingness of the general public and politicians to question the actions of medical professionals, and to see health care delivery as a product and to demand a high standard of service delivery. One of the main aspects to this model is that the consumer also is able to choose between 'garages'. Equity within this model is not so much that all patients are equal, but rather that by transferring resources to them they are able to 'shop around' for the health care provision that they think is best or most appropriate - thus maximising (in theory at least) 'consumer choice'. This shift from 'patient' to 'consumer' might also explain the rising tide of complaints both about poor service provision and complaints about the performance of doctors, which some have concluded is a result of the 'fall from grace' of the medical profession and a rise in the knowledge and assertiveness of the consumer. This in turn might be attributed to a gap between consumer expectations and the NHS's standards, or perhaps more accurately, rising consumer expectations, due to a whole variety of causes such as constant government reorganisations of the NHS, each of which promised a better and more efficient service, and media encouragement of consumer activism, which has lead to expectations which simply could not be met by the NHS. However, the decline in the cultural and professional authority of the doctor can also be linked to other factors such as the rise of alternative medicine, challenges from other healthcare professions, particularly nursing (Nottingham and O'Neill, chapter twelve) and the formation of self-help groups which are often formed around the perceived failings of orthodox medicine in dealing with particular medical conditions. But the most remarkable thing of all is that even though consumers were more likely than ever to complain, large scale criticism has not been directed primarily at the doctors or staff working within the service or indeed upon the premise of an NHS. Rather, flaws or shortcomings were attributable largely to government failure, and falling standards or service inadequacies were blamed on ministerial mistakes or inefficiencies.

What emerges from the chapters in this volume, is that any analysis of health policy must take place from within the context of political, social and economic changes and pressures. Perhaps the most important role of health policy analysis is the framing of the questions rather than with finding the answers. What has become clear is that the faith in managed competition as a way to solve the many and varied problems of the NHS has faded while other possible solutions have been grasped at. Such things as evidence based medicine, managed care and a shift away from hospitals to primary care settings clearly have a role to play in solving some of the problems, but they are far from being a miracle cure. If policy makers are to have any success at all in determining which policies or innovations have (or are likely to) succeed or fail, it is essential that a body of academic knowledge exists which critically analyses the development and working of health policy. The existence of dissenting voices in policy subsystems tend to counter a tendency for government elites to 'group think', and exposes the process of policymaking and change to stronger critical analysis. Such groups or individuals may be uncomfortable to have around but they are an essential component in the generation of debate and the process of policy learning. Individuals such as the late Petr Skrabanek, (1994), who took great pains to publish unpopular and critical views of some of the health services most fundamental philosophies and services, have done much to provoke discussion and widen debate. While the authors in this volume may not claim that their work is unpopular, they certainly criticise and evaluate government policy and the implementation of its policies. Thus health policy research is of crucial importance, and should be supported both from within academic institutions and from outside them in the broader context of health related research initiatives and research grant giving organisations. While the Health Politics Specialist Group is not in a position to fund research, it can at least support its members in other ways, and through the pages of this volume, bring their work to a broader audience.

# References

Baggott, R. (1994), *Health and Healthcare in Britain*, Macmillan Press, London.

Butler, J. (1992), *Patients, Policies and Politics: Before and After Working for Patients*, Open University Press, Buckingham.

Department of Health (1989), *Working For Patients*, Cm 555, HMSO, London.

Department of Health (1992), *The Health of the Nation*, Cm 19, HMSO, London.

Department of Health (1997), *Primary Care the Future: Choice and Opportunity,* HMSO, London.

Klein, R. (1993), 'The Goals of Health Policy: Church or Garage?' in A. Harrison (Ed) *Health Care in the UK*, Kings Fund, London.

Klein, R. (1995), *The New Politics of the NHS*, Longman, London.

Skrabanek, P. (1994), *The Death of Humane Medicine*, Routledge, London.

# 2    New Labour, New Health Policy?

CALUM PATON

## Introduction

The architects of the original NHS reforms under the Conservative government were in essence those policy advisers close to Mrs Thatcher in the late 1980s. Speaking in retrospect after the election of the Labour Government nearly ten years later, David Willetts MP (who had been in the mid-1980s the member of the No. 10 Policy Unit responsible for health, then the Director of the Centre for Policy Studies, a right-wing think tank) summarised the aims as: stimulating the 'supply side' in health care by the spectre of competition; transferring power to GPs but in the context of giving them budgets within which they had to manage; building on the Griffiths Report in 1983 which had created the institution of general management and the aspiration of clinician-led management;  the related objective of bringing about a cultural change towards explicitness of objectives and services; and  replacing the NHS's 'culture of denigration' (bad-mouthing services in order to get more money) with incentives to stress the positive. (Willetts, 1997).

This account underplays the ideological verve of the late 1980s towards markets, individualism and hostility to the public purse.  Indeed the aims as listed above (with the partial exception of the first) would no doubt be endorsed by New Labour. Nevertheless it is a summary of intentions which both proponents and opponents of the NHS changes could recognise (at least the intentions of those even remotely sympathetic to the NHS, as opposed to those on the Right who wished to undermine its legitimacy). Intentions are not outcomes, however. It is arguable that any increased productivity on the supply side was outweighed by bureaucratic costs; that decentralisation of purchasing made contracting for specialised services and services for large catchment areas a cumbersome process; that reconciling GPs' new entrepreneurialism with service planning was problematical; and that any 'culture of denigration' was replaced with its equally pungent opposite, a culture of Panglossian sunshine stories enforced by politically-appointed regional Chairmen and senior managers on short-term contracts and performance-related pay.

## The Market Inherited by Labour

The notion of the market, in any pure economic sense, was in any case problematic for the NHS for a variety of reasons. Thus, the market system has been variously referred to as a quasi-, 'internal' or 'managed' market. Le Grand (1994) saw the NHS market as **attempting** to mimic a true market system and by its design, to try to achieve the benefits of better quality services, more efficient provision, greater user choice and more responsive services. The corollary of this was generally not so clearly understood: that the so called 'quasi market' policy was designed to **stimulate** markets where they did not exist; and was not primarily a policy to **restrict** markets for social or public purposes (Paton, 1995b). The key question remains, therefore, as to whether (in the provision of public services) a market system is appropriate at all.

Klein (1991) suggested that one test of the NHS reforms was the way in which purchasing authorities were commissioning services and monitoring their delivery — crucial in determining what is being provided to whom. To this however might be added: is the 'new purchasing' essentially different from effective planning as was sought in the NHS without, and before, a market? Our own investigations (Paton et al, 1998) suggested that reshaping services had been carried out at a level higher than the health authority — and that the new 'purchasing health authority' has usually been just a mouthpiece for centrally-stated 'government priorities'. 'Planning' was often perceived by HAs and Trusts as ensuring that local services reflected national priorities or even direct orders from on high — ranging from new hospitals to the Patient's Charter — irrespective of whether these were felt locally to be appropriate:

> "all too often we end up putting far too much emphasis onto the things that are highlighted as being nationally important in order to either get five stars in the league table or get the tick in the box in relation to the Patient's Charter . . . you have to do this . . . in an ideal world we wouldn't place such a high priority on some of these aspects . . ." (Chief Executive, 1995) .

A common picture emerging from our research was the marginalisation of the purchaser in service planning — squeezed between (often changing and even contradictory) government policy and provider

11

autonomy, ironically as the result of the purchaser/provider split. Government policy after 1992 stressed, initially, competition and, later, collaboration — often indeed together! In Sheffield, for example, the two main hospital trusts (covering the Royal Hallamshire and the Northern General respectively) were at first forced to compete 'across the board' and then (more sensibly) encouraged to work with the purchaser in rationalising services. But the Conservative government was schizophrenic on this issue, causing waste and confusion 'on the ground'.

In addition to the separation of provider units from Health Authorities, GPs were also given the option of becoming fundholders, with (initially) limited budgets from which to purchase certain services on behalf of their patients. The emergence of GP fundholding was referred to as the 'wild card' in the government reforms (Glennerster, Matsaganis et al 1994), possibly because of its potential for unseen consequences but more probably because — by giving direct purchasing power to GPs, as independent contractors — there was greater potential for disruption to current patterns of health care provision. It is important to recognise that the costs of fundholding were beyond the GPFH practice, and were incurred by providers who, inter alia, have to prepare individual invoices and letters to GPs, to ensure payment.

The various forms of block, volume and cost per case contracts between health authorities and providers were negotiated annually. This was widely criticised as making it impossible for providers to plan services for the longer term (for example, to plan for growth or contraction). It was yet more difficult for hospitals to manage (even in the short term) when faced with a myriad of GP contracts. Some economists have taken a different view — that short-term contracting does not actually hamper hospitals' ability to plan for the future, as it is not the contracting process but a higher level of planning process which decides upon the configuration of services. Contracts merely alter terms and conditions of various sorts, year on year or for longer periods. The question then arises however — how useful is contracting **at all**? Is it a cumbersome process out of proportion to any benefits?

**Specific Outcome of 'The Market'**

So what were the trends associated with the development of the internal market? Firstly our research highlighted that it was rarely the case that the money followed the patient — allegedly one of the benefits of the reforms. The reasons for this are complex. To begin with, the statement itself was always born more in political rhetoric than in a forward-looking analysis of the likely consequences of the reforms. The language of consumerism was used to justify an increasing stress upon markets and the whole panoply of the reforms, although our survey highlighted that local populations played little part in determining purchasing priorities. This leads to the conclusion that 'local voices' was more about communication of the inevitable to the public than about participatory purchasing. Another reason that the money did not generally follow the patient, is that the problem of "underfunding" remained.

Again at the level of rhetoric, it was claimed that the incentives introduced through the market and the reforms generally would diminish shortages, somewhat contradicting the view that the reformed NHS would make rationing more overt. This was because the extra productivity would diminish the pressure. In practice however, there was a strong sense, by 1997, of "this is where we came in". The under-funding remained, and the reforms had not altered the nature or size of the public demand for healthcare. Money may follow the patient if and when fundholders refer patients to their desired place of treatment and pay on a cost per case basis, up front. This was the phenomenon seen in early versions of fundholding, often generously funded by comparison with the rest of the referred case load paid for under Health Authority contracts, although this was not exclusively the case (Glennerster and Matsaganis, 1994). As fundholding embraced more of the population however, it was often fundholders who were increasingly having to make the hard choices themselves. In consequence, as they formed consortia and became mini health authorities' (even before Labour's new policy), patients had to follow their contracts also.

Secondly, anything resembling a functioning market, was the exception rather than the rule. While the institution of the purchaser/provider split naturally created changed behaviour, it was not in the direction of a recognisable market. As one Chief Executive commented *"we're not really a business, lets not pretend that we're running a business when we're not . . ."*. This had implications for both the behaviour of providers and the allocation of resources. It also had implications for purchasers. Just what were purchasers up to? Providers allegedly competed for contracts, although direct competition between providers was found to be limited for the majority of trusts.

But what drives purchasers? Are they the conscience of the NHS; are they hell-bent on 'bureau-shaping' influence without responsibility for operations (Dunleavy, 1991); or is **central diktat** the stick which drives them? Our study concluded that the mechanisms for determining service contracts were crude (largely based on historical data) and that health authorities' priorities reflected national concerns with little specific locality purchasing. Furthermore, in contracting for services, localism predominated in terms of where purchasers placed their contracts. The typical HA was likely to allocate about half of its budget to a single, local provider. At least 70% of the HA's budget went to three providers only (all of which may have been local, including community and other trusts as well as acute). Consequently, competitive markets, involving a range of providers, both local and non-local, were largely absent.

Thirdly, our survey highlighted that the purchaser/provider split itself had significant 'transactions' costs and rather more intangible or variable benefits. The term "transactions costs" is borrowed from behavioural economics to explain the costs of conducting business through contractual processes rather than what the textbooks call administrative hierarchies. In the context of today's NHS, this phrase has virtually reached the newspapers, although of course it has to be carefully distinguished from management costs more generally. The transaction costs of both GP fundholding and of the 'short termist' market (including annual contracting) were high. These costs were not simply in terms of the resources required to run an institutional distinction, however. The purchaser/provider split also created certain types of behaviour and incentives, many of which are perverse (Paton, 1995a). This raises a problem with 'economic' models. They may assume certain types of human behaviour, and thereby bring it about. One man's science is another's ideology. Assuming that NHS actors are 'selfish maximisers' may change reality in that direction.

It was expensive to create and manage the institutions of a market within a public service such as the NHS, and the final irony in this process was the political anxiety at the genuinely high costs of running market — resulting in persistent directives to all health authorities and trusts to cut management costs. Another suggestion of our research was that GP fundholders would increasingly commission in parallel with the Health Authority, but at high cost. From April 1st 1996, GP fundholders as well as other GPs were 'accountable to' the new Health Authorities (Department of Health, 1996). This in fact was to be used by Labour to build its 'evolutionary' model of 'primary-care commissioning' yet accountability to the health authority on the part of GP purchasing groups. Another development to be 'moulded' by Labour was the Total Purchasing Pilot (TPP) (Mays et al, 1998). These pilot projects consisted in budgets for all health services being given *jointly* to the GPs covering a locality (say, of 60,000 to 100,000 people); thus they were an extension of GP fund holding (in two ways — covering more services; and more GPs). Yet they were to be used by Labour in devising the Primary Care Group (see below) — to become the linchpin of Labour's policy. Already, therefore, the question appeared: was New Labour simply copying and moulding existing policy for the NHS?

## Labour's Evolving Policy

Labour's policy throughout and indeed after the Conservatives' period of rule was one of grudging adoption of the new realities perhaps grudging in public; philosophical or even enthusiastic in private. Labour was never intrinsically hostile to the Griffiths Report in 1983, for example, but sounded grudging in order to respond to concerns expressed especially by the nursing profession and of course lower paid workers in the NHS, who were already threatened by compulsory competitive tendering. Labour was more hostile to the NHS Reforms of 1989/1991, following *Working for Patients (1989)*. Nevertheless, their loss of the 1992 General Election meant that the eggs contained in the White Paper, *Working for Patients*, had become an omelette which apparently could not be unscrambled by 1997.

On winning the 1997 election, Labour had to act before its plans for the health service could be assembled into a White Paper, (and certainly before legislation, which, eventually came before Parliament for its second reading in 1999). The first announcement geared to equity, in early July, concerned the establishment of common waiting lists for patients whether or not they were with fundholding general practitioners. This was aimed at avoiding 'queue-jumping' by purchasers with more money (normally but not always fundholders). But what was to stop fundholders or their successors sending their patients to other trust hospitals, where waiting times were shorter for all purchasers? This would be likely to leave the local trust with less cash, and actually worsen waiting times for local patients funded by the local health authority rather than fundholding GPs. It could be argued that waiting times locally would also come down, with less people to be treated — but only if the local trust could afford to keep all its staff and services. Alternatively, it could be argued that all purchasers could seek the shorter waiting times elsewhere. But this assumed that the popular hospitals can expand elastically in response to demand, exactly the sort of unrealistic market assumption which persuaded Labour to 'abolish the internal market'. So Labour had to follow up partial instructions with more instructions — that all patients had to be treated equally. Yet if all purchasers within an HA area were to be regulated so that one does not refer its patients to shorter waiting-lists, what was the point of local purchasing in the first place?

Next, Labour sought to 'claw back' extra funds from GP fundholders. Yet when they simply threatened to spend less on community services (and the district nurses and health visitors contracted from community trusts), Labour again had to regulate further. The signs were there early on, that 'micro regulation' rather than rethinking was to be the order of the day. This was strange: Labour had had many years to shape its policy, yet seemed to be floundering early on.

Another announcement, concerning hospital rationalisation, at the NHS Confederation conference a little earlier in 1997, seemed to suggest that Health Action Zones (HAZ) would co-ordinate hospital closures, mergers and new developments. The (logical) reason was that local purchasers cover too small areas and numbers to do what is a sub-Regional or Regional job. Unfortunately Labour's favoured policy of primary care commissioning runs right against this, for the latter policy devolves key decisions even lower.

Confusingly, HAZs were later defined as something different — as 'anti-deprivation' multi-agency task forces in selected areas of the country. Although HAZs are now at last clear as to their mission (if not their rationale) it seems the policy evolved 'on the hoof' — with an apparent coining of 'initiatives' and acronyms before the content had been decided. This was analogous to the Conservative policy, which had let 'one hundred flowers bloom' in the hope that 'something would turn up'.

Regarding the purchaser/provider split, Labour in office was now pledged to keep it. This sounded to some like an ideological acceptance of 'the market'. The new soundbite was that Labour would abolish the market, but keep the split. But, on reflection, if there is not really a market, it means little change — and only little changes — from Tory policy. Or, turning it round the other way, if a purchaser/provider split means a bias to as much of a market as the politicians will allow (as purchasers are allowed to choose providers, presumably on market criteria), it means not abolishing the market after all. Labour accepted advice from 'experts' (who in many cases had been advising the Conservatives) that the purchaser/provider split was the one aspect of the Tory reforms which **was** clearly worthwhile. This was based on no evidence, however. The contrary hypothesis — that, separating 'planning' from 'management' or 'implementation' makes policy less coherent — may equally be true. At the end of the day, however, Labour was keen to advertise a policy of 'abolish the market; keep the purchaser/provider split'. This meant little in practice, but sounded good — and had the advantage of allowing Labour to accept the inherited reforms **de facto** while proclaiming the abolition of the market as a genuflection to those among their ranks unimpressed by 'New Labour' and those among the public (a majority) who distrusted the Conservatives' reforms.

## The White Paper, The New NHS: Modern and Dependable

Prior to this White Paper's emergence on December 9th 1997, the Labour Government had announced 42 GP Commissioning Group pilot projects, which were to 'go live' on 1st April 1998. These were to be monitored and evaluated by independent researchers, and were to embrace a number of different approaches to GP commissioning (now called Primary Care Group commissioning, in the White Paper.) Labour had debated whether to 'go for' GP commissioning or locality commissioning (a wider concept.) They wanted one of the two, because they wanted to offer GP fundholders a pivotal role in the newer arrangements to 'sweeten the pill' of fundholding's abolition. Thus returning to full Health Authority control — although it could have helped Labour 'cut management costs' — was off the agenda. This was actually politically weak (with a parliamentary majority of nearly 200!): many GP fundholders did not object to fundholding's demise; and New Labour's alleged belief in 'hard choices' should surely have made them sanguine about failing to please all of the people all of the time!

In the end **Primary Care Groups** — comprised of GPs and more — were to be 'the answer' (to a question never clearly put!).

Concerning the range of models, there were to be four options for Primary Care Groups (PCGs). These were:

1. The minimalist role — supporting the health authority in commissioning, and acting only in an advisory capacity.
2. Taking devolved responsibility for managing the budget, but as part of the health authority.
3. Becoming freestanding bodies — Trusts — (but accountable to the health authority), contracting for secondary services.
4. Becoming freestanding bodies as in three but with the added responsibility for providing community health services for the

population (by implication as an alternative to contracting with community trusts for this purpose).

The White Paper was unclear as to whether the ultimate intention was that all Primary Care Groups would become freestanding bodies — or Primary Care Trusts, as the White Paper called them. Indeed the original intention had been that the pilot projects would be assessed to find the most appropriate model or models in the light of the objectives of providing effective care and also reducing administration and management costs by comparison with the previous government's internal market. But there was a sentence in the new White Paper, which pointed out that Primary Care Groups " . . . will be expected to progress along (the spectrum) so that in time all Primary Care Groups assume fuller responsibilities". Later still, (former) Minister of State for Health Alan Milburn made it clear **all** PCGs were to become Trusts.

At the end of the day, the practical questions to be resolved included: whether or not real money for all care would be devolved to groups of GPs operating through Primary Care Groups; and the extent to which all GPs should be involved in decision-making as part of such groups. If one subscribes to the view that the GP is the closest health service decision-maker to the patient, then there is a quasi-democratic argument for so devolving budgets. Unfortunately the management costs of such a policy are likely to be high, and furthermore there is no evidence that GPs are either willing or able to carry out such a fundamental role themselves. Ultimately, such a policy came to mean devolution to *management agencies* operating under the aegis of the Health Authority, and the ultimate outcome of the policy might well be more management tinkering rather than a truly innovative policy.

As with the previous government's reforms, the main question which arises concerns incentives and whether they are benign or perverse. What are the key incentives embodied in the White Paper, *The New NHS,* and are they likely to bring improved relations between primary care and hospital care on an affordable basis? The new **philosophy** is collaboration, but its means of realisation are not clear, even if one (rightly) goes beyond economics in considering incentives. One can have sympathy with the senior Department of Health official who said (off the record) in some frustration, "we were criticised under the Tories for stressing economic incentives as 'the answer'; now we're being criticised for **not** having adequately clear incentives"! And arguably new arrangements are at least likely to provide a more stable basis for NHS decision making than the predecessor arrangements — as long as there is a fruitful reconciliation of the respective roles of Regions, Health Authorities and Primary Care Groups.

It is useful to compare the English White Paper with the Scottish White Paper. In Scotland, market mechanisms had not developed so far. GP fund holding, in particular, was more limited. As a result, the Scottish White Paper heralded a new (Scottish) NHS which was to be more 'integrated'. As well as the Health Boards (health authorities), there were to be (in the areas of most Boards) one acute hospital Trust and one Primary Care Trust. The latter were however different from the English Primary Care Trusts, which were to be **first** purchasers and **second** providers. In Scotland, Primary Care Trusts were to be providers: they were to contain all GP practices, and all community and mental health services. Instead of Primary Care Groups doing the purchasing, as in England, 'local health-care co-operatives' of GPs (LHCCs) were to advise the Health Board (Authority). What is more, it seemed that Health Boards (authorities) in Scotland would have a more direct role in the affairs of Trusts in Scotland — for example in capital allocations and services plans.

The problem for New Labour is two-fold. Firstly, to govern the NHS pragmatically while re-integrating it. This actually requires structural change — which the New Labour government denies. (Otherwise, Labour is simply administering a Conservative-shaped NHS). In practice, Labour *is* implementing structural change: the 'iron law of NHS reform' is that, the more governments deny structural change, the larger that structural change is likely to be! The problem for Labour is that its structural changes (PCGs et al) are not well geared to its objective of cost-effective management.

The worst-case scenario is that, in seeking to 'reintegrate the NHS without structural reorganisation', Labour will incur a huge structural reorganisation without reintegrating the NHS.

For Labour, modernisation in health policy could have been 'radical' in dismantling the new fragmentation inherited from the Conservatives, rather than adapting it. As things stand, there is the danger of inappropriate structures and policies to combine equity, effectiveness and economy. As Anthony Crosland had put it many years before, 'Labour had always been split between radicals and modernisers. The trouble was, the radicals lived in the past, whereas the modernisers were no longer radical'. Despite Blairite rhetoric about the radical centre, this may well be the epitaph for Blairite health policy.

## Evolving and Implementing Policy

The White Paper, *The New NHS*, and subsequent policy announcements contained other, more 'technical' elements. A National Institute for Clinical Excellence (NICE) was to promulgate best practice in clinical effectiveness, technology and even **service frameworks** (i.e. blueprints for how to organise services locally and regionally). A Commission for Health Improvement (CHImp) was to be constituted as a 'special health authority', an inspectorate to enforce quality and cost-effectiveness.

Quality was to be addressed through the concept of 'clinical governance': hospitals, community providers and primary care groups were to designate a Board-level officer (normally the Medical Director, in hospitals), responsible to the Chief Executive for clinical quality. This meant that individual clinicians would have to be more 'accountable' to their departmental heads (Clinical Directors of specialities), who in turn would be responsible to the designated officer.

Some of this came from the analogy with 'corporate governance', which became an obligation for Trusts under the Conservatives after the fashion of the Cadbury Report which had been covered to provide an 'ethical' code of practice for the private sector. (The worry was that the newly 'commercialised' NHS might go off at a tangent in the direction of sharp or lax practice, as exemplified by scandals in Wessex concerning Information Technology procurement and the West Midlands concerning management services.)

Thus clinical governance was to be about seeking to 'avoid scandals' — but more than that, it was intended to promote 'organisational development' to promote quality across the board.

Later announcements concerned the actual shape of PCG Boards. They were to be controlled by GPs, who would have an in-built majority (assuming they wanted it) — following the so-called 'Chisholm letter' to the Minister of Health (from John Chisholm of the BMA) setting out GPs' demands, in the light of the scepticism of many (both fundholders and non-fundholders, many of the latter not wishing to control cash-limited budgets even where they wanted to be involved in 'commissioning' — whatever that meant). (Our earlier research had revealed that about 90% of GPs 'thought GPs should be involved in commissioning', but that only a minority **wanted** to be involved **themselves**, and that there was no consensus at all about what it meant, although generally a convenient assumption that it was about GPs getting what they wanted!) (Paton et al, 1998, p129).

As the instructions concerning PCGs grew in volume, making The New NHS the harbinger of arguably the biggest reorganisation yet, it became clear that PCGs would be 'mini health authorities', responsible to the present Health Authority through the local 'Health Improvement Plan' (HIP), which could also include Trusts and non-NHS 'collaboration' in the locality.

Overall, the rhetoric of the 'Third Way' — collaboration, rather than the 'market' of 1991 or the allegedly pre-1991 'command and control' — was belied increasingly in practice by the reality of 'command' (even if control was difficult, given the multifarious organisations and committees spawned by *The New NHS* and the inevitable 'policy-making on the hoof' which followed it).

### New Labour, Old Tory?

Standing back from all this, is the Labour Government continuing the previous government's reforms by extending them (in some cases amending them) or changing course? Some significant pointers had emerged by 1999 to suggest that New Labour was increasingly replicating the health policy of the Conservatives.

### The PFI

Firstly, the Private Finance Initiative (private capital to finance public services) was revived and extended.

In 1995, Shadow Secretary of State for Health Margaret Beckett had given intimations it would be abolished. When Sheila Masters, a Conservative appointed member of the Private Finance Panel, had suggested that the PFI would be retained under Labour, Mrs Beckett let it be known she was speaking out of turn. Yet Mrs Beckett herself was moved from the health portfolio soon after.

The PFI had ironically been slow to get off the ground under the Conservatives. Firstly, the private sector had feared that PFI projects agreed with NHS Trusts were **ultra vires** in that NHS Trusts had a dubious legal status (were they 'independent' or were they creatures of the Secretary of State?) Secondly, there had been no planning of what the priority developments were for which 'PFI' funding would be sought. In 1997 Labour passed the NHS (Private Finance) Act to remove the former problem, and claimed it was identifying projects by order of priority. (In reality, this was a sleight of hand — Labour simply speeded up projects already in the pipeline.)

The PFI is a dangerous road for the NHS to travel down. Government borrowing is nearly always cheaper than privately borrowed capital. Unless Trusts have land or property to 'give away' (and why should they? why should they not derive the profits?) in return for — say — a privately constructed hospital (which the NHS Trust still has to lease, not own), the PFI is generally a 'bad deal' financially.

Next it is argued (e.g. by Chris Elliott, a Managing Director of Barclays Capital, in *The Times*, Feb 17, 1999) that even although public capital would be cheaper, private partners 'design, build and operate' the hospital as well as finance it. But this is illogical. Why should not the NHS use public capital for finance and then seek the best means of 'designing, building and operating'? And even if public capital is not available for everything, it could often be cheaper to get a 'high street loan' than enter a tortuous PFI scheme with more strings attached than Soviet bureaucracy, let alone the traditional public sector.

The PFI has a bias to 'bricks and mortar' — it is not good for non-hospital developments. (Ways of making it so are arguably more problematic than the problem!) Equally the need for significant profit to be 'paid back' by the NHS, with often a lot of front-loading and high interest rates or pay-back rates, means that the revenue (running cost) budget of the NHS is constrained for years to come. That is why PFI schemes to replace hospitals involved bed cuts, size cuts and service cuts. Professor Alyson Pollock, of St. George's Hospital, London continues to carry out detailed research into this issue.

For New Labour to embrace the PFI is to store up trouble for the future: the PFI's embrace will in turn crush New Labour's aspirations to 'rebuilding' the NHS and providing a comprehensive service. It is interesting to note that, in Scotland, the Scottish National Party has made opposition to PFI a major plank of its campaign for the May 1999 elections to the new Scottish Parliament.

**Local Pay**

Labour virulently attacked the Tories' policy of (limited) local pay in the early to mid-1990s. They (rightly) saw it as getting (from the viewpoint of the Tories' objectives) the worst of both worlds — only limited local variation (and not even that, in the end) yet huge bureaucratic cost and lowered staff morale. The issue of performance-related pay had also caused problems under the Tories. Management theory tends to suggest that individual performance-related pay (as opposed to, say, team or group-determined pay) is impossible to decide rationally or fairly, as improved outcomes to be rewarded cannot be traced to individuals — not least in a complex, multi-professional service.

Yet New Labour began in 1999 to copy elements of the previous government's policy. A consultation document *Agenda for Change* proposed to merge the many existing pay scales into three national pay scales — for doctors and dentists; nurses and other caring staff; and other staff. In itself this could be sensible. Further suggestions included that specific pay bands were to be decided in negotiations between employers and unions, and that both a local element and a performance-related element would be introduced. To be fair, this plan was less for local pay than for **amended** national pay. But the amendments included ideas which had caused problems for the previous government. Rewarding 'top performing teams' might just be a good idea, and was included. But **individual** 'performance pay' had generally failed. Paying extra in areas where recruitment and retention was difficult may be sensible. The jury is out on whether 'local pay' is limited to this or not.

Labour was copying, for the NHS, its initiative of 'merit pay' in education — as so often, the education service provided a breeding-ground of ideas for the health service. The origin of the policy was at root pragmatic — there was not enough money to pay everyone more, so there was an attempt to pay more to **some** to seek (for example) to get over the nursing recruitment problem using a blend of limited cash and PR.

**Incentives for good performance**

Time would be better spent seeking to increase organisation-wide incentives for good performance (both increased quantity and quality). To be fair, the original problem to which the internal market was a (inappropriate) solution was the fact that hospitals and other providers which improved efficiency **et al** got extra workload but not extra money. Instead of generating extra 'real' money, they got extra responsibilities. In an altruistic world, one might say — so what? But admittedly, in the context of shrinking hospital budgets, such a situation can be galling even for altruists.

The internal market sought to relate 'reward' to workload — but contracts did not take this form (except where they were very bureaucratic and expensive to administer). Furthermore, the atmosphere of aggressive competition was a disincentive to 'sharing good practice' between rival provider Trusts.

Instead, therefore, providers should be funded in proportion to what they accomplish, both quantitatively and qualitatively. This would necessitate a large enough 'purchaser'/planner to distribute money over a large enough area, to reward variations in performance from a pot large enough to cope with such variations.

Whether one calls this 'Regional planning' or a 'public market' is a matter of theology. And local priorities within a national framework can be helped by avoiding national 'Charters' (Dyke, 1998) and monolithic, one-dimensional 'priorities' such as reducing waiting lists without considering priorities within.

Again, to be fair, New Labour is seeking to mobilise co-operative behaviour through clinical governance, and to reward-improved practice or outcomes in a variety of (non-material) ways.

## Moral Panics

To this commentator, it is quite extraordinary how 'panics' about NHS funding have increased in frequency over the last twenty years — despite repeated 'fundamental reviews' both by governments and self-appointed gurus. Agonising about alternatives to the NHS model are in inverse proportion to their appropriateness. The trouble is that there *is* no magic answer. Public financing is both fairest **and** most efficient. So if we want to spend more at all equitably, we should do it publicly. Otherwise, a 'vicious circle' sets in whereby — if the better off pay more privately — they will have less to redistribute to even a minor degree to help the poor through public taxation. A service for the poor is a poor service, for fiscal as well as sociological reasons.

Yet just as New Labour has launched its *New NHS*, the agonising has begun again, generally but not exclusively in the pages of the right-of-centre broadsheets. Business leaders who have recently turned their minds to the NHS are rediscovering (often imagined) problems and re-honing inappropriate solutions — to such an extent, now, that one wonders if good sense and stability can continue to hold the fort. To amend a famous phrase, the price of protecting the NHS is eternal vigilance. (One recent suggestion in the pages of *The Times* is that we copy the Singaporean model for financing healthcare, and therefore adopt a hierarchy of access according to the generosity of one's coverage.)

Alongside such instigated 'moral panics' we find increasing interest by New Labour in gearing the NHS to the needs of the economy, rather than maintaining its core value of meeting need for healthcare equitably. In February 1999, the government was reviewing an idea to put those on incapacity benefit to the top of waiting lists ('queue jumping'), to save on the welfare budget. This is despite the implication of pushing children, the elderly, and the unemployable further down the list. (This adds grist to the mill of those who argue, in a 'Marxist' manner, that the priority of investing cheaply in workers' health on behalf of industry makes the NHS a 'middleman' for industry — which generally contributes less to healthcare costs than in Continental Europe, especially with British general taxation being significantly less progressive than at the end of the 1970s.)

Had such an idea been put forward by Mrs Thatcher, it is likely that (Secretary of State for Health) Frank Dobson and others would have proclaimed the end of civilisation as we know it.

**Power in the Post-1991 National Health Service**

Power relationships in the British National Health Service, changed after the reforms which were implemented from 1991 onwards by the Conservative Government. The Labour Government elected in May 1997 soon signalled that further change would be incremental, and that root-and-branch removal of the institutions of the 'new' NHS would not occur. As a result, many of the new power relationships and incentives brought about by the 1991 reforms would remain. In particular, the use of purchasing agencies to prioritise and ration care remains as the theoretical cornerstone of the purchasing function (despite rather bizarre protestations by the Minister of Health in December 1997 that Labour was ending rationing rather than beginning it). This means less power to patients and 'front-line' doctors, (i.e. doctors, **qua** doctors) and more power to politicians and managers (even if the latter wear white coats) and even if Labour claims to be re-empowering doctors.

While the abolition of the 'internal market' was heralded by the Labour government, the 'mobilisation of bias' (Schattschneider, 1960) effected by the institutions of the post-1991 NHS has had more impact upon incentives and culture than will Labour's policy prescriptions. In particular, while the market was always limited (and arguably short-lived, from 1992 to around 1995), the culture of 'divide and rule' between purchasers and providers of health care remains as the cornerstone of the 'reformed' NHS, despite rhetoric about collaboration. The following paragraphs expand upon these points.

The reforms promulgated by the Thatcher Review of the NHS had allegedly created an 'internal market' within and around the NHS. This quasi-market was less about creating widespread competition in supply than in setting up a 'purchaser/provider split' which created separate agencies with responsibility respectively for provision (hospitals and other types of service) and for purchasing services from providers via contracts (health authorities and groups of general practitioners with budgets, GP fundholders). The 'fall out' from the various reforms has meant that power has shifted in various directions within, and around, the NHS.

Purchasers have more financial power than the pre-reform health authorities, which has resulted in pressure upon providers to 'do more for less'. Yet the separation of purchasers and providers has resulted in this being power without responsibility (for shaping and managing services), and has furthermore given providers a separate, autonomous power based upon information and knowledge about services. There is an asymmetry in both these types of power between purchasers and providers.

Labour has now 'cash limited' **all** NHS budgets — including GPs prescribing budgets for the first time. By giving 90% of the NHS budget (all but the most specialised services) to PCGs (which GPs will control), Labour is possibly creating a dynamic of conflict between GPs and hospitals/hospital doctors, which will go 'against the grain' of the new collaborative **ethos** — and also perhaps create a **sharper** 'market' than the Tories managed to do!

Labour is probably right to avoid formal or 'explicit' criteria for rationing (Hunter, 1997). It is sometimes claimed that such criteria should be explicit at the level of national government and even the local Health Authority, but that individual clinicians should have leeway within guidelines to use their judgement. Nevertheless, allowing local clinicians judgement may indeed undermine 'explicit' criteria for rationing. Even if costs are well known over time, outcomes vary —for the same procedure and for different procedures — across individual patients. Even therefore by economists' quality-orientated criteria as related to cost (such as the quality adjusted life year), generalisations — and therefore explicit criteria for rationing — are often difficult. (This is a layman's way of stating that explicit criteria of rationing in fact involve interpersonal comparisons of utility, allegedly outlawed by classical welfare economics).

Planning health services requires a planning agency above the level of the health authority (and certainly above the level of groups of GPs). Today's NHS lacks such an authority, and (by default in some cases and by design in others) central government — sometimes acting through Regional Offices, sometimes not — now is responsible for planning, which involves closing and opening hospitals and other providers; merging and reconfiguring groups of providers; and articulating priorities to be implemented by purchasers and providers (more than before). That is, planning must be distinguished from purchasing (and the associated term, 'commissioning', which — to the extent it means anything — covers the 'grey area' between the two). Purchasing involves contracts for services once their nature and location has emerged from the planning process. This is even more true under Labour, which has implemented a policy of mergers and rationalisation of providers — in pursuit of clinical specialisation; economies of scale; and avoidance of duplication of management costs. Labour had promised to reinvigorate Regional Health **Authorities**, but seems to have abandoned that (perhaps awaiting the birth of Regional assemblies in England, in the longer run).

The complexity and fragmentation inherent in implementing policy, in the new NHS, has led central government to rely more (not less) upon 'command and control' — as a means of seeking to circumvent complexity and replicate informally the often-absent formal lines of responsibility for implementation. Such 'commands' are however single-issue, and such 'control' is by complex regulation which mirrors the plural sources of decision within the NHS. In this way, the NHS, and policy towards it, is becoming a little more like U.S. social policy (incapable of complex planning owing to unsuitable political institutions) than traditional British social and health policy. But 'command and control' seeks to counteract this. By the end of 1998, the profusion of 'commands' by Department of Health circulars and executive letters was testing the patience of even the most willing senior managers. To characterise this as a 'Third Way' seemed dubious.

The 'third way' is allegedly between the Scylla of 'hierarchy' and the Charybdis of the 'market'. One can detect a fusion of academic analysis about hierarchies, markets and networks, on the one hand, and popular slogans about the same, on the other hand. Thus it is sometimes argued that the NHS before the market was a kind of Weberian hierarchical bureaucracy, with command and control its popular expression. After the internal market, some analysists depict an amalgam of market and networks as the source of both structure and agency. (Ferlie et al, 1996).

To the present author, however, this is fashionable but misleading. The 'market' was in practice the latest variant of command and control, and represented the **deepening** of hierarchy — not its negation. (Jenkins, 1995). New Labour's policy is tidying up the often-unintended fragmentation of the market, and continuing with command and control. The so-called collaborative networks established in *The New NHS* are in fact mandatory mechanisms for implementing central policy. (A clear example is on clinical quality, where the limited discretion left to hospitals on this matter in *The New NHS* has already been removed by a Ministerial edict from Alan Milburn, Minister of State for Health, on April 13th, 1998.)

The 'third way' is mostly rhetoric. Almost all New Labour policies are announced as a 'third way'; but one must look at the particular context to see which two alternatives the alleged 'third way' is coming between. On the economy generally, it appears to be between **laissez-faire capitalism** and **redistributive welfare capitalism**, with the 'third way' a rather limited supply-side tinkering. On welfare reform, it is between collectivism in financing and universalism in provision, on the one hand, and pure individualism, on the other hand.

The general thread is that the 'third way' rejects social democracy (never mind socialism) while asserting community, responsibility, and opportunity rather than relying on laissez-faire in its purest form. In health, however, the special status of the NHS ensures that more direct government control continues, which makes talk of a 'third way' rather superficial. What is more, rather than diminishing bureaucracy, the new health care state can validly be categorised as an example of the 'new bureaucracy'.

## Labour, The Market and The State

One school of thought argues that a public National Health Service is rendered both more inequitable and more cost-ineffective through the introduction of market mechanisms, even in the limited form of the internal market as originally proposed. The present author is of this school — and therefore argues that Labour is right to abolish the internal market in the NHS.

Another school of thought argues that the market **mechanism** may be appropriate, but that it was never systematically tried. Our research results suggest the latter part of this claim to be true, but we do not argue that market mechanisms — if systematically attempted — would produce benign results. Nevertheless, political interference with the policy of the internal market, over the years from 1991-1997, endeavour to produce the worst of both worlds — diminution of coherent planning, yet also failure to reap any benefits of the market, hypothetical or real.

To the extent that Labour is unequivocal about ending the market of the NHS, it could be considered to make health an exception to its 'policy rethink' and therefore to be more like old Labour at least in the aspiration

28

of ending the market.

New Labour has argued, however, for the centrality of market forces in the economy as a whole, even to the extent of altering Clause 4 of its constitution to stress inter alia the vigour of market forces. In areas of social policy such as health and education, however, the approach in practice is central control plus inspectorate — performance management backed up by central sanctions, in the pursuit of objectives.

In macro-economic policy New Labour is following a policy of economic orthodoxy which would be recognisable in the 1920s and 1930s. Indeed new Labour is so very old Labour that its post-Keynesianism is closely analogous to the pre- Keynesianism of Ramsay Macdonald, Philip Snowden and the others in the 1920s. The obsessive desire to appear electable and to placate the City brings to mind Marx's dictum (after Hegel) about history repeating itself, the first time as tragedy and the second time as farce. Thompson, (1996) rather convincingly suggests the poverty of economic thought in the current Labour party, by placing it in historical perspective. The question is, will pro-market orthodoxy eventually extend even to the NHS, diminishing even the timid critique of market forces in the NHS made by Labour?

Seeking to replicate the distributional incentives of the textbook perfect market has an honourable place in socialist economic theory. To that extent, designing sensitive reimbursement mechanisms for providers in health care for use in a planning system may reasonably align itself with this approach. Yet going beyond this to institute actual market forces is to follow a current in neo-conservatism rather than to design a genuinely 'new welfare state' which synthesises social objectives and the market to produce either something new or a whole greater than the sum of the parts.

It is not so much a question of markets versus hierarchies. Internal markets in public services of the nature of the National Health Service **require** hierarchies and more 'command and control' than a modern, flexible planning system. The phrase derived from organisational economics, 'hierarchy', confuses two elements. Firstly, there is the control of resources and organisations at a high enough level to prevent the perverse incentives of decentralised market forces in a public service — which some of our recent research has noted. (Paton et al, 1998). Secondly, there is 'hierarchy' in the often-pejorative sense of centralised bureaucratic control of operations within organisations. Disadvantages within the latter may be minimised without removing the former — and certainly without instituting internal markets.

Finally, it is worth considering theories of the state as relevant to New Labour. The role of the state, according to New Labour, is not 'social democratic' in the sense of 'taming' capitalism, but pro-market — to enable survival (and more) in the global capitalist economy. In this environment, even 'post Fordist' regulation (Jessop, 1990) is too ambitious for the state, the further disempowerment of which is accepted by New Labour, in its acceptance of and indeed eulogy for globalisation.

Such a neo-liberal 'non state', as we might call it, might be expected to eschew direct provision of health services for all. Indeed, some countries are following this path (slowly, given the complexity and popularity of 'socialised medicine', whatever it is called in practice). Britain however has a ready-made instrument for investing in the **health of the productive, cheaply** — the NHS. The NHS is not **only** cheap in the sense of good value — it is parsimonious in provision, and also exploitative of its workers in the Marxist sense of reduced costs and therefore increased profits for companies by comparison with the alternative of these companies contracting for their workers' healthcare in an open market (Paton, 1997). New Labour seeks to have it both ways — it supports the NHS because it is the expression of solidarity and equity, yet also because the NHS is cheap: and (not always) cheerful, New Labour's strategy is to proclaim its continuing adherence to 'health and education for all' while construing that adherence as the core of the state's diminished responsibilities in the age of globalisation. In that age, the state's role, according to New Labour, is both to give global capitalism a 'human face' and also to facilitate economic absorption of the dictates of globalism. To that extent, the new healthcare state is about direct investment in productivity. Countries with more diffuse healthcare systems (as in France or the USA) can only envy the economy of the British healthcare state.

New Labour's ideal of community (which could be construed as necessitating yet resistance to globalisation) is likely to be skin-deep, as productivity supersedes equity. Yet its support of the NHS will continue, in a strategy which is 'playing it both ways' rather than embodying a third way. Or, to put it another way, Britain will invest in the productive **within** the public sector rather than (as in the US) leaving it to corporations to invest in productive workers and reward productive workers with generous health benefits.

# References

Department of Health (1989), *Working for Patients* (Cmnd 555), HMSO, London.

Department of Health (1992), *The Health of the Nation*, HMSO, London.

Department of Health (1996), *Functions and Manpower Review*, Department of Health. London.

Department of Health (1997), *The New NHS: Modern and Dependable*, HMSO, London.

Dunleavy, P. (1991), *Democracy, Bureaucracy and Public Choice*, Harvester Wheatsheaf.

Dyke, G. (1998), *The New NHS Charter, A Different Approach*, Department of Health, London.

Ferlie, E., et al (1996), *The New Public Management in Action,* Oxford University Press, London.

Glennerster, H., Matsaganis, M., et al (1994), *Implementing GP Fundholding — Wild Card or Winning Hand*, Open University Press, Buckingham.

Hunter, D. (1997), *Desperately Seeking Solutions: Rationing Health Care*, Longman, London.

Jenkins, S. (1995), *Accountable to None: The Tory Nationalisation of Britain,* Hamish Hamilton, London.

Jessop, B. (1990) *State Theory: Putting Capitalist States in their Place,* Polity Press, Cambridge.

Klein, R. (1991), 'The politics of change', *British Medical Journal*, vol. 302, no 6785, pp 1102-1103.

Le Grand, J. (1994), 'Introduction', in Bartlett, W. and Le Grand, J. (eds.) *Quasi-Markets in the Public Sector*, Policy Press, Bristol.

Mays, N., Goodwin, N., et al (1998), *What were the achievements of first-wave total purchasing pilots?*, King's Fund, London.

Paton, C. (1995a), 'Present Dangers and Future Threats: some perverse incentives in the NHS reforms', *British Medical Journal*, vol. 310, 13 May, pp 1245-8.

Paton, C. (1995b), 'Contriving Competition', *Health Service Journal*, vol. 105, no 5460, 6 July, pp 24-25.

Paton, C. (1997), 'Necessary Conditions for a Socialist Health Service', *Health Care Analysis*, vol. 5, no 3, Autumn 1997.

Paton, C. et al (1998) *Competition and Planning in the NHS, 2nd Edition: The Consequences of the NHS Reforms*, Stanley Thorne's, Cheltenham.

Schattschneider, E.E. (1960) *The Semi-Sovereign People: A Realist's View of Democracy in America*, Holt, Rinehart and Winston, New York.

Thompson, N. (1996), *Political Economy and the Labour Party*, UCL Press, London.

Willetts, D (1997), *Address to the Royal Society of Medicine*, London, 6 October.

# 3    New Labour's Health Policy: A 'Third Way' to Organise?

STEVE HARRISON and BRUCE WOOD

## Introduction

This chapter is concerned with changing approaches to the making of policy for the organisation (or, more precisely, reorganisation) of the English National Health Service (NHS) over the last thirty years. In summary, there has been a shift away from the presentation of a blueprint as the intended endpoint of reorganisation, and its replacement by the 'bright idea': a rather unspecific vision of how to proceed. However, the election in 1997 of a new Labour government has brought at least some reversal of this trend, which prompts the questions about its own rhetoric: what is the content of the self-proclaimed 'third way' in health policy, and how 'modern' is new Labour health policy? What follows is divided into four main sections. The first describes the 1974 Reorganisation of the NHS, a moment which we take to represent the high point of health policy as a blueprint. The second describes the creation in 1989 to 1991 of the so-called 'internal market' in the NHS, which we take to represent the high point of health policy as a 'bright idea'. (We have considered the process of transition between these states, and the reasons for it, elsewhere; see Harrison and Wood, forthcoming.) The third section examines the NHS organisation policy developed by the post-1997 Labour Government. In our concluding remarks we discern sufficient of a reversion to the 'blueprint' approach to partly justify new Labour's own frequent description of itself and its policies as 'modern'.

## The 1974 Reorganisation

The antecedents of the April 1974 reorganisation of the NHS are to some extent traceable back to the Service's earliest years. The Conservative Governments of 1951 to 1964 were responsible for both the development of the *Hospital Plan* (which, as will be seen below, profoundly affected the 1974 structure) and several reports on the administrative structure of professions and institutions (for a summary, see Harrison 1988 pp12-14). The Labour Governments of 1964 to 1970 exhibited a more sustained and integrated emphasis on questions of management and organisation (a theme continued by the succeeding Conservative Government). First, they instituted, and accepted the recommendations of a number of further reports on such topics. The Salmon Committee, established in 1963 by the Conservatives, recommended a comprehensive, hierarchical management structure for hospital nursing (Ministry of Health 1966), and similar principles were extended to community nursing by the subsequent Mayston Report. A series of joint reports of the (then) Ministry of Health and the medical profession (usually termed the 'Cogwheel' reports after the logo on their cover) urged physicians to recognise their interdependence with each other and with the organisation, and proposed a series of committees within hospitals as the means of integrating specialities and relating them to the local administration (Joint Working Party 1967). The subsequent Zuckerman (1968) and Noel Hall (1970) Reports recommended career structures for NHS scientists and technicians, and pharmacists respectively (Watkin 1975 pp341-9).

The second manifestation of the Labour Government's interest in management and organisation was their concern with the macro-level organisation of the NHS. Consideration of possible reorganisation of general purpose local government had begun in the mid 1960s (Wood 1976) and extensive efforts were made to ensure that the design of a reorganised NHS was both consistent and integrated with parallel changes then being planned for. This design had been carefully developed over a period of several years. The process of its development included extensive consultation via two Green Papers (Ministry of Health 1968; DHSS 1970), both of which discussed organisational design and the various functions of each tier in some detail, and an equally detailed White Paper (DHSS 1972a). The reorganisation was preceded by several years of extensive conceptual and design work by the management consultants Messrs McKinsey and by the Health Services Organisation Research Unit at Brunel University, which produced rather distinctive formal organisational arrangements (see for instance Rowbottom *et al* 1973; Jaques 1978). The plans which took shape over this period survived changes of government from Labour to Conservative in 1970, and back in January 1974, with only minor changes such as the Conservatives' even more explicit emphasis on management (Klein 1983 p91). They were bipartisan attempts to design a 'rational' organisational framework.

The new form of organisation adopted health districts as the operational level of the new service, which was to run hospitals, clinics and community services; they were largely designed around the (nominally 250,000) 'catchment' populations of existing District General Hospitals. Such hospitals, designed and located in accordance with the Conservatives' earlier *Hospital Plan* (Ministry of Health 1962) normally contained an accident and emergency department, all the main medical specialities (with at least two consultants in each) and often a maternity unit. Above the District level of organisation was the Area level, whose mainly planning function for a population of some 400,000 to 800,000 was logically reinforced by its boundaries being coterminous with local government, which continued to be responsible for environmental health and personal social services. (In about one third of cases, these two levels were conflated into 'single district areas'.) Above the Area level were Regions, retained at the insistence of the 1970 to 1974 Conservative Government, but now responsible for oversight of what hitherto had been treated as three virtually separate services (the so-called 'tripartite structure' of 1948): hospitals; GPs, dentists and pharmacists; and community and domesticity services.

These and further details of the new organisation were conveyed to the NHS in a document which became known as the 'Grey Book' (DHSS 1972b), a detailed and densely packed 174 page organisational prescription of structures, and institutional, managerial and professional roles and relationships, including elaborate consultative mechanisms and formal powers of veto. It is difficult to convey the character of this volume in a few sentences, but to describe it as a 'blueprint' is not an exaggeration. Successive chapters discuss organisation in general and of particular skill groups, and management and planning processes. The document contains sixteen detailed diagrams of different segments of DHSS and NHS organisation, specifying functions and relationships between statutory bodies, and managerial and professional relationships within and between them; a key element of this was the system of 'consensus decision making' which was to operate within the various multi-disciplinary top management teams (Harrison 1982). An appendix contains 27 detailed role specifications, together with definitions of key terms such as 'manager', 'accountable', 'monitor' and 'co-ordinate'. The blueprint was uniformly implemented throughout the Service on 1 April 1974, at the same time as corresponding changes to the structure of local government.

The character of the Grey Book was to some extent the reflection of a specific approach to organisation, developed in the Health Services Organisation Research Unit at Brunel University (Rowbottom *et al* 1973).

This approach seems to have been built on the assumption that most organisational problems were, at root, problems of misunderstanding of role; consequently, its prescriptions very much emphasised clarity of definition of roles and relationships. But the Grey Book's approach was also consonant with contemporary received wisdom which stressed planning, integration of social policy and the various health and social services (what became known as the 'joint approach to social policy': Glennerster 1981), professional specialisation (other than in social work) and large-scale institutional operation (Committee on the Functions of the District General Hospital 1969), and eschewed any need for the kinds of experimentation or pilot studies then taking place in other sectors of social and urban policy (Burch and Wood 1983 pp200-3). For whatever reason however, the history and outcome of the 1974 reorganisation of the NHS manifest a clear policy/action distinction; there was a long period of careful planning and design of the new policy, which transcended changes of government and was then adopted almost in its entirety by the government of the day, and implemented nationally and uniformly.

**The 1991 Reorganisation**

The 1991 introduction of the quasi-market was very different from that of the 1974 reorganisation in several respects which constituted a new style of policymaking. The key differences were as follows. First, the process of initial design of the reforms was shorter and more closed than for 1974. The 1991 reorganisation was the product of a Prime Ministerial Review of the NHS, announced by Mrs Thatcher in 1988 as a response to a perceived financial crisis; during the review, its agenda seems to have drifted away from a direct response to this crisis and towards the question of NHS organisation. Moreover, it was conducted informally, largely in secret and uninformed by expert opinion from the field (Lee-Potter 1997), all the review team members being politicians with the exception of Sir Roy Griffiths, the Managing Director of a supermarket chain who had previously advised the government on the management of the NHS (Harrison 1994).

Second, the resultant White Paper *Working for Patients* (Department of Health *et al* 1989), though some 102 pages long, devoted substantial space to Scotland, Wales and Northern Ireland and had a generously spaced and repetitive text containing only the barest account of the proposed 'internal market', the role of Health Authority purchasers, NHS Trusts (providers) and General Practice (GP) Fund Holders. It promised further details in a forthcoming series of working papers on organisational and financial matters. Eleven eventually appeared, some with as few as twelve generously spaced pages, and many (see, for instance Department of Health 1989) also largely innocent of substantive content. As Klein has summarised it 'the White Paper's proposals were little more than outline sketches, even when supplemented by a series of working papers' (1995 p198).

Third, and presumably as a result, even by the formal implementation date of April 1991 aspects of the reorganisation fundamental to the purchaser/provider split, not least the contracting process, had not been thought through, in some cases with disastrous results for individual institutions (Harrison *et al* 1994). Relationships between institutions were adapted as perceived to be necessary and some of these amounted to far more than minor adjustments in government thinking; for instance the relative importance given to competition and co-operation, the importance of GP fund holding rather than health authority purchasing, and the ideal service configuration for Trusts (that is, whether acute and non-acute services should be combined in one institution) all varied substantially between 1991 and 1996. Indeed it is highly significant for our thesis that the 1991 reorganisation permitted the appearance of two separate and logically inconsistent models of purchasing (Harrison 1991), that is by Health Authorities and by GP Fund Holders.

Fourth, the implementation arrangements were not uniform, but rather centred upon a process of annual waves of volunteers for (as the case may be) Trust or Fund Holding status. The criteria for admission of volunteers to the new status were developed 'on the hoof' in parallel with the application process. This allowed ongoing adjustments; thus initial criteria for acceptance of volunteers were relaxed over time to ensure the apparent success in implementation terms of the approach. By 1995, all provider units in England had achieved Trust status, despite considerable evidence that managers had frequently pressed ahead in the teeth of opposition from clinical staff (see, for instance, Peck 1991). By 1996, some 60% of English GPs had become fund holders (Audit Commission 1996), despite considerable initial professional opposition and the known reluctance of many actual 'volunteers' (Harrison and Choudhry 1996). In addition, the Government became quick to seize upon local initiatives, such as 'total' GP fund holding (Mays *et al* 1997) and Trust mergers, and to then recycle them into further nationally defined options for volunteers.

Indeed, there were incentives for managers and senior professionals not only to acquiesce in the innovations, but to volunteer to participate in their development. Early adopters of Trust or Fund Holding status stood themselves to gain, to contribute to the plausibility of the project's success, and to diffuse the perception that this was the direction which others would either be compelled to follow, or would suffer deprivation for not following (Lee-Potter 1997). Some of these incentives were material. Early 'waves' of fund holders were more generously funded than strictly required to achieve equity of purchasing power with Health Authorities (Harrison and Choudhry 1996), and fund holders could retain budget underspends for investment in their practices. Early Trust managers were able to secure higher salaries than those available in other hospitals or paid to Health Authority chief executives. Other incentives may have had more to do with actors' perceptions of enhanced freedom in respect of their work roles (Glennerster *et al* 1994), for instance (in the case of GP fund holders) to employ financial leverage to change the kinds of services provided by hospitals or (in the case of Trust managers) to use the threat of external competition to change medical behaviour in hospitals (Harrison and Pollitt 1994 pp121-5). And there is evidence that yet another incentive for managers was the feeling of being part of a great endeavour, engendered partly by the heavy marketing of the reforms; Day (1992) has graphically, if uncritically, described the mood of excitement shared by those managers present at the teleconferenced launch of *Working for Patients*.

These differences characterise the 'bright idea' approach to NHS reorganisation under the Conservative Governments of 1987 to 1997: secrecy of initial development; a deliberate eschewing of blueprints in favour of the promulgation, in vague terms, of a core set of ideas; and an invitation to relevant actors (which they could not easily refuse) to constitute the formal institutions which would embody these ideas. In terms of implementation, this approach can be seen as highly successful. The absence of a blueprint allowed unannounced policy adjustment to emerge when deemed necessary; for instance early policy emphasis on the role of Trusts gave way to emphasis on Health Authorities' purchasing role after the 1992 General Election campaign in which the 'War of Jennifer's Ear', arising from the reported refusal of the NHS to authorise what was argued to be ineffective surgical treatment in a girl suffering from 'glue ear', played a prominent media role. The absence of a blueprint also blunted potential opposition to the reforms by making it difficult for opponents to seize on concrete proposals to criticise, and the volunteer arrangements both allowed time for the reluctant to become used to the idea of the new status (of Trust or Fund Holder) and to feel that nothing was compulsory. A 'bandwagon effect' was rapidly created. Yet the 1991 reforms were not without conscious direction, and despite the approach described above, they can be seen as having retained a number of central features of Conservative ideology, including incentives for (narrowly-defined) efficiency, a means of challenging the perceived unity of the medical profession, and a broadly anti-statistic preference for markets, rather than planning, as the means of resource allocation.

## Post-1997 Labour policy for NHS organisation

Shortly before the May 1997 general election, the then Conservative Government enacted legislation (the NHS Primary Care Act 1997) which sought further to continue the new style of policy making by its core provision for volunteers to make proposals for breaking down the existing rigid division between primary and secondary care, including the strict financial regime of separate budget heads which underpinned it. Unspecified new organisational forms could be proposed, and initial approval by the Secretary of State on a case by case basis could later be replaced by blanket approval to generic new developments. Early in its office the new Labour Government made limited use of the 1997 Act by approving minor schemes (such as for salaried GPs) in some localities (*Health Service Journal* 18 June 1998, p28), but greater government attention was given to a further NHS reorganisation to replace the 'internal market' system which had been bitterly criticised by the Labour Party while in opposition.

The initial proposals appeared in a White Paper *the New NHS: Modern, Dependable* (Secretary of State for Health 1997) which, despite 86 pages and several diagrams, is actually quite insubstantial. Considerable repetition of central ideas is accompanied by only the sketchiest details of key institutions and processes such as the management of the new Primary Care Groups, the proposed National Institute for Clinical Excellence, the development of local systems of 'clinical governance', arrangements for integrating with the work of local authorities, and funding for patients who receive care outside their home district. The retention of NHS Trusts is implicit acknowledgement of the success of some of the Conservative's reforms, and the phrase 'go (ing) with the grain' of trends is used no less than seven times. The 1997 White Paper was far from a blueprint of the 1974 variety and, as in 1989, was to be fleshed out by further committees (Maynard 1998). The two main elements of new Labour health policy are 'clinical governance' and the creation of 'primary care groups'.

## Clinical governance

A consultation document *A First Class Service: Quality in the New NHS* (NHS Executive 1998) was issued some seven months after the original white paper. This is another physically substantial (87-page) document, which does move nearer to providing a blueprint for certain aspects of NHS organisation policy than has been the case since 1974. Clinical governance is there defined as

> "a framework through which NHS organisations are accountable for continuously improving the quality of their services and safeguarding high standards of care by creating an environment in which excellence in clinical care will flourish" (NHS Executive 1998 p33).

Taken alongside the use of the term 'governance' rather than 'government', this formulation is perhaps calculated to be anodyne: in any event, it conveys little of substance. In the official literature, the term is mainly used to refer to measures *within* hospitals but since such measures cannot be understood other than in relation to the activities of a number of new external institutions, 'clinical governance' is used here to cover both. Within hospitals, the key element in the new arrangements is that chief executives will effectively become responsible for the clinical, as well as the financial performance of their institutions; legislation is proposed which will place upon Trusts a statutory duty for the quality of care. Outside hospitals, the three key institutions will be the National Institute for Clinical Excellence (NICE), the Department of Health, and the Commission for Health Improvement (CHImp).

NICE will be established in 1999 with the role of undertaking 30 to 50 evidence-based appraisals per annum of new or existing clinical interventions (such as drug treatments, surgical procedures or physiotherapy treatments), at least some of which are likely to be subcontracted to existing academic centres with relevant expertise. Such appraisals may result in the production of 'clinical guidelines' for the management of relevant medical conditions, or in recommendations to the Department of Health that particular treatments should not be introduced to the NHS without further trials. It is made clear that such appraisals will include evidence of *cost*-effectiveness as well as clinical effectiveness. NICE will also be responsible for giving its *imprimatur* to particular models of clinical audit for use in hospitals.

In addition to this central specification by NICE of *clinical* models, there is to be central specification of *service* models, beginning with coronary heart disease and mental health. 'National Service Frameworks' (NSFs) will be developed as a means of defining the pathway through primary, secondary and tertiary care which a particular type of patient will be expected to pass. Although developed in consultation with experts and consumers, NSFs will be nationally promulgated by the Department of Health, and compliance will be a dimension of NHS performance management.

Third, CHImp will be established as a statutory body 'at arm's length from government' (NHS Executive 1998 p51), a model which appears to borrow from that of the Audit Commission. CHImp will 'conduct a rolling programme of reviews, visiting every.... Trust over a period of around 3-4 years' (p53). Such reviews will include local compliance with clinical guidelines issued by NICE, and with NSFs. In addition to routine reviews, the Secretary of State, regional offices of the NHS Executive or health authorities will be able to initiate inquiries where local problems are suspected.

The activities of these external institutions to which, given the new responsibilities of chief executives outlined above, there will presumably be a managerial motivation to respond, have clear implications for the *internal* control of hospitals (Black 1998). For each NICE guideline, a local 'lead clinician' will be identified as having responsibility for leading local implementation. Departures from NICE recommendations will 'be challenged locally' (NHS Executive 1998 p22). Although the previous Conservative government decreed that all doctors should take part in medical audit, this seems not to have been enforced; however, from 1999 all hospital doctors will be required to participate in national speciality-based audit programmes as well as in the existing voluntary confidential enquiries into maternal mortality, preoperative mortality, stillbirths and infant mortality, and suicide and homicide by persons with mental illness.

**Primary Care Groups**

Originally promulgated whilst Labour was still in opposition through an unusually detailed speech in December 1996 by the then Shadow Secretary of State for Health, Chris Smith, Primary Care Groups (PCGs) will federate groups of general practices so as to produce aggregate practice populations of from 46,000 to 257,000. PCGs may take one of four forms. At level 1, the least developed form, PCGs support the HA in commissioning care for its population, acting in an advisory capacity. At level two, PCGs will take devolved responsibility for managing the budget for health are in their area, formally as part of the HA. At level 3, PCGs become more independent of the HA, and are therefore to be solely accountable for the budget, and from April 2000 PCGs will be able to acquire the status of NHS Trusts (level 4). Where a budget is held, it will be a cash-limited unified budget for providing primary health care and purchasing hospital and community services, though HAs will continue to commission highly specialised services such as transplant surgery.

Unlike GP Fund Holding (which is to be abolished), membership of a Primary Care Group (operational from April 1999) will be compulsory for all GPs, and there will be strict rules about the geographical coverage of such groups. PCGs are intended to develop around 'natural communities' rather than groups of like-minded GPs. Although the self-employed status of GPs apparently will not change, PCGs will have governing bodies accountable to HAs and required to enter into annual 'accountability agreements' with them. There will be a requirement to produce a (public) annual accountability report, presumably relating to the preceding year's accountability agreement. Whilst there are potential non-material incentives resulting from the proposal of four different entry levels to Primary Care Group status, and some GPs certainly perceive an incentive to achieve the highest level as quickly as possible in order to maximise their independence from the Health Authority, GP enthusiasm for PCGs is far from general (*Health Service Journal* 28 May 1998, p3; 2 July 1998, p11; *British Medical Journal* 28 March 1998, p1025).

**Concluding Remarks**

Three of the key elements of the 'bright idea' approach practised by the Conservative administration in respect of 1991 reorganisation initially applied to Labour policy. The White Paper was developed in a secret process and gave only bare details of policy but largely abandoned the fourth element, that is the strategy of implementation by volunteers, underpinned by material incentives. Subsequently published instructions, however, have left considerably reduced scope for policy to be developed 'on the hoof'. This altogether more 'top-down' flavour, can be seen in the specificity of both policy content and intended policy outcomes. The *content* of policy handed down to the NHS has become more specific, with less scope for NHS actors to shape it for themselves. For instance, PCG membership is compulsory, albeit with some initial choice of entry level, and much of the apparatus of clinical governance is built round national institutions with centrally determined functions. The *intended outcomes* are also less interactive than were those of Conservative policies in the sense of eschewing markets in favour of planning. Expressed more crudely, there are signs of significant centralisation at work. In the discourse of academic politics, the term 'governance' is commonly used to contrast with the term 'government': that is to signify a mode of co-ordination based on networks rather than on hierarchy (see, for instance, Rhodes 1996). It is ironic therefore that the term has been officially appropriated to refer to a set of rather hierarchical arrangements for controlling members of the medical profession.

What sort of a 'third way' does all this represent? Every new Labour policy field seems to have its own usage of this slogan; for the NHS the claim is that the reforms avoid both 'the old centralised command and control systems of the 1970s' and 'the divisive internal market system of the 1990s' (Secretary of State for Health 1997 para 2.1). Yet in proposing what looks very much like a new form of centralisation, more like hierarchy than network, the supposed NHS 'third way' trades on the myth of an earlier system of NHS command and control which does not correspond to the findings of contemporary empirical studies of NHS management, which clearly revealed managers as 'diplomats' rather than controllers (Harrison 1988; Harrison *et al* 1992). The direction of new Labour health policy is as yet far from clear. We have indicated that, in comparison with the Conservatives, there are some continuities but important discontinuities in both the process of policymaking and the content of policy. And of course it is far from self-evident that these policy differences will produce differences in outcome; the impact on the medical profession also remains to be seen.

# References

Audit Commission (1996), *What the Doctor Ordered: A Study of GP Fund Holders in England and Wales*, HMSO, London.

Black N. (1998), 'Clinical Governance: Fine Words or Action?' *British Medical Journal* 316: pp 297-8.

Burch M., Wood B. (1983), *Public Policy in Britain*, Martin Robertson, Oxford.

Committee on the Functions of the District General Hospital (1969) *Report*, HMSO, London.

Day P. (Ed) (1992), *Managing Change: Implementing Primary Health Care Policy*, University of Bath Centre for the Analysis of Social Policy, Bath.

Department of Health (1989), *Self-Governing Hospitals: An Initial Guide*, HMSO, London.

Department of Health, Welsh Office, Scottish Home and Health Department, and Northern Ireland Office (1989), *Working for Patients*. Cm 555. HMSO, London.

DHSS (1970), *The Future Structure of the National Health Service* (the Crossman Green Paper), HMSO, London.

DHSS (1972a), *National Health Service Reorganisation: England*, Cmnd 5505, HMSO, London.

DHSS (1972b), *Management Arrangements for the Reorganised National Health Service*, HMSO, London.

Glennerster H. (1981), 'From Containment to Conflict: Social Planning in the Seventies' *Journal of Social Policy* 10(1), 31-51.

Glennerster H., Matsaganis M., Owens P., Hancock S. (1994), *Implementing GP Fund Holding: Wild Card or Winning Hand?* Open University Press, Buckingham.

Harrison S. (1982), 'Consensus Decision Making in the National Health Service: A Review' *Journal of Management Studies* 19(2), 377-94.

Harrison S. (1988), *Managing the National Health Service: Shifting the Frontier?* Chapman and Hall, London.

Harrison S. (1991), 'Working the Markets: Purchaser/Provider Separation in English Health Care' *International Journal of Health Services* 21(4), 625-35.

Harrison S. (1994), *Managing the National Health Service in the 1980s: Policymaking on the Hoof*, Avebury, Aldershot.

Harrison S., Choudhry N. (1996), 'General Practice in the UK National Health Service: Evidence to Date', *Journal of Public Health Policy* 17(3), 331-46.

Harrison S., Hunter D. J., Marnoch G., Pollitt C. (1992), *Just Managing: Power and Culture in the National Health Service*, Macmillan, London

Harrison S. and Pollitt C. (1994), *Controlling Health Professionals*, Open University Press, Buckingham.

Harrison S., Small N. and Baker M. R. (1994), 'The Wrong Kind of Chaos? The Early Days of a National Health Service Hospital Trust' *Public Money and Management,* 14(1), 39-46.

Harrison S., Wood B. (forthcoming), 'Designing Health Service Organisation in the UK, 1968 to 1998: from Blueprint to Bright Idea and 'Manipulated Emergence', *Public Administration*.

Jaques E. (Ed) (1978), *Health Services: Their Nature and Organisation and the Role of Patients, Doctors and the Health Professions*, Heinemann, London.

43

Joint Working Party on the Organisation of Medical Work in Hospitals (1967) (Chairman Sir George Godber) *First Report*, HMSO, London.

Klein R. E. (1983), The Politics of the National Health Service, Longman, London.

Klein R. E. (1995), *The New Politics of the National Health Service*, Longman, London.

Lee-Potter J. (1997), *A Damn Bad Business: the NHS Deformed*, Gollancz, London

Lyon D. (1994), *Postmodernity*, Open University Press, Buckingham.

Maynard A. K. (1998), 'Curbing Private Enterprise' *Health Service Journal*, 12 March p21.

Mays N., Goodwin N., Bevan G., Wyke S. (1997), *Total Purchasing: A Profile of National Pilots*, King's Fund, London.

Ministry of Health (1962), *A Hospital Plan for England and Wales*, Cmnd 1604, HMSO, London.

Ministry of Health (1968), *National Health Service: The Administrative Structure of the Medical and Related Services in England and Wales*, HMSO, London.

Ministry of Health and Scottish Home and Health Department (1966), *Report of the Committee on Senior Nursing Staff Structure*, HMSO, London.

NHS Executive (1998), *A First Class Service: Quality in the New NHS*, Department of Health, London.

Peck E. (1991), 'Power in the National Health Service: a Case Study of a Unit Considering NHS Trust Status' *Health Services Management Research* 4(2), 120-30.

Rhodes R. A. W. (1996), 'The New Governance: Governing Without Government' *Political Studies* 44(4): 652-57.

Rowbottom R., Balle J., Cang S., Dixon M., Jaques E., Packwood T., Tolliday H. (1973), *Hospital Organisation*, Heinemann, London.

Secretary of State for Health (1997), *The New NHS: Modern, Dependable*, HMSO, London.

Watkin B. (1975), *Documents on Health and Social Services: 1834 to the Present Day*, Methuen, London.

Wood B. (1976), *The Process of Local Government Reform 1966-74*, Allen and Unwin, London.

# 4 Variations on a Theme: New Labour, Health Inequalities and Policy Failure

MARK EXWORTHY and MARTIN POWELL

## Abstract

The New Labour Government of 1997 has stated that they wish to achieve fair access within the NHS and reduce the health gap between rich and poor. Labour's variation on a theme is to turn the Conservative policy failure regarding health variations to a policy success in reducing health inequalities. This paper examines the relevance of a model of policy failure (Wolman 1981) to New Labour's claims. It seeks to determine whether the Wolman framework can provide clues to the probability of policy success. In particular, does New Labour's approach constitute a paradigm change so as to turn previous policy failure into policy success? It is claimed that Wolman's (1981) framework does have some efficacy in generating pertinent questions about New Labour's desire to address health inequalities. It suggests although there are hints of a paradigm change in some areas, many problems still remain and policy success might depend on whether political priorities will enable the expensive scattergun approach of waiting list reduction to be employed.

## Introduction

The prominence of health inequalities has varied throughout the fifty or so years of the NHS. In the early years policy making and expenditure allocation were largely incremental, with the result that the health inequalities followed the broad patterns inherited from the period before the NHS. These inequalities started to be recognised and addressed in the 1960s and 1970s (Klein 1995; Powell 1997). However, some received more attention than others. For example, there were major attempts to address geographical and client group inequalities. Social class inequalities were highlighted in the Black Report, set up by the 1974 Labour Government but

45

rejected by the incoming Conservative Government of 1979 (see Townsend et al 1992). Inequalities of race and gender tended to receive little attention by policy makers (Powell 1997, 1998).

During the years of the Conservative Governments of 1979-1997, the 'I' word — inequalities — was little mentioned in government circles, with the preferred term being health variations. Causes of these variations were seen to result from individual, behavioural rather than structural, materialist reasons (DH 1992, 1995: see Wainwright 1996). The New Labour Government of 1997 has stated that they wish to achieve fair access within the NHS and reduce the health gap between rich and poor. In other words, Labour's variation on a theme is to turn the Conservative policy failure regarding health variations to a policy success in reducing health inequalities.

This paper examines the relevance of a model of policy failure (Wolman 1981) to New Labour's claims. It seeks to determine whether the Wolman framework can provide clues to the probability of policy success. In particular, does New Labour's approach constitute a paradigm change so as to turn previous policy failure into policy success?

This paper is divided into three sections. The first examines the means and ends of New Labour's approach to reducing health inequalities. Does New Labour seek new policy goals? Is it pursuing these with new policy mechanisms? The second section introduces Wolman's (1981) model of policy failure. The third section examines whether Wolman's model provides useful insights into New Labour's policies regarding health inequalities.

**New Labour; New Paradigm?**

New Labour claims that fairness will be at the top of its health agenda (e.g. Goddard and Smith 1998; Bevan 1998). For example, the 1997 Labour Election Manifesto (Labour Party 1997) stated that over the five years of a Labour Government the NHS would be rebuilt. 'Labour commits itself anew to the historic principle: that if you are ill or injured there will be a national health service there to help; and access to it will be based on need and need alone.' Certainly, the new government made some rapid moves on equity. Within two weeks of the Election, the new Minister for Public Health, Tessa Jowell claimed that Labour had a 'New mission to tackle inequalities that lead to ill health' (DH 1997b), recognising the impact that poverty, poor housing, unemployment and a polluted environment have on health. In July 1997 the former Chief Medical Officer, Donald Acheson, was commissioned to produce a 'second Black Report', with an inquiry into inequalities in health.

According to the NHS White Paper (DH 1997a) one of the six principles of the 'new NHS' is to renew the NHS as a genuinely national or 'one nation' service characterised by 'fair access' to services, ending the unfairness, 'unacceptable variations' and 'two-tierism' of the Conservative internal market. The 'New NHS' advances a number of mechanisms to achieve greater equity. At the national level, there will be national service frameworks, and new institutions of the National Institute for Clinical Excellence (NICE) and the Commission for Health Improvement (CHImp). It has been claimed that the 'one nation NHS' may be achieved by the centralising tendency and emphasis on hierarchy evident elsewhere in Labour's policy, illustrated by 'naming and shaming' and centrally appointed 'hit squads' (see e.g. Boyne 1998; Klein 1998; Clarence and Painter 1998; Powell 1999).

At local levels, the new Primary Care Groups (PCGs) will be the main commissioning agents in the NHS. PCGs are organisations with an executive board led by GPs, covering an average of 100,000 population. Health Improvement Programmes (HIPs) will be the local strategy for delivering health and health care. One of the main objectives of the new Health Action Zones (HAZs) will be to reduce health inequalities (see DH 1999). HAZs are area-based policies located in some of the areas of worst health, which have certain flexibilities not enjoyed by other areas. There is a strong emphasis on local partnership — or the 'collaborative discourse' (Clarence and Painter 1998) — as the means of reducing inequalities. As many of the causes of inequality lie beyond the control of the NHS alone, partnerships must include not only alliances within the NHS, but also embrace organisations outside the service. There will be a new statutory duty of partnership placed on NHS bodies and local authorities.

The Green Paper 'Our Healthier Nation' (DH 1998a) is seen as the follow-up to the first strategy for health (as opposed to health care) in England of the Conservatives, entitled the 'Health of the Nation' (DH 1992). It seeks to improve the health of the population as a whole and to improve the health of the worst off in society in order to narrow the health gap. This document extends the earlier notions of partnership and co-operation upwards to include central government and downwards to include individuals, families and communities. Subsequently, Secretary of State for Health, Frank Dobson announced that the Government was committed to a 'public health crusade against inequalities' (DH 1998b). The Green Paper claims that 'connected problems require joined up solutions'. The strategy involved a so-called 'contract for health' in which stakeholders — government, public agencies and individuals were required to meet their 'responsibilities to improve health'. The 27 targets of the Health of the Nation were abandoned and replaced by four targets on heart disease and stroke, accidents, cancer and mental health. These national targets could be supplemented by local targets. The Green Paper did not set targets to reduce the health gap, but they may be introduced by a later White Paper set to follow the Acheson Report.

The Acheson Report (1998) produced 39 recommendations — 'the 39 steps'. Like Black, Acheson pointed out that many of the factors which influence health such as poverty and unemployment and poverty lie outside the NHS. Indeed, the one section in the report on the NHS might be contrasted with the eleven sections dealing with issues outside the service. Welcoming the Report, Frank Dobson stated that 'The whole Government...is committed to the greatest ever reduction in health inequalities'. He claimed that many of the recommendations were (already) being addressed through current policies (DH 1998c).

**Wolman's Model of Policy Failure**

There is an extensive literature examining policy failure, focusing on why great expectations centrally are dashed locally (Pressman and Wildavsky 1973; see Rothstein 1998 for a recent review). Wolman's (1981) framework for evaluating 'programme performance' or, in a more anglicised version, 'policy outcome', is a potentially useful device but has hitherto been neglected in policy analysis. Like any model, it needs to be applied and adjusted (as Wolman himself recognises) in order to determine a sense of what strategies designs or patterns of behaviour are likely to lead to policy success. According to Wolman, policy formulation consists of five sequential stages:

- problem conceptualisation,
- theory evaluation and selection,
- specification of objectives,
- programme design and
- programme structure.

Similarly, Wolman argues that policy implementation consists of five stages:

- resource adequacy,
- management and control structure,
- bureaucratic rules and regulation,
- political effectiveness and
- feedback and evaluation.

Criticism can be aimed at Wolman's distinction between policy formulation and implementation, the sequential nature of policy formulation and the clear-cut division between activities. It is often accepted that the distinction between policy formulation and implementation is a false dichotomy because of the autonomy enjoyed by street level bureaucrats (e.g. Lipsky 1980; Hill 1997). Since there are several sites at which policy is 'made' (both centrally and locally), policy is formulated and re-formulated and also implemented and re-implemented at multiple sites. Inevitably, much of this debate rests on clear definitions of what constitutes policy, formulation and implementation. Wolman offers a highly linear and rationalist view of policy process as well as overlooking the wider structural forces acting upon the policy process and stakeholders. However, this framework does offer a broad set of issues which appear to have some relevance for New Labour's attempts to reduce health inequalities. Although the dichotomous distinction between formulation and implementation is simplistic, it is maintained here for its heuristic value. We focus on Wolman's first five stages of formulation as it is premature at this stage to examine implementation.

## New Labour, Health Inequalities and Policy Failure

*Problem Conceptualisation*

Wolman (1981: 436) argues that the way in which a 'problem' is conceptualised affects policy objectives and the nature and design of policies intended to cope with the problem, resulting in vagueness and lack of direction throughout the entire formulation and carrying out process. The end result is perceived to be a program which has failed to solve a problem even though no one is quite sure what the problem is.

Hence, why are health inequalities viewed as a problem? Is there agreement on the role of the NHS in reducing health inequalities, given that it is generally agreed that the key determinants of health are located outside the service? The work of Kingdon (1984) is a useful starting point in addressing these issues. Kingdon (1984) argues that whether issues floating in the 'primeval soup' become translated into decisions, actions and policy depends on the conjoining of three policy streams. The 'problem stream' concerns the ways in which issues become problems that organisations decide to tackle. The 'politics stream' concerns the mechanisms and dynamics of pressures groups and public opinion and changes in government or post-holder. The 'policy stream' concerns not simply the official policies sanctioned by government in response to specific issues but also the range of proposals offered by the broader policy community and academia.

It has been known that gradients in health status have existed for at least 150 years since Chadwick's Report on the Sanitary Condition of the Labouring Population of Great Britain of 1842 (Klein 1988; Macintyre 1997; Acheson 1998). More recent evidence is summarised in the Black Report and the Health Divide (Townsend et al 1992) and the post-Black avalanche of studies (e.g. summaries in Davey Smith et al 1994; Benzeval et al 1995; Macintyre 1997). It is generally argued by Labour politicians and academics that the Conservative Governments saw such gradients as 'differences' and 'variations', which were not a legitimate area for government action, rather than 'inequalities' which are a legitimate area for government action. For example, Frank Dobson claimed that the previous government pretended that the problem of health inequalities did not exist, and banned the term (Hansard 1998: col. 1225). According to Tessa Jowell, 'for years we've had a few warm words, no action and an outright denial from some that there even are such things as inequalities in health' (DH 1999). In other words, the policy window remained closed due to a lack of political will (e.g. Wainwright 1996; Black 1996; Saltman 1997). This is not a completely accurate view. First, recognition of 'variations' *did* lead to some response such as the setting up of a DH working group (DH 1995) and the ESRC Programme into 'Health Variations'. It would be more accurate to say that the discourse of variations influenced the *type* of response, which tended to be in terms of exhortation to individual behaviour rather than in government action (cf Macintyre 1997; see below). Second, it is far from simple to deconstruct the term 'inequality' in terms of an operational policy definition (see below). Certainly, New Labour claims that it will take the problem of health inequalities (rather than variations) more seriously than the Conservatives. This is reflected in the setting up of the Acheson Inquiry, and possibly greater links with the 'policy networks' concerning health inequalities. However, while the problem and politics streams suggest a greater propensity for action, the policy stream is arguably still less clear (see below).

Wolman (1981: 437) claims that the better the understanding of the causal processes, the more likely it is to devise policies to deal with it successfully. The most obvious starting point is the Black Report's explanations of health inequalities. The report offered four possible explanations: artefact, natural selection, cultural and structural (Townsend et al 1992; Davey Smith et al 1994; Macintyre 1997; Green and Thorogood 1998). Note that this framework does not allow any role for health care in reducing health inequalities (but see Mackenbach et al 1989; Benzeval et al 1995; DH 1995). A variation on the structural theme has been provided by Wilkinson (1996) who has argued that health inequality is explained by income differentials and levels of social integration; in terms of relative rather than absolute levels of resources. The Green Paper on public health (DH 1998a) recognised that the causes of ill health are complex and many of the factors are still not clear. The Acheson Report (1998) argued that 'the weight of scientific evidence supports a socio-economic explanation of health inequalities'. However, this 'model' is composed of different 'layers' including individual lifestyle and the socio-economic environment. This is in line with recent accounts which attempt to move beyond the dichotomy between structure and agency, and stress the interaction between different explanations (Davey Smith et al 1994; Benzeval et al 1995; Macintyre 1997; Bartley et al 1998).

New Labour claims that its explanatory framework varies from the Conservatives in recognising structural factors such as poverty in addition to individual, behavioural factors (DH 1997b, 1998a,b,c Warden 1998; but see Wainwright 1996). In the House of Commons Debate on the public health Green Paper (Hansard 1998) Frank Dobson argued, while the previous government concentrated on lifestyle and factors beyond the control of individuals, our Green Paper (DH 1998a) intends to tackle the root causes of bad health (col. 1225). Conservative health spokesman, John Maples responded that New Labour was building on the Conservative Health of the Nation (DH 1992), but then seemed to undermine his case by stating that 'I believe that far more ill health is caused by smoking, the overuse of alcohol, bad diet and lack of exercise'. He continued that people can and must take more responsibility for their own health. The government must not give people an alibi for their bad habits by allowing them to blame circumstances for everything...Getting people to improve their lifestyle is the key (cols. 1228-9). As Labour Chair of the

Parliamentary Health Committee, Dave Hinchcliffe put it, the public health policy appeared to consist almost entirely of insulting remarks by Mrs Edwina Currie about northern males (col. 1230). Labour claims that its 'third way in public health' involves a balance between individual and collective responsibility in a 'contract' between government and the people (DH 1998a). While Labour claims to be, paraphrasing a famous Blairism, tough on ill health and tough on the causes of ill health, some MPs such as the distinctly 'Old Labour' Hinchcliffe and the Liberal Democrat Peter Brand implied that having embraced the 'I word' (inequalities), New Labour should rediscover the 'r word' (redistribution) (cols. 1230-1). New Labour's public health policy may well be charting a middle course as it has been attacked from both left (see Warden 1998; Chadda and Limb 1998; Moore 1998) and right (Waugh 1999).

*Specification of Objectives*

According to Wolman (1981: 439), without clear objectives it is difficult to design a programme, to administer it completely, or to assess its performance. Vague and/or unobtainable objectives make a successful programme impossible. Are some health policy objectives more important than others? Are all desired objectives feasible? What is the nature of the trade-off between desirability and feasibility?

For evidence of inequity to be admissible, there must be some agreement of what would constitute equity. Such an agreement has never been reached by academics or policy-makers. Equity is a contested concept (Le Grand 1982; Klein 1988; Powell 1997; Saltman 1997). Perhaps the most common form is that equity is composed of 'equal $x$ for equal $y$' (Sen 1992). In other words, equity consists of equality statements. In terms of health policy the relevant dimensions are what and whom. The 'equality for whom' issue addresses age, sex, class, ethnicity and geography whilst the 'equality of what' issue concerns expenditure, access, provision, use and outcome. These two dimensions can be brought together to form an equity matrix (see Powell 1997: 129). Terms such as equal outcomes by social class (Townsend et al 1992) are thus partial notions, and can be seen in terms of individual cells within this matrix. Rather than a single notion of equality, there are a multiplicity of possible measures. In short, equality becomes equalities (Rae et al 1981). It follows that stating that 'Equity was a founding principle of the NHS and is central to Government policy' (Acheson 1998) does not advance analysis very far. Before equity can be audited (Benzeval et al 1995; Acheson 1998), it must be defined and operationalised. Consequently, progress towards monitoring equity is at a rudimentary stage (Oakley et al 1996; Macintyre 1997).

It has recently been concluded that much of the literature on equity in health is more complex than was previously thought (e.g. Macintyre et al 1996; Smaje 1995, 1998; Powell 1997; Goddard and Smith 1998). Moreover, the precise equity objectives of the NHS remain unclear (e.g. Le Grand 1982; Benzeval et al 1995; Powell 1997; Bevan 1998). The NHS has sought different equity objectives at different times and even different objectives at the same time. For example, the Designated Area Policy for GPs throughout the period of the NHS and the Hospital Plan of the 1960s sought equal provision. On the other hand, the Resource Allocation Working party (RAWP) of the 1970s specified their objective in terms of 'equal access for equal need', but allocated in terms of equal expenditure for equal need (see e.g. Beech et al 1990; Powell 1997; Bevan 1998). Consequently it is difficult to come to any clear verdict on the level of equity achieved by the NHS (e.g. Benzeval et al 1995; Powell 1997).

Despite (or perhaps because of) Labour's emphasis on fairness, there is little indication of the desirability of individual concepts of equity from the many possible types (above). Within the NHS, the gold standard soundbite seems to be 'fair access' (DH 1997a). Outside the NHS, the Green Paper on public health (DH 1998b: 5) aims 'to narrow the health gap'. Frank Dobson has stated that 'Poor people are ill more often and die sooner. And that's the greatest inequality of them all — the inequality between the living and the dead' (Warden 1998). We interpret this to mean that the most important inequality is that of outcome between social classes (cf Townsend et al 1992)! The operational definitions of equity which flow from these concepts are not fully clear. The White Paper (DH 1997a) argues that we need new measures of NHS performance. It outlines six dimensions including health improvement, fair access, effective delivery of appropriate services, efficiency, patient/care experience and health outcomes of NHS care. However, these do not seem particularly valid or reliable. The effectiveness dimension is redundant, since if health care does not affect outcome (the final measure), it is ineffective. There is no suggestion of how to operationalise the measures. For example, how exactly is 'fair access' measured? The White Paper (DH 1997a) states that the 'NHS contribution must begin by offering fair access to health services in relation to people's needs, irrespective of geography, class, ethnicity, age or sex. For example, ensuring that black and minority ethnic groups are not disadvantaged in terms of 'access to services'. However, few studies have examined the criterion of 'equal access for equal need', not least due to the continuing problems of measuring access' (see Powell 1995, 1997; Goddard and Smith 1998). Outside the NHS, a possible paradigm shift can be pointed out. Frank Dobson speaks of 'our unprecedented commitment to tackle inequalities in health. No previous Government has ever set itself such ambitious targets' (DH 1998c). Dobson is correct that, contra Black, no government has made an explicit commitment to reduce inequalities of health status, but critics pointed out that the Green Paper - despite the rhetoric - avoided setting such targets (see below).

*Programme Design*

Wolman (1981: 440) notes that it may not be possible to design an acceptable programme to solve every problem. This may be because we do not understand the causes of the problem and/or the problem is too complex; because we do not know how to intervene or have the means of doing so; or because the programme may be impracticable or contain negative side effects. Wolman focuses on a number of issues such as causal efficiency; political feasibility; technical feasibility; and secondary consequences.

It has been suggested above that we do not have a clear understanding of the causes of health inequalities. As Davey Smith et al (1994: 141) put it, 'The central question- why are there inequalities in health? remains unanswered'. Moreover, it is often forgotten that one of the reasons for Conservative Secretary of State for Social Services, Patrick Jenkin's rejection of the Black Report was concerned with uncertainty over the effectiveness of Black's call for greater expenditure in dealing with the problems identified (in Townsend et al 1992). Solutions are often posed at high levels of generality. For example, Green and Thorogood (1998: 75) claim that 'global explanations...may be of value in thinking about policy at the macro level'. However, as Klein (1988: 10) pointed out a decade previously, no one since the days of Chadwick has attempted to deny that there is a link between social conditions and health: the challenge is to identify with precision which aspects of deprivation are crucial. Broad-brush solutions such as 'improving housing' or 'reducing income differentials' are likely to be expensive. They are likely to have *some* effect on reducing health inequalities, but other policies may be more cost effective. An analogy might be hitting a target with a blunderbuss as opposed to a rifle. The evidence base for evidence-based policy making remains limited; we do not know which policy levers are the most effective in reducing health inequalities (Powell 1998). It appears that our knowledge of the *precise* mechanisms to reduce health inequalities are still limited (Arblaster et al 1995; Benzeval et al 1995; Oakley et al 1996; Mackenbach and Gunning-Schepers 1997; Macintyre 1997; Goddard and Smith 1998). In short, in spite of New Labour's emphasis on 'what counts is what works' we know neither what counts nor what works.

There may be a trade-off between the desirability of equity goals and the feasibility of achieving them. For example, equal outcome *may* be a desirable aim but it may be easier to achieve equal access. In other words, policy makers may 'own' or control equal access more than equal outcomes (Carter et al 1992).

Moreover, as with other organisations, the goals that the NHS pursues are multiple and often conflict (Carter et al 1992; Maxwell 1984). There is little recognition of the potential trade-offs between concepts such as equity and efficiency; or between health gain and reducing inequality. For example, many traditional health education campaigns tend to increase inequalities as the most 'cost-effective' success is usually achieved when targeted at the middle class (Klein 1988; Acheson 1998; Waugh 1998). It is well known that equal access is impossible because we cannot occupy the same unit of space. Everyone cannot live next door to a hospital. There would be a significant loss of efficiency if all remote Scottish islands had teaching hospitals (Maynard 1988; Powell 1995). The NHS has never been, and could never be, a *perfectly* equitable service (Klein 1988; Powell 1997). The dilemma between equity and other goals is unlikely to be a simple binary division, between equity *or* another goal but rather between degrees of equity and degrees of efficiency (or any other objective). However, the knowledge base is insufficient to calculate the precise trade-off.

Finally, technically feasible policies may be politically impossible. For example, Acheson's 'socialist-style programme for redistributing resources from the rich to the less well off' (Laurance 1998) is unlikely to appeal to New Labour. Similarly, New Labour has rejected the 'nanny state social engineering' ascribed to the 'old left' (DH 1998a). New Labour claims that it wishes to end *unacceptable* variations (DH 1997a), but provides no identification or justification for these (see Klein 1988; Maynard 1988).

Behind the rhetoric, it appears that Labour does recognise some of the problems associated with feasibility. According to the public health Green Paper (DH 1998a), 'The Government does not propose at this stage to set national targets to narrow health inequalities between social classes, different parts of the country, ethnic groups and men and women...Because the causation is complex and many factors inter-react, it is not possible to set realistic quantified targets for greater health equality at this stage'. Many commentators accused the government of 'bottling out'. Criticising the failure to set targets, David Player of the Public Health Alliance argued that 'This is the litmus test — if they fail on this, they fail entirely' (Chadda and Limb 1998; Moore 1998). According to Light (1998: 442-3) the government shows no interest in reducing the large income gaps that have grown extensively over the past 15 years. There are serious limits to how egalitarian any health care system can be in an increasingly inegalitarian society. It is unclear whether New Labour's reluctance to set targets is due to ignorance about policy levers or concerns about the financial and electoral cost of redistributive policies.

*Programme Structure*

The main concern here is whether the administrative structure through which the programme design is to be carried out facilitates or frustrates the accomplishment of programme objectives (Wolman 1981: 446). Applied to health, the most important problem appears to be the efficacy of co-ordination. Are there problems of inter-agency co-ordination between NHS agencies and/or between NHS and outside agencies?

New Labour has emphasised a collaborative discourse (Clarence and Painter 1998), with 'joined up government' at the centre and governance (Rhodes 1997) at the periphery. The various health policy outlets in central government which have addressed health inequality complicate the notion of a single 'centre'. These include the Social Exclusion Unit (run by the Cabinet Office), the Department of Health and the NHS Executive. New Labour aims to end 'Departmentalism' and argues that complex problems require joined-up solutions. For example, it is acknowledged that reducing health inequalities will require action across areas such as education, employment and housing (SEU 1998; DH 1998a,b,c). In her first major speech as Health Minister, Tessa Jowell argued that big factors cannot be changed by single Government departments, but require 'shared agendas' across Government (DH 1997b). She later claimed that 'In previous times, all too often it appeared that the Department of Health had policies for the NHS and social services on the one hand, a separate policy for public health on the other, and "never the twain shall meet". Those days are over. Now we have one, coherent and mutually reinforcing agenda'. (DH 1999).

Similarly, at the local level there are numerous sites at which policy is formulated and/or implemented such as Health authorities, NHS trusts local authorities, community and voluntary organisations and the independent sector. Governance has been defined as 'self-organising, inter-organisational networks' (Rhodes 1997). It denotes a fundamental change from government in which hierarchical relationships previously provided the transmission mechanism between the centre and the periphery towards network structures which have enabled local agents to be more autonomous, creative and entrepreneurial (Hoggett 1996). The Conservative 'health of the nation' policy stresses the need for local coalitions or 'healthy alliances', but the shift towards governance has at least rhetorically been accelerated under New Labour. Hudson (1998: 26) argues that 'the Labour Government's concept of partnership distinguishes it from the Conservatives' approach. Certainly, there is great stress on partnership and co-operation in the White and Green Papers on health. However, Higgins (1998) points out the nature of partnerships are not clear. It may be difficult to achieve such 'partnership'. Mere exhortations to 'add value through creating synergy between the work of different agencies' will not be enough. As Light (1998) puts it, waving a big stick, Ministers growl 'The Government will establish a new statutory duty for NHS Trusts to work in partnership with other NHS organisations' as if partnerships can come from legal coercion (cf Clarence and Painter 1998). 'Paper partnerships' and statutory meetings can be enforced, but effective partnerships are unlikely to result simply from legislation, imposed by administrative fiat. The history of joint working between health and social care is not encouraging (Hudson 1998). Health Minister Milburn recognised that joint working will not be easy, with different cultures-accounting, funding and legal frameworks and so on between the NHS and LAs (Davies 1997). On the other hand, new partnerships may break up old relationships. Many individual organisations have close working relationships and are closely bound together in mutual dependence (Exworthy 1998). These embedded relations effectively limit the degree of independent action by any single organisation or individual. Hasty partnerships of organisations with different goals, styles, cultures and structures of accountability could have parallels with some of the more unsuccessful pairings of 'Blind Date'.

It is possible that New Labour envisages a new paradigm of partnership. First, 'joined up government' at the centre through initiatives such as the Social Exclusion Unit may reduce 'departmentalism'. Second, local partnership may be viewed in a more totalising sense, as more than a synonym for public sector — private sector collaboration. Opportunity and responsibility, community and empowerment are central to New Labour rhetoric: individuals, families, communities, local authorities, voluntary and private organisations must all play their part in a national 'contract' for health (DH 1998a). HAZ bids subscribe to an idea that partnership seems to be simultaneously both bottom-up and top-down; individuals, their problems and their diagnoses of solutions are valued equally alongside the views and actions of state and voluntary agencies. North Staffordshire Chief Executive, Richard Priestley has summarised the new perspective on empowerment succinctly: 'it is not a question of doing it *for* people. That is passé...A lot of it is about empowerment of individuals and communities ... (the) aim is eventually to get residents taking part in commissioning services across the agencies' (quoted in Chadda 1998: 15; cf SEU 1998). It is not yet clear that HAZs will offer anything different beyond the standard form of NHS empowerment which rarely extends beyond tokenist involvement of a community elite (Winkler 1987). Finally, the emphasis on partnership in HAZs seem to be an admission that there is something lacking in the partnership arrangements for non-HAZ areas.

## Conclusion

Wolman's (1981) model does have some efficacy in generating pertinent questions about New Labour's desire to address health inequalities. This aim is certainly more problematic than some of the rhetoric implies. The nature of the problem, and the role of the NHS remain uncertain. For all the work addressing the explanatory framework of inequalities in health, knowledge of causes remains deficient. The goals to be achieved are not clear, or set in the context of trade-offs among multiple goals or feasibility. Knowledge regarding mechanisms to reduce inequalities are still unclear in terms of causal and efficiency and political feasibility. Finally, 'partnership' and 'joined up government' is still at the 'apple pie' stage. There seems to have been little thought devoted to policy mechanisms beyond the soundbite. Labour does not appear to have learned the lessons of previous policy failures. In this sense, Labour is still finding the transition from opposition to government difficult.

On the other hand, there are hints of a paradigm change. At least in the rhetorical sense, New Labour views tackling health inequalities as a higher priority. The 'third way' in public health has shifted the balance between individual and collective responsibility, and sees a more extensive role for government. The importance of achieving equity in health and health care is stressed, even if operational definitions are vague and targets have not (yet) been set. Joined up government at the centre and the new partnerships of governance may yet prove to deliver a winning hand. Policies to combat social exclusion, including the welfare to work initiatives, may pull appropriate policy levers almost by mistake. In the last analysis, whether health inequalities are reduced may depend on their political priority. New Labour is determined to deliver its commitments on issues such as hospital waiting lists. This is proving to be more difficult than the initial rhetoric suggested, and eventually the option which was first ruled out, throwing more inputs at the problem, was taken up. If Labour is equally determined to reduce health inequalities, it may be achieved by the expenditure blunderbuss rather than the policy rifle, but some shots will still hit the target.

**Acknowledgements**

The research upon which this paper is based is funded by the Economic and Social Research Councils Health Variations Programme (phase 2) (award ref. no. L128251039). We are grateful for their support.

59

# References

Acheson, D. (chair) (1998), *Independent Inquiry into Inequalities in Health.* The Stationery Office, London.

Arblaster, L. et al (1995), *Review of the Research on the Effectiveness of Health Service Interventions to Reduce Variations in Health* CRD, University of York, York.

Bartley, M. et al (1998, Ed), *The Sociology of Health Inequalities,* Blackwell, Oxford.

Beech, R. et al (1990), Spatial Equity in the NHS in A. Harrison (Ed) *Health Care UK 1990,* Policy Journals, London 44-61.

Benzeval, M. et al (1995, Ed), *Tackling Inequalities in Health,* Kings Fund, London.

Bevan, G. (1998), Taking Equity Seriously, *British Medical Journal,* 316, 3 January, 39-42.

Black, D. (1996), Inequitable Variation, *Journal of the Royal College of Physicians of London,* 30(1), 8-9.

Boyne, G. (1998) Public Services under New Labour: Back to Bureaucracy?, *Public Money and Management,* 18(1), 43-50.

Carter, N. et al (1992), *How Organisations Measure Success,* Routledge, London.

Chadda, D. (1998), 'Using Their Initiative', *Health Service Journal,* 22 January, 15.

Chadda, D. and Limb, M. (1998), Anger as Green Paper Falls Short on Inequalities and Funding Pledges, *Health Service Journal,* 12 February, 9.

Clarence, E. and Painter, C. (1998), Public Services under New Labour: Collaborative Discourses and Local Networking, *Public Policy and Administration,* 13(1), 8-22.

Davey-Smith, G. et al (1994) Explanations for Socio-Economic Differentials in Mortality, *European Journal of Public Health,* 4, 131-144.

Davies, P. (1997) 'Slaying the Paper Tigers', *Health Service Journal,* 23 October, 10-11.

Department of Health (1992), *The Health of the Nation.* HMSO, London.

Department of Health (1995), *Variations in Health. What Can the DH and the NHS Do?* DH, London.

Department of Health (1997a), *The New NHS,* Stationary Office, London.

Department of Health (1997b), *New Mission to Tackle Inequalities That Lead to Ill Health — Tessa Jowell.* Press Release 97/95, 15 May.

Department of Health (1998a), *Our Healthier Nation.* Stationary Office, London.

Department of Health (1998b), *Government Committed to Public Health Crusade against Inequalities — Dobson.* Press Release 98/298, 20 July.

Department of Health (1998c), *Government Committed to Greatest Ever Reduction in Health Inequalities Says Dobson.* Press Release, 98/547, 26 November.

Department of Health (1999), *Health Action Zones are the Frontline in the War on Health Inequalities.* Press Release 99/38, 21 January.

Exworthy, M. (1998), 'Localism in the NHS Quasi-Market. *Environment and Planning C; Government and Policy,* 16, 449-462

Goddard, M. and Smith, P. (1998), *Equity of Access to Health Care,* CHE, University of York, York.

Green, J. and Thorogood, N. (1998), *Analysing Health Policy: A Sociological Approach.* Harlow: Longman.

Hansard (1998), House of Commons Debates, 5 February (Debate on 'Our Healthier Nation').

Hill, M. (1997), 'Implementation Theory: Yesterdays Issue?' *Policy and Politics,* 25(4), 375-385.

Hoggett, P. (1996), 'New Modes of Control in the Public Service', *Public Administration*, 74, .9-32.

Higgins, J. (1998), 'HAZs Warning', *Health Service Journal*, 16 April, 24-5.

Hudson, B. (1998), 'Prospects for Partnership', *Health Service Journal*, 16 April, 26-7.

Kingdon, J. W. (1984), *Agendas, Alternatives and Public Policy*. Little Brown, Boston.

Klein, R. (1988), Acceptable Inequalities in D Green (Ed) *Acceptable Inequalities*, IEA, London, 3-20.

Klein, R. (1995), *The New Politics of the NHS*, Longman, Harlow.

Klein, R. (1998), Why Britain is Re-Organising Its National Health Service — Yet Again, *Health Affairs*, 17(4), 111-125.

Labour Party (1997), *New Labour Because Britain Deserves Better* (Election Manifesto), Labour Party, London.

Laurance, J. (1998), Children at Risk as Health Inequality Between Rich and Poor Increases, *Independent*, 27 November, 6.

Le Grand, J. 1982. *The Strategy of Equality*. George Allen and Unwin, London.

Light, D. (1998), Managed Care in a New Key: Britain's Strategies for the 1990s, *International Journal of Health Services*, 28(3), 427-444.

Lipsky, M. (1980), *Street Level Bureaucracy*. Russell Sage Foundation, New York.

Macintyre, S. et al (1996), Gender Differences in Health: Are Things as Simple as They Seem? *Social Science and Medicine*, 42, 617-624.

Macintyre, S. (1997), The Black Report and Beyond, *Social Science and Medicine*, 44(6), 723-45.

Mackenbach, J. et al (1989) The Contribution of Medical Care to Inequalities in Health, *Social Science and Medicine*, 29(3), 369-376.

Mackenbach, J. and Gunning-Schepers, L. (1997), How Should Interventions to Reduce Inequalities in Health be Evaluated, *Journal of Epidemiology and Community Health*, 51, 359-364.

Maxwell, R. (1984) Quality Assessment in Health, *British Medical Journal*, 300, 919-922

Maynard, A. (1988), Inequality in Health Care is in General Desirable in D. Green (Ed) *Acceptable Inequalities?*, IEA, London.

Moore, W. (1998), Action Stations, *Health Service Journal*, 22 January, 16.

Oakley, A. et al (1996). *Variations in Health. Report of a Research Consultation Exercise*, Institute of Education, London.

Powell, M. (1997), *Evaluating the National Health Service*, Open University Press, Buckingham.

Powell, M. (1998), Policy Evaluation in the Past, Present and Future of the NHS in R. Skelton and V. Williamson (Eds) *Fifty Years of the National Health Service*. University of Brighton, Brighton, 87-101.

Powell, M. (1999) New Labour and the Third Way in the British NHS, *International Journal of Health Services*, 29(2), 353-370.

Powell, M. A. (1995), On the Outside Looking in, *Health and Place*. 1(1), 41-50.

Pressman, J. and Wildavsky, I. (1973), *Implementation*. University of California Press, Berkeley.

Rae, D. et al (1981), *Equalities*, Harvard University Press, Cambridge, MA.

Rhodes, R. (1997), *Understanding Governance*, Open University Press, Buckingham.

Rothstein, B. (1998), *Just Institutions Matter*, Cambridge: Cambridge University Press.

Saltman, R. (1997), Equity and Distributive Justice in European Health Care Reform, *International Journal of Health Services*, 27(3), 443-453.

Sen, A. (1992), *Inequality Reexamined*, Clarendon Press, Oxford.

Smaje, C. (1995), *Health, 'Race' and Ethnicity*, King's Fund Institute, London.

Smaje, C. (1998), Equity and the Ethnic Patterning of GP Services in Britain, *Social Policy and Administration*, 32(2), 116-131.

Social Exclusion Unit (1998) *Bringing Britain Together*, Cm 4045. Stationery Office, London.

Townsend, P. et al (1992), *Inequalities in Health*. Penguin, Harmondsworth.

Wainwright, D. (1996), The Political Transformation of the Health Inequalities Debate, *Critical Social Policy*, 16(4), 67-82.

Warden, J. (1998), Britain's New Health Policy Recognises Poverty as Major Cause of Illness, *British Medical Journal*, 316, 14 February, 495.

Waugh, A. (1998) The Rich Must Eat Sawdust, *Sunday Telegraph*, 18 October, 41.

Wilkinson, R. (1996), *Unhealthy Societies*, Routledge, London.

Winkler, F. (1987), Consumerism in Health Care: Beyond the Supermarket Model, *Policy and Politics*, 15, 1-8.

Wolman, H. (1981), 'The Determinants of Program Success and Failure', *Journal of Public Policy*, 1(4), 433-464.

# 5  GP Independence under Threat? The First Wave Primary Care Act Pilot Site Contracts

ROD SHEAFF and ANDREW LLOYD-KENDALL

## The Changing GP Contract

In creating the NHS the fundamental policy objective was to extend free access to healthcare to the whole population. Policy makers took for granted that general practice would remain the first point of access for non-emergency patients in the new system. To secure GPs' participation in the NHS the then Labour government thought it necessary to guarantee that GPs would remain 'self-employed' medical contractors, either individually or as partnerships (Honigsbaum 1979). Independent contractor GPs would provide all primary medical care except for hospital accident and emergency services, sexually transmitted disease and school clinics.

Establishing the NHS also necessitated more substantial public funding for healthcare. The Beveridge Report had anticipated that healthcare would be publicly financed by extending the National Insurance scheme through which general practice had partly been financed since 1911 (Beveridge 1942). Such a method readily accommodated independent-contractor general practice. From the early 1950s, however, governments tacitly recognised that it was futile to expect the NHS to be financed predominantly from National Insurance, which had effectively became a supplementary income tax. By 1994-5 it represented only 13.4% of NHS income (Appleby 1996). By then, however, NHS methods for paying GPs and the General Medical Services (GMS) contract under which this was done had already settled into a pattern which strongly reflected the pre-1947 system and the (now outdated) assumption that the NHS general practice would be funded in a similar way. With adaptations, this pattern has endured ever since. The NHS has continued to pay GPs by a complicated mixture of capitation fees and 'item of service' (fee-for-service) payments. These payments were nationally uniform and minutely specified in the 'red book' — the *General Medical Services Terms and*

*Conditions of Service* (Department of Health, annually). Formally these arrangements made GPs directly accountable to the Secretary of State.

Not that this meant that NHS managers tightly controlled the GPs. NHS managers had only three formal channels through which to influence what GPs did in return for these payments. A GP could be disciplined for breaching the terms of his or her General Medical Services (GMS) contract but these terms covered practice administration and finance rather than the nature or quality of clinical activity, about which they stipulated almost nothing. In extreme — and rare — cases it was possible to report a GP to the General Medical Council for unethical or grossly incompetent practice. Equally rarely, patients could sue a GP through the civil courts. Otherwise GPs exercised clinical autonomy much as NHS hospital consultants did but were even more insulated from NHS management. GMS payments for medical care itself were not cash limited (although reimbursements of the costs of running the GPs' surgeries became cash-limited in the 1980s). So British general practice continued for forty years.

By the 1990s this system was coming under challenge. The terms of the national GMS contract were extended in 1990 to include target payments for achieving specified levels of health promotion activity (vaccination and immunisation levels, child health surveillance and, initially, anti-smoking advice); an attempt to offer GPs direct financial incentives for implementing national health policy. NHS general medical services themselves were not cash limited, unlike hospital and community health services. Consequently non-cash limited GMS spending grew faster that other categories of NHS spending during the 1990s (OHE 1996), a growth and freedom from control increasingly incongruous with financial management practice elsewhere in the public sector (including the NHS). A government 'listening exercise' in 1996 revealed that some GPs and HA managers had also become dissatisfied with the rigidity of the GMS contract (Department of Health 1996). The GMS contract was proving an obstacle to attracting GPs into under-doctored urban areas and to removing some of the unevenness in the quality and availability of NHS primary healthcare. The incentives for a GP to work in an urban area evidently did not compensate for the increased workload and (sometimes) an unattractive practice environment. Changes in the hospital sector were also placing increasing demands on primary healthcare, in particular demands for higher levels of community care resulting from shortening lengths of hospital stay and a shift away from inpatient care for chronically ill and elderly patients. Meanwhile the spread of GP fundholding had enabled GPs to start extending practice-based primary health services and shifted the balance of medical power away from hospitals towards general practice.

One of the Conservative government's last acts was the *NHS (Primary Care) Act* of 1997, 'designed to allow those who wish to have flexibility to explore different models for the provision of Personal Medical Services (PMS) to test the practical implications of these models and the benefits they could bring' (Department of Health 1997c, p5). The 1997 Act permits three fundamental changes to the 1911 system of general practice built into the NHS. First, it permits independent practitioner GPs (both individuals and partnerships) to make locally tailored, 'practice-based' contracts with their Health Authority (HA). These Personal Medical Services (PMS) contracts replace the national GMS contract and can differ from it in whatever ways the GPs and HA agree, provided that the amount and quality of GP services are no worse under the PMS contract than they were under GMS arrangements and that certain national requirements for information-collection are still met. Unlike GMS payments for medical care itself, PMS contracts are cash limited. Secondly the Act permits HAs to commission general medical services from other NHS providers besides independent-contractor GPs, breaking the independent-contractor GPs' monopoly. Alternative providers include NHS community health service (CHS) trusts) and 'nurse-led' organisations. Thirdly, independent-contractor GPs are permitted to employ salaried GPs, as are NHS trusts and other new providers including nurse-led providers. In April 1998 a first wave of Primary Care Act Pilot Site (PCAPS) projects began operating experimentally under these new arrangements.

The 1997 Act made these provisions on a pilot basis only but the 1999 *Health Bill* makes them permanent, allowing Primary Care Groups (PCGs) to make PMS contracts with independent contractor GPs, to employ salaried GPs and to obtain personally medical services from other NHS sources. Further, PCG membership is mandatory for GPs and most NHS primary healthcare will eventually be provided through the primary care trusts (PCTs) into which PCGs will develop. The *Health Bill* thus opens the way for PCGs to replace HAs as the body to whom GPs are contracted and for PCGs to make PMS contracts with PCAPS-like providers their preferred form of governance in primary healthcare.

Some BMA Council members among others have seen these developments as threatening GPs' independent status (Anon 1999A) in two ways. One is that 'A salaried option will become increasingly attractive to many GPs and unavoidable for many others' (Reggler 1998, p7). Dr. Reggler may be anticipating that PCGs which have had difficulty recruiting

GPs or want to 'buy out' GMS contracts will do so by offering GPs salaried status on relatively generous terms but not GMS contracts in future. The other putative threat is that GPs will become more subject to lay control (Anon 1999B) even though they remain independent contractors. The Department of Health anticipated that under the 1997 Act PHC providers' 'accountability to local communities and to health authorities will be delivered via the explicit contractual and consultation arrangement on which the pilot schemes will be based' (Department of Health 1997c p5). Current health policy documents are understandably coy about defining explicitly what 'GP accountability' specifically means. However an obvious reading is as 'GP accountability to the government, via NHS management, for implementing those of the government's current health policy objectives which depend on the GPs'. Of the two mechanisms for accountability, consultation only occurs when a GP or practice initially transfers from a GMS to a PMS contract or when HAs plan substantial changes in services. Their contracts are the more permanent and routine medium of GP accountability to NHS management and other lay bodies, above all the government. The most cogent interpretation of the perceived threat to contractor GPs' independence is to see 'loss of independence' as the obverse of GP 'accountability', with PMS contracts as an important means of realising that accountability. PMS contracts will be means of constructing and managing a 'principal-agent' relationship (cp. (Williamson 1975, Niskanen 1979, Smith et al. 1997, Walsh 1995) with the HA as principal and the GP its agent. This threat to GPs' independence is therefore as great as the PMS contracts' mechanisms for stipulating what GPs will do and ensuring that they do it are powerful.

This chapter therefore examines the first wave of PMS service contracts as one source of evidence about how far these two putative threats to GP independence have been realised to date.

**The Content of Contracts**

A 'classical' conception of contracting holds that a contractual system for ensuring provider accountability for policy implementation must be so designed that:

1.  The benefits which the contract requires the agent to provide do actually help to realise the principal's (here, the government's health policy) objectives.
2.  The agents accept such contracts.

3. The agents actually implement the contract, hence:

3a. Payments to the agent must be conditional upon the agents actually providing the specified benefits to the principal; otherwise payment, or some non-financial benefit, will be withheld, reduced or renegotiated.

3b. To motivate the agents, the payments and penalties must make a non-trivial practical difference to them.

3c. Before paying the principal must verify that the agent has actually satisfied the contract (or, if the agent is paid prospectively, there must be a mechanism to check the agent's performance after the event and to recoup the payments if the contract has not been satisfied).

For present purposes the main limitation of the classical conception is that contracts are not necessarily the only *de facto* incentives that NHS healthcare providers face. Informal relationships such as trust between principal and agent (here, HA and GP) and professional organisations coexist alongside the contractual relationship. These additional relationships are likely to influence whether and in what ways contracts are actually implemented, besides influencing GPs' accountability and independence in their own ways. Many contextual assumptions (e.g. about local epidemiology or service deficiencies) would be redundant for purely contractual purposes and not necessarily appear in the finished contract even though they gave rise to the objectives and fees, terms and conditions that are explicit. Contract documents are bound to overlook any unwritten terms, conditions, or agreements ('understandings'). They do not need to repeat other, concurrent written agreements or statutory requirements, for instance the regulations limiting non-GPs' freedom to prescribe. Neither does a contract taken alone show how far either party actually exercises the rights which it gives them (Smith 1998). Contracts state minimum requirements which can be exceeded. For example only two of the contracts analysed below stipulated monthly financial monitoring. Yet monthly monitoring of budgets is normal management practice in NHS Trusts and the authors have independent evidence that such monitoring occurs in at least two sites whose contracts are less onerous. Recognising these limitations in mind, contracts are nevertheless one of the most important sources of documentary evidence about whether PMS contracts do in practice threaten GP independence as has been alleged.

Eighty-five PCAPS projects began in 1998. Some HAs and PCAPS sites made 'PMS-plus' contracts. These are also cash limited but the contractor provides a wider range of services than under GMS and PMS-only contracts. We obtained 66 contract documents from the sites and NHSE Offices. They cover 71 projects (84%) because in one NHSE Region all PCAPS projects but one used the same contract, altering only the dates, signatories' names, addresses, sums of money etc. [1] We analysed these contracts to discover how far they stipulate what the GP is to do and what arrangements are established to ensure that the GPs have satisfied the contract. We also investigated how far the contracts created scope for salaried general practice and for alternatives to independent-contractor GP provision of primary healthcare. We noted:

a. Who the PCAPS providers are, especially whether any new types of provider were emerging to contest the independent-contractor GPs' monopoly.
b. What benefits the PCAPS providers are to provide for the HA.
c. How far the contract objectives reflect objectives stated in contemporary (1998) health policy documents.
d. Financial and non-financial incentives and penalties for the PCAPS providers, and any conditions thereof.
e. What provision the contracts make to monitor the provider's performance and for the principal to respond accordingly (Sheaff & Peel 1993).

**Is GP Provision Being Contested?**

Of the 100 English Health Authorities 45 had first wave PCAPS sites, 16 of them more than one. Table 1 shows what kind of providers the first wave PCAPS were. (In all tables N = number of contracts. Percentages are rounded and do not total 100% when contracts fall into more than one category.)

Table 1: PCAPS Providers

| Main Provider Contractor | N | % |
|---|---|---|
| General Practice | 39 | 55 |
| NHS Trust | 28 | 39 |
| Nurse-led Practice | 3 | 4 |
| | | |
| New Professional Roles | | |
| Nurse Practitioner | 10 | 14 |
| Salaried GP | 44 | 62 |

Only 31 sites (43%) involved new forms of provider organisation although a slight majority of contracts allowed salaried general practice. All contracts save one permitted 'subcontractors' (meaning above all out-of-hours treatment of patients by deputising services or GP co-operatives) although 37% of the contracts required the HA to be notified of or approve any subcontracting. Despite recent policy emphasis on collaboration with Social Services (Department of Health 1997a, 1998) only one contract (1%) explicitly named them as a co-provider, although 5 (7%) stipulated that PCAPS providers would offer patients advice on how to access social services.

## What Services Are GPs To Provide?

As noted, one condition for being a PCAPS scheme is that the range and standard of services be no less than under GMS contracts. The main activity of all PCAPS sites is still providing primary medical care. PMS contracts are of two types. By implication PMS-only contracts retain general medical practice in its GMS form without adding or subtracting services. Over two thirds (69%) of first wave PCAPS contracts were of this kind. For general practice itself only a change of contractual form occurs, although not a trivial one; for one thing, GP medical care becomes cash limited. For another, a PMS contract can specify such requirements as surgery hours. 32 contracts (45%) stipulated hours of GP or other service provision whilst 15 (21%) only required that providers should abide by whatever hours of service were stated in their practice leaflet. From the contracts it was impossible to tell whether hours of service had changed from previous levels. Further, a PMS contract can specify how general practitioner medical services will relate to other providers' services, as table 2 shows for the PMS element in all the contracts we analysed.

Table 2: PMS Element

| Community Health Services to be Available | N | % |
| --- | --- | --- |
| Community Nursing | 22 | 31 |
| Physiotherapy | 9 | 13 |
| Impacts on Other Services | | |
| Social Service Access | 16 | 23 |
| Reduced Hospital Utilisation | 15 | 21 |
| Increase CHS Utilisation | 7 | 10 |

Contracts mentioning the impacts on other services tended to so in broad terms (e.g. 'to reduce the number of older people admitted to hospital and nursing homes') rather than quantified targets. Just over a third (30) of the contracts expressly specified services for priority care groups (table 3).

Table 3: Priority Groups

| Care Groups | N | % |
|---|---|---|
| Elderly | 10 | 14 |
| Homeless | 6 | 8 |
| Young Families | 5 | 7 |
| Disease Groups | | |
| Chronic Disease | 31 | 44 |
| of which: | | |
| Diabetes | 14 | 20 |
| Asthma | 10 | 14 |
| Mental Health | 15 | 21 |

Forty-two contracts (59%) claimed to be based on a needs assessment (either existing or in progress) but few indicated why these groups were chosen nor gave any other evidence of a needs assessment beyond the bare claim.

All the foregoing points apply to both PMS and 'PMS-plus' contracts. 22 sites (31% of those) analysed had 'PMS-plus' contracts. Table 4 shows what additional services the PMS-plus contracts covered

Table 4: 'Plus' Elements in PMS+ Contracts

| | N | % |
|---|---|---|
| Social Services Advice | 5 | 14 |
| Health Promotion | 4 | 6 |
| Endoscopy | 3 | 4 |

Few contracts mentioned integrated working between district nurses, health visitors and practice nurses. None specified any division of clinical labour even where a nurse practitioner was to be introduced.

Quality of clinical work is a matter in which one might expect GPs to be acutely sensitive to threats to their independence. Table 5 indicates how the contracts specified the quality of primary medical care.

Table 5: Quality Specifications

|  | N | % |
|---|---|---|
| Complaints procedure | 56 | 79 |
| GP Qualifications | 46 | 65 |
| Guidelines, Protocols, Pathways | 43 | 61 |
| Standard of Premises | 40 | 56 |
| Clinical Audit | 32 | 45 |
| Non-medical Healthworkers' Competence | 31 | 44 |
| Evidence-based practice | 22 | 31 |
| Expert Consensus on Good Practice | 11 | 15 |
| Patient-defined Outcomes | 3 | 4 |

Clinical guidelines, protocols, or pathways were frequently mentioned only as a requirement that the provider should develop them during the contract term. In these cases the introduction of clinical guidelines, protocols or pathways (assuming it occurs) can be attributed to the use of PMS contracts. Specifications for patient complaint procedures ranged from baldly stating the requirement to pages of detail.

The NHS Executive have already stated that they will evaluate the first wave of PCAPS in terms of the policy objectives of 'quality', 'fairness', 'accessibility', 'responsiveness' and 'efficiency' in primary healthcare (Department of Health 1997c). 'Quality' is increasingly understood in terms of healthcare effectiveness and evidence-based medicine. 'Efficiency' includes measures to relieve demand on NHS hospitals and to contain NHS costs. 'Equity' or 'fairness' includes increasing access to GMS for under served populations (in city centres, for certain ethnic minorities, homeless people, travelers) (Department of Health 1997b). HAs will increasingly be encouraged to pursue these objectives in partnership with other local agencies such as social services (Department of Health 1998). Table 6 counts the contract objectives related to current health policy.

Table 6: Contract objectives

|  | N | % |
|---|---|---|
| Effective Service Delivery | 52 | 73 |
| Good Employment Practice | 48 | 68 |

| | | |
|---|---|---|
| Fair Access | 46 | 65 |
| Public Involvement | 40 | 56 |
| Improve Population Health | 38 | 54 |
| Improve Patient and/or Carer Experience | 35 | 49 |
| Efficiency | 32 | 45 |
| Implement HA Strategy | 30 | 42 |
| PHCT Skill Mix Changes | 30 | 42 |
| Implement HImP | 4 | 6 |
| (None) | 16 | 23 |

The new NHS stipulates that HA should make Health Improvement Plans as a strategic framework within which to contract service provides (Department of Health 1997a). Such plans barely existed in 1998 so it is hardly surprising that few contracts mentioned them. Other national policy objectives tended to be mentioned briefly and in broad terms. Specific, operationalised objectives such as Gray and Donaldson (1996) recommend were rarer than the above counts suggest. Health objectives were seldom translated into outcome indicators. The level of detail about patient involvement in deciding and monitoring services ranged from simply stating a requirement to do it to specifying methods; occasionally surveys or focus group, more often (10 contracts, 14%) by consulting the Community Health Council (CHC). 'Efficiency' was almost always expressed verbally as 'value for money', not quantified. Mostly the contracts concentrated on inputs, transposing existing GMS guidance on methods of payment, GP qualifications and contract administration into the PCAPS settings and stating GPs' right of return to pre-PCAPS status. Many sites simply photocopied parts of national guidance documents into the contract. The management consultancy's contract document was in these respects similar.

**Incentives for GPs**

Whether strong incentives for new ways of working really constitute threats to GP independence is debatable. But supposing for the sake of argument that they do, what incentives did the PCAPS contracts offer? 55 contracts (77%) provided for block payments, usually calculated by totalling the previous year's capitation and other GMS payments but then making marginal adjustments (e.g. to reflect known population changes). Since the levels and quality of general medical services were to be no lower than before, and since providers' other costs (surgery premises and staff, pharmaceuticals etc.) were more-or-less unchanged, this approach implicitly retained 'red book' levels of payment to the GP(s). In 18 contracts (25%) the block payment excluded the additional incentive payments for GPs to reach the vaccination and immunisation targets which were introduced in the 1990 GMS contract. These were still on offer as before. Seven contracts (10%) stated a figure for GP salary but without comparing it to the doctors' income under GMS. Table 7 summarises conditions under which payments to the provider would be renegotiated.

Table 7: Payment Renegotiation

|                                    | N  | %  |
|------------------------------------|----|----|
| Contract Unworkability             | 54 | 76 |
| Force Majeure                      | 29 | 41 |
| List Size Changes                  | 28 | 39 |
| 'Uncontrolled Events'              | 28 | 39 |
| Inflation                          | 20 | 28 |
| Provider Fails to Satisfy Contract | 10 | 14 |
| Provider Activity Volume           | 5  | 7  |

'Uncontrolled events' usually meant changes in nationally agreed GMS payments.

Only three contracts (4%) prescribed penalties and two (3%) a bonus, all attaching to administrative activity (data provision) not healthcare targets. 17 contracts (24%) anticipated that the provider might achieve savings on the cost of providing the contracted services after the GPs had received a specified personal income (typically last year's income plus nationally recommended yearly uplift). 15 (21%) let providers keep all savings. In seven cases the savings could only be spent on purposes that the HA approved, in eight only on developing patient services. No contracts forbade spending savings on GPs' premises although both the Audit Commission (1995) and the press have criticised GP fundholders for doing so because the GP would benefit personally when he or she eventually sold the premises. No contracts differentiated savings due to efficiency gains from savings due to over-estimating costs and payments initially.

**Monitoring Provider Performance**

Table 8 outlines monitoring requirements in the contracts.

Table 8: Monitoring

| Frequency | N | % |
|---|---|---|
| Annual report | 23 | 32 |
| Three-monthly | 24 | 34 |
| Monthly | 2 | 3 |
| Monitor | | |
| HA Only | 53 | 75 |
| HA & CHC | 6 | 8 |
| HA & Provider | 5 | 7 |
| HA & Users | 4 | 6 |
| Dispute handling | | |
| NHS Arbitration System | 54 | 76 |
| Informal Discussion then Independent Arbitration | 36 | 51 |

Surprisingly, no contracts stipulated exception reporting (i.e. that providers report any cases where services were not provided as specified). 15 contracts (21%) required nationally recognised data formats (which include a few internationally recognised formats). However, many providers were probably already supplying monitoring data in standard formats before 1998. 15 contracts (21%) proposed to compare PCAPS data with historical data for the same services, and another three (4%) with other providers' activity and costs. Most contracts (52, i.e. 73%) stipulated a formal evaluation of the PCAPS project to which they applied, although several of the 29 contracts (41%) that mentioned external evaluation simply reprinted documentation supplied by the Kings Fund without amendment. In general, therefore, PCAPS contracts required more monitoring data than GMS contracts.

Contracts which mentioned such matters at all stated that if the provider was at fault in failing to satisfy the contract, the first resort would be contract renegotiation. Most contracts mentioned the NHS arbitration, preceded in some cases by informal discussion and arbitration. Surprisingly, 17 contracts (24%) did not mention NHS arbitration system at all; possibly this was a piece of context which they simply took for granted.

## GP Independence Threatened?

In the light of this evidence from contracts, how realistic is it for GPs to expect either that they will become more subject to lay control even whilst remaining independent contractors, or that salaried practice will gradually overtake independent contracting?

The results above indicate that in 1998 salaried general practice was still a rarity. The 44 contracts allowing for salaried practice have to be seen as a proportion of over 25,000 English GPs in over 6000 practices. Even these figures may overstate the scale of salaried general practice because the fact that the contract permits salaried general practice does not mean that the option has actually been implemented. Recall that only seven contracts stated a precise salary for salaried GPs. On the other hand, rare and small pockets of salaried general practice do exist outside PCAPS. Nurse-led schemes are rarer still. Defining 'nurse-led' as 'a nurse filling a contractor role similar to that of an independent-contractor GP', there are just three. 28 NHS Trusts have become small-scale GMS providers.

Scarce though they be, these experiments nevertheless suggest that specific alternative organisational models to independent medical contractor provision of PHC appear to be practicable, although a final judgement has to be reserved until it becomes clearer that non-GP providers can satisfy their contract objectives to the same extent that independent-contractor GPs do. They offer prototypes which PCTs, indeed government, could decide to promote more widely. They therefore make general practice more contestable; for the first time in fifty years independent practitioner GPs face the possibility of competition or substitution by other forms of PHC provision beside community pharmacies and private general practice. So that 'threat' does now exist, although on a tiny scale yet.

A more immediate question is therefore whether the above evidence suggests that PMS contracts threaten to make formerly independent GPs the agents of HAs and the government? A majority of first wave PCAPS contracts do appear to have changed the governance of general practice rather than services or levels of GP income. The contracts mostly do reflect current national policy and service objectives for NHS primary healthcare in a much more specific and targeted way than in the GMS contract. Where any are stated, financial incentives tend to be for providers to contain or reduce the costs of service provision. The contracts allow for annual adjustments, renegotiation, or premature cancellation. Superficially these results might seem to suggest that PMS contracts do serve to some extent as a medium for constraining GPs to act as agents implementing HA, and thereby national, policies. However this conclusion assumes that if necessary the HAs can apply these constraints effectively. The contracts usually stated national policy objectives so briefly and broadly as to prevent specific monitoring of providers' achievements. Payments and incentives were rarely linked to these objectives, or to specific changes in the nature or quality of clinical practice. Whilst many of the contracts make early attempts to specify the quality of clinical services, they commonly rely on GPs to write the specifications. The contracts betray fragmentary and underdeveloped monitoring practices and information systems, which are supposed to be made good as the PCAPS projects proceed. Cancelling contracts is likely to be of limited use to HAs as a response to providers' non-compliance. Returning to GMS status would not be a major change for many PCAPS providers. HAs have few alternative providers for most services involved, except perhaps for community health services which other NHS Trusts could supply.

In two respects GPs under first-wave PMS contracts find themselves in a similar position to that first-wave NHS Trusts in 1991, although the similarities lie more in the absence rather than the presence of threats to independence. Stipulations of the health impact of GPs' clinical work are virtually non-existent in the first wave PMS contracts, stipulations of the quality of general practice and evidence-based medicine far from universal. Through such contracts it would be it virtually impossible for HAs to monitor and manage GPs' clinical activity in much detail even they wanted to and even if the necessary information systems existed which, on evidence from the contracts, they largely do not. A second similarity is that mostly the first cycle of PMS contracts differ little from their GMS predecessors in terms of payment structures, monitoring and how they define established as opposed to new services. Often the new contracts only 're-label' existing arrangements (cp. Bennet & Ferlie 1996). They seem to serve the limited purposes of an insurance for GPs that the PCAPS experiments will not jeopardise their practice and personal incomes, and for HAs that service levels will not decline. Wittingly or not, HAs and GPs seem to be replicating the 'smooth take-off' and 'no surprises' policy of the first year of HCHS contracting (1991-2).

PMS contracts therefore appear to threaten non-salaried GPs' independence only in the sense that rather weak instruments of management have replaced a near vacuum; not much of a threat yet.

These conclusions only reflect the first wave of PMS contracts. A second has already been announced and if *The new NHS* and the *NHS (Primary Care) Act* are implemented in a similar way to *Working for*

*Patients* others are likely to follow. Neither should we forget that informal relationships between GPs and HAs are likely to become stronger as a consequence of PMS contracting. Professional organisations are also likely to play a larger role in these relationships as clinical governance develops in primary healthcare. The mechanisms by which NHS managers will in future be able to influence GPs are therefore likely to become stronger than they now appear from PMS contract documents taken alone.

If PMS contracts for independent-contractor GPs eventually become the norm in NHS general practice, the NHS internal market will in effect have been extended into primary care (although for electoral reasons the process will certainly not be described that way). HAs were the principal in the first wave PMS contracts. The 1999 *Health Bill* also allows Primary Care Trusts to make PMS contracts with GPs. Both the government and many GPs expect GP representatives to play a prominent role in PCT management. GPs would then participate on both sides of PMS contract negotiations. Public health doctors also seem likely to play an increasing role in making and monitoring service contracts. Opinions differ as to whether such 'restratifications' of the medical profession strengthen (Freidson 1994) or weaken (Coburn 1995; Light 1995) its independence. If rank-and-file GPs' independence is indeed threatened in such conditions, the question then arises; by whom?

**Note**

1. At least 13 sites used a standard draft contract sold by a management consultant but amended it locally. We therefore analysed these contracts individually; making the unit of analysis is the individual PCAPS site with its corresponding contract. For regulatory reasons one HA had to issue the same contract to nine general practices severally instead of making one contract with them all as a single PCAPS as it had first intended. For consistency this case is counted as one site with one contract in the results that follow. At September 1998, 31 contracts were marked 'draft' and unsigned. 30 were signed, leaving 10 in (presumably) final form or nearly so but unsigned. In the event contracts were missing from just over 19% of PCAPS where the provider was a general practice and just under 19% of sites where the provider was an NHS Trust; from 18% of sites with a PMS contract and the same percentage of sites with a PMS+ contract; from 12.5% of the nurse-led sites and from 21% of the others. The results below are therefore not substantially biased towards any particular type of provider or contract. Our data cannot indicate whether the proportions of

draft and signed contracts were the same among responders and non-responders. One NHS region has only two PCAPS and we could only obtain the service contract for one of them. Otherwise the missing contracts are geographically distributed more-or-less equally.

# References

Anon (1999A), 'BMA to debate GP fears over independent status', *Pulse* (6th March) p15.

Anon (199B), 'GP anger at lay majority in primary care trusts', *Pulse* (6th March) p19.

Appleby, J. (1996), 'Financing the NHS' in Merry, P (Ed.) *1996/97 NHS Handbook* Tunbridge Wells, JMH.

Audit Commission (1995), *Briefing on GP Fundholding,* HMSO, London.

Bennett, C. and Ferlie, E. (1996), 'Contracting in Theory and Practice: Some Evidence from the NHS', *Public Administration* LXXIV, 49-66.

Beveridge, W. (1942), *Social Insurance and Allied Services*, HMSO, London.

Coburn, D., Rappolt, S. & Bourgeault, I. (1997), 'Decline vs. Retention of Medical Power through Restratification: an Examination of the Ontario Case', *Sociology of Health and Illness,* XIX (1) 1-22.

Department of Health (1996), *Choice and Opportunity. Primary Care: the Future,* HMSO, London.

Department of Health (1997a), *The New NHS. Modern, Dependable,* HMSO, London.

Department of Health (1997b), *Evaluation of Primary Care Act PMS Pilots. Research Brief,* (DoH; unpublished), Leeds.

Department of Health (1997c) *Personal Medical Services under the NHS (Primary Care) Act 1997*, NHSE , Leeds.

Department of Health (1998), *Partnership in Action* DoH, London.

Ferlie, E. (1994), 'The Creation and Evolution of Quasi Markets in the Public Sector: Early Evidence from the National Health Service', *Policy and Politics,* XXII (2) 105-112.

Freidson, E. (1994). 'The Changing Nature of Professional Control', *Annual Review of Sociology,* X 1-20.

Granovetter, M. (1992) 'Economic Institutions as Social Constructions: a Framework for Analysis', *Acta Sociologica,* XXXV 3-11.

Gray, J. D. & Donaldson, L. (1996), 'Improving the Quality of Health Care through Contracting', *Quality in Health Care* V 201-5.

Honigsbaum, F. (1979), *The Division in British Medicine,* Kogan Page, London.

Light, D. (1995) 'Countervailing Powers: a Framework for Professions in Transition' in Johnson, T., Larkin, J., & Saks, M. (Eds.) *Health Professions and the State in Europe,* Routledge, London.

Niskanen, W.A. (1979), *Bureaucracy,* IEA, London.

Office of Health Economics (OHE) (1996), *Compendium of Health Statistics* OHE, London.

Reggler, J. (1998), 'My Point-by-Point Rejection of Deal' *Pulse* (27th June), p7.

Sheaff, R. & Peel, V. (Eds.) (1993), *Best Practice in Health Care Commissioning,* Churchill Livingstone, Harlow.

Smith, P. C. (1997), *Devolved Purchasing in Health Care. A Review of the Issues,* Nuffield, London.

Walsh, K. (1995), *Public Services and Market Mechanisms,* Macmillan, Basingstoke.

Williamson, O. E. (1975), *Markets and Hierarchies,* Free Press, New York.

# 6   At the Sharp End: Implementing Community Care in a Cutback Environment

DAMIEN RILEY

A well-known pastiche of 'Volvo' car adverts once observed that the cars crashed because they were 'designed by robots, driven by dummies'. One might observe that in recent years, similar attitudes have prevailed in the relationship between central government policy-makers, and local government departments responsible for implementing policy. Although differences of opinion would doubtless emerge over who was the 'dummy' responsible for policy 'crashes', this somewhat glib observation suggests an important truth; policy outcomes are usually a compromise. A compromise between the preferences of those who design a policy, and the preferences of those who implement it. The 1990 NHS and Community Care Act was no exception to that truth. This paper analyses the implementation of this legislation in three local authorities, in the period 1989-1997. It adopts a rational choice framework — the bureau-shaping model — to explain the approach to implementation observed in the three cases, identifying the preferences of senior officials within local government, and the constraints placed upon them by central government, as the key explanatory variables. Section One outlines the core elements of the community care reforms; recognising that they were both a pragmatic attempt by central government to make financial savings, but also fitted into a broader agenda of public sector reform designed to encourage an 'enabling state' — the state as a purchaser, rather than a provider of services. Sections Two and Three examine the reorganisations that have taken place within three case study authorities, in response to the reforms. Section Four provides a bureau-shaping analysis of the implementation of the reforms. Finally, Section Five assesses the extent to which key aims of the 1990 NHS and Community Care Act have been achieved in the case study authorities. Has the 'enabling state' resulted in more efficient and effective local government?

# 1. Policy Background: The 1990 NHS and Community Care Act

Changes to the financing and organisation of community care were essentially a response to the surge in social security claims, arising from the statutory regulation of financial assistance for those resident in private nursing home care in the early 1980s. Ironically (as it turned out), the statutory regulations introduced in 1980 were an attempt to limit bureaucratic discretion in the administration of supplementary benefits payments, and thus help to contain costs. In fact, the changes created an open-ended 'quasi-voucher' system, whereby patients — typically elderly people — could be transferred out of long-stay hospitals into private residential care, and the Department of Social Security rather than local authorities or the NHS, would pick up the bill. The costs of provision rose from £10m in 1979 to £500m by the mid 1980s, reaching £2,000m by 1991 (Glennerster and Lewis 1996; Harrison and Wistow 1997).

Clearly, this was embarrassing for a government committed to cutting public spending, within which social security was a prime target. It was also patently at odds with the broad thrust of community care policy that was being developed at the time — theoretically at least — by central and local government. One of the basic tenets of the policy was that service users should be enabled to remain in their own homes for as long as possible before entering hospital or residential care. This was assumed to be both more cost-effective and a preferable form of care for service users. The reality on the ground was that because of the perverse effects of the social security system, home care and other alternatives to residential care were left under-developed. Cash-constrained local authorities and the NHS were transferring users to private residential and nursing homes, and letting the social security system pick up the bill (Audit Commission 1986; Glennerster and Lewis 1996: pp.2-6).

Thus central government was left with two problems. To find a way of checking the rising residential care bill, and reverse the growth in this form of provision, which was seen to be contrary to a community care policy built around the provision of high quality home care and day care facilities as professional best practice in meeting user needs. The Government brought in Sir Roy Griffiths to 'sort the money problem'. He recommended substantial changes to the way in which community care was to be financed and administered (Griffiths, 1988). Most of his suggestions were incorporated into the 1989 White Paper 'Caring for People' and were enacted in the 1990 NHS and Community Care Act. Budgetary responsibility for residential care was transferred directly to social services authorities through the revenue support grant, forcing local authorities to operate within budgets determined by central government, enabling central control on spending. Additionally, a locally administered assessment system was introduced that guaranteed consumers a right to an assessment of care needs rather than services, which would be provided within available resources. Assessors could avoid committing authorities to expensive forms of care, by setting an 'ideal' level of service provision which could be used for planning future services, and an 'actual' level of provision given to users based on what the social services authority could currently afford to finance (Secretary of State for Health 1990: 23-34; Glennerster and Lewis 1996: 13-15).

Substantial sums of new money were also made available to local authorities, sweetening the bitter pill of their new responsibilities: the community care transitional grant. The grant was designed to help 'pump-prime' the necessary care services. It was originally envisaged that it would be available for the first three financial years after the implementation of the reforms, but has recently been renewed until 1999/2000. However, its use was tightly prescribed by central government's '85% rule'; local authorities were required to spend 85% of this 'new' money on independent sector purchasing. Another catch was the way in which the grant was distributed. Central government attempted to appease two different groups of interested parties when deciding how the grant should be allocated. In order to appease the private sector residential care lobby, the Government allocated half of the total 1993/94 grant to those authorities with large numbers of private sector care homes, and the other half according to the Standard Spending Assessment (SSA) formula that favoured local authorities with a high proportion of elderly people in their population. In order to appease local authorities with large numbers of elderly people (typically — though not exclusively — Conservative-controlled counties), the grant for 1994/95 onwards was simply allocated according to the SSA formula. Overall, there were wide variations in the degree to which different local authorities benefited from this new source of funds (Glennerster and Lewis 1996: 28-42).

Alongside these fiscal changes, the 1990 Act and subsequent policy guidance sought to promote functional changes within social services departments. There was an affirmation of the lead role to be taken by social services authorities as 'enablers'. They were expected to move away from their historical role as direct service providers, and develop their management and information systems in assessment, contracting and monitoring in a social care market, retaining a residual role in direct service provision. Whilst a rigid purchaser/provider split was not imposed, there was a strong expectation that this sort of restructuring would be necessary for social services departments to discharge their new responsibilities (Secretary of State for Health 1990: 37-38).

Overall, the 1990 community care reforms were in many respects a pragmatic solution to the need to stop the haemorrhage in the social security budget. However, they should also be understood as part of a broader agenda of public sector reform, which resulted in a substantial reconfiguration of both central government and local government during the late 1980s and early 1990s. Frequently referred to as the application of 'New Public Management' methods, proponents of these reforms believed that the disaggregation of large public sector bureaucracies, coupled with the introduction of incentivisation in personnel management and competition in the provision of services such as health and social care, would lead to a more efficient and effective public sector (discussed in Dunleavy & Hood 1994). In the context of community care, there was an assumption that with the extension of contracting out of service provision and the development of the social services authority as an 'enabler', cost containment could be achieved alongside a shift in the balance of care, from residential care to home care. Therefore, three elements of the reforms will be the focus of the following analysis:

- The extension of contracting out as an alternative to 'in-house' delivery of social care;
- The extent to which the legislation encouraged cost containment in care provision;
- The extent to which there was a shift in the balance of the forms of care provided; away from residential care and towards home care alternatives.

Whilst central government's priority in reforming community care was primarily to make financial savings, the details of policy implementation — how best to 'manage up' a social care market and shift the balance of care provision from residential care to home care — were largely left to local authorities themselves. In analysing how local authorities have chosen to implement the reforms, the remainder of this paper applies the bureau-shaping model, which provides an empirical 'map' of the changes in the structure of three case study authorities, and offers an institutional rational choice account of the implementation of the reforms in these cases.

## 2. Analysing Organisational Change: The Bureau-Shaping Model

The bureau-shaping model is composed of two distinctive, related components. First it offers a descriptive typology of agency and budget types. Second, it develops a rational choice account of bureaucrats' behaviour that is critical of the budget-maximising model popularised by Niskanen (1994) (Dunleavy 1991; Dunleavy and Biggs 1995). The typology will be outlined below, whilst the model's explanatory component will be developed in section four.

The bureau-shaping typology focuses on analysing linkages between the makeup of a bureaucracy's budget, and its function. Dunleavy argues that an organisation's total budget is constituted by four elements, the precise proportions of which will vary across different types of agencies:

- The core element represents the administrative overheads and
- Staffing costs of the agency.
- The bureau element encompasses funds channelled to private contractors and individual recipients.
- The program element represents funds channelled to lower tiers of government for policy implementation by them, via contracts or transfer payments.
- Finally the folio element constitutes funds controlled by the agency which it passes on to other agencies at the same tier of government.
- Taken together these elements constitute an agency's program budget, displayed in Figure 1 (Dunleavy, 1991: 181-183; Dunleavy and Biggs 1995: 8-9).

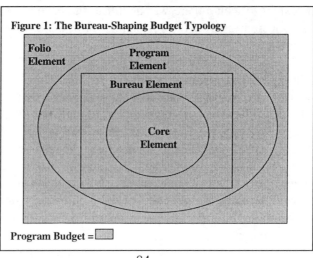

Figure 1: The Bureau-Shaping Budget Typology

Folio Element

Program Element

Bureau Element

Core Element

Program Budget =

It is suggested that the composition of the program budget provides an indicator of an agency's functional type. Four distinct types are identified (Dunleavy 1991: 183-188; Dunleavy and Biggs 1995: 12-15):

Delivery agencies are direct service providers and are usually labour-intensive organisations, with correspondingly high core element levels, and residual bureau and program elements.

Transfer agencies are involved in the payment of subsidies or entitlements to private individuals or firms. Consequently, the bureau element absorbs the bulk of their program budget, whilst the core and program elements are low.

Contract agencies develop and supervise the tendering of capital or service projects, for implementation by private sector bodies. Once again, their bureau elements are high, and they maintain staff for R and D, project specification and contract management, thus having moderate core elements, and low program element levels.

Control agencies channel funding to bodies at other tiers of government, in the form of grants or through 'quasi-contracts' such as service level agreements. Thus the program element absorbs the majority of their program budget.

Dunleavy claims that the application of this common typology allows one to make meaningful comparisons across a plurality of local government structures, and to analyse and assess the changes that have taken place in these structures in recent years. Essentially, he argues that reorganisations can be characterised by their effects on departmental budget structures, and thus on changes in organisational type. For example, the contracting-out of social care provision formerly undertaken 'in-house' is represented by a resource shift from the core element to the bureau element. If a social services department primarily concerned with service delivery implements a purchaser/provider split, then this will be evidenced as a shift of resources from the core element to the program element; the agency is transformed from a delivery agency to a control agency type (Dunleavy and Biggs 1995: 23). In the section that follows, the model is operationalised through an examination of the reorganisation of three social services departments following the implementation of the community care reforms in 1993.

## 3. The reorganisation of community care: An empirical analysis

Budgetary data has been compiled for three social services authorities, covering the years 1989/90, 1993/94, and 1996/97, and focused on community care services. These years have been chosen because the community care reforms were implemented in 1993; the time slices allow a 'pre-test — post-test' assessment of the effects of the reforms on the budget structures of these authorities. The data sources used were the local authorities' own estimates for these years.

The data distinguish between administrative costs, direct service delivery, agency/transfer spending and transfers to other departments. This most closely follows the distinctions made by the authorities in their own spending estimates. For the purposes of analysis, core element resources equate to administrative costs plus direct service provision. These costs are incurred in the provision of local authority residential and day care for example, and administrative overheads. Bureau element resources are derived from agency/transfer spending. This refers to all care contracted out to the independent sector, whether voluntary or private, for residential or home care services for example. It also incorporates individual transfer payments such as concessionary travel for the disabled. Program element resources equate to transfers made to other public sector departments, for services provided by other authorities or by other departments within the same authority, such as education or leisure services, which is paid for by social services departments. Where a purchaser-provider split is introduced, resources transferred from the purchasing authority to 'arms-length' statutory providers would also count as program element resources. The results are displayed in Figure 2.

Figure 2: Case study authority budget structures 1989-97

| Authority A | 1989-90 | 1993-94 | 1996-97 |
|---|---|---|---|
| Core element | N/A | 77 | 59 |
| Bureau Element | N/A | 17 | 36 |
| Program Element | N/A | 6 | 5 |
| | | | |
| Authority B | 1989-90 | 1993-94 | 1996-97 |
| Core element | 86.8 | 72 | 58 |
| Bureau Element | 12.7 | 27 | 42 |
| Program Element | 0.5 | 1 | <0.1 |
| | | | |
| Authority C | 1989-90 | 1993-94 | 1996-97 |
| Core element | 75 | 73 | 63.4 |
| Bureau Element | 25 | 27 | 36.2 |
| Program Element | <0.1 | 0 | 0.4 |

In Authority A the expansion of the bureau element at the expense of core element levels between 1993/4 and 1996/7, is distinctive. Such expansion represents a shift away from in-house service provision and the extension of the use of the independent sector for care delivery, as the authority expanded its contracting function at the expense of its delivery function after the introduction of the reforms. Note that a substantial core of direct services remain under local authority control. Authority B resembled a delivery agency with a residual contracting function before the implementation of the reforms. The growth of the bureau element relative to the core element throughout the period studied indicates a similar shift in the authority's function from a delivery to a contracting role. The trend in Authority C is similar although less marked, with a smaller increase in contracted-out services as a proportion of total service provision from 1989/90-1993/94, and a more marked increase from 1993/94-1996/97.

The direction of change in the budget structures of all three authorities is clear. Core element cuts have occurred as the bureau element expands to reflect the substantial increases in the contracting out of service delivery to the independent sector. The rate of this expansion has increased following the implementation of the community care reforms in Authorities B and C. Of equal importance is that the effect of the reform process on the program element component has been minimal. The relative stability of program element levels across all three authorities indicates that they have chosen not to introduce a formal purchaser/provider distinction within their organisations. However, new evidence gathered on more recent reorganisations indicates that in all three authorities, there has been a senior management decision to introduce a functional separation between 'commissioning' and 'operations' — a purchaser — provider split. The implications of these decisions will be discussed in Section Four below.

Before evaluating some possible explanations for these findings, some further analysis is necessary. The shift from in-house provision to increased independent sector provision is hardly surprising given the constraints on spending of the community care transitional grant; the '85% rule' described in Section One. It could be construed that the change reflects central government controls placed on local authorities' spending on social care services, rather than local authority-level policy decisions. To control for this the data in Figure 3 show the authorities' budget structures with the transitional grant element removed.

Figure 3: Case Study Authority Budget Structures 1993-97
(Minus Community Care Transitional Grant)

| Authority A | 1993-94 | 1996-97 |
|---|---|---|
| Core element | 83 | 69 |
| Bureau Element | 11 | 24 |
| Program Element | 6 | 7 |

| Authority B | 1993-94 | 1996-97 |
|---|---|---|
| Core element | 78 | 60.5 |
| Bureau Element | 21 | 39.3 |
| Program Element | 1 | 0.2 |

| Authority C | 1993-94 | 1996-97 |
|---|---|---|
| Core element | 78 | 79.8 |
| Bureau Element | 22 | 19.7 |
| Program Element | 0 | 0.5 |

Here the evidence is less clear-cut. In two out of the three Authorities the figures suggest an increase in the use of the independent sector beyond that prescribed by central government spending constraints. The shift from core to bureau element resources in Authority A is less pronounced but a shift is still in evidence — the bureau element has expanded by 13% from 1993/4 to 1996/7. In Authority B, the trend is also still strongly in evidence — the bureau element has grown by 18.3% from 1993/94 to 1996/97. However, Authority C's figures indicate the bureau element shrinking by 2.3% accompanied by a small increase in the core element. This shrinkage points to the significance of central government spending constraints in encouraging the increase in contracting-out of services by Authority C after 1993/4.

Despite this latter finding, the bulk of the evidence indicates that these three authorities are engaged in shifting resources away from their core elements towards the bureau elements of their spending. In terms of the bureau-shaping typology, they are reorganising themselves from delivery agencies to contract agencies, although currently could be more accurately described as having a mixed delivery/contract function. The next section outlines the explanatory component of the bureau-shaping model, which can provide valuable insights into why these authorities have pursued these forms of reorganisations.

## 4. Explaining Organisational Change: Bureau-Shaping in a Cutback Environment

These findings suggest that contracting-out of service delivery functions has emerged as a definite trend within these social services authorities; they are clearly moving away from a provider function towards an 'enabling' role. This change is taking place at different speeds and the authorities are starting from different baselines. Authority C might be characterised as the most 'reluctant' contractor, although the figures also indicate it was making most use of non-statutory sources before the implementation of the reforms. The bureau-shaping model has provided a useful empirically grounded way of establishing the progress made by the local authorities studied here.

However, the model also aspires to contribute to explanations of the reconfiguration of the public sector in recent years, of the sort observed in Section 3. It employs an institutional rational choice approach that focuses on the preferences of senior bureaucrats about the budget structure and agency types described above, and the constraints placed upon bureaucrats by their political principals. The model suggests that public sector reorganisations provide opportunities for senior officials to restructure their work environments in ways advantageous to them. (Dunleavy 1991: 210-248; Dowding 1995; James 1995; Cope 1997).

In the past rational choice models focused on senior bureaucrats' attitudes to their departmental budgets. In common with the first principles of public choice and much 'folk-wisdom' surrounding public sector officialdom, bureaucrats are considered to be self-regarding, with a clearly-defined utility function, and seek to maximise their utility in their activities. Niskanen viewed their preferences as analogous to those of managers within neo-classical firms, who seek to maximise profits to boost their own pecuniary rewards and reinforce their own positions within the firm against possible internal and external rivals (Niskanen 1994: 36-38). Since bureaucrats operate within publicly funded agencies without a profit-making capacity, he argued they will focus on maximising their budgets. He suggested that bureaucrats' utility functions are composed of salary, perquisite acquisition, public reputation, power, output of the bureau, ease of making changes and easing management tasks within the bureau (Niskanen 1994: 38). He contended that:

'All of these variables except the last two, are a positive, monotonic function of the total budget of the bureau during the bureaucrat's tenure in office'.

Thus Niskanen argued that within the constraints imposed by politicians, senior bureaucrats in the public sector seek to maximise their organisation's budget (Niskanen 1994: 38-39).

In a thorough critique Dunleavy argues that this focus on the maximisation of total budget levels is misplaced, and has limited empirical support. Employing the bureau-shaping typology, he suggests that it is principally the core element which is the source of the utilities Niskanen describes, since this part of the budget includes expenditure on running costs which can most easily be diverted into generating slack resources, acquiring perks, maintaining plusher offices, etc. He also posits an additional behavioural assumption, namely that senior bureaucrats are more concerned with their work tasks and the promotion of a congenial work environment, than merely with large budgets. Citing evidence from studies in administrative sociology, he suggests that senior officials are interested in policy-making rather than 'hum-drum' implementation tasks, and working within smaller-scale work units with a proximity to political power centres. Furthermore, he argues that these latter interests are likely to be better served in contracts and control agencies which are more concerned with policy formulation and monitoring, and have less responsibility for direct service provision. The management of delivery agencies provides higher core element levels, but involves precisely the kinds of hands-on management work that senior officials dislike. Thus he concludes that rather than attempting to maximise their budgets, senior bureaucrats are far more likely to adopt bureau-shaping strategies. These involve internal departmental reorganisations that seek to marginalise service delivery and implementation functions whilst expanding policy-making functions, or more radically the contracting-out or hiving-off of implementation work to the independent sector through competitive tendering, or the introduction of internal functional divides between purchasing and provision activities, such as 'internal trading models' in local government (Dunleavy 1991: 162-209).

The model has been applied with some success to understanding reorganisations in central government departments over the past decade (Dowding 1995; Dunleavy 1991; James 1995). In the context of community care, it provides an attractive — if simplistic — explanation for the acceleration of contracting out in the three case study authorities.

Namely, that senior officials in the three authorities under study wished to divest themselves of responsibility for direct service provision, and focus on strategic policy-making activities. However, the model requires some modification before it can be applied to a local government context. Firstly, its behavioural assumptions — a preference amongst senior officials for 'hands-off' policy work rather than policy implementation and direct service delivery — do not provide an wholly accurate motivational picture of senior officers in local government. Local authorities have always been implementation-level bureaux, comprising professionalised departments that have been primarily concerned with direct service delivery. 'Doing', and expansions in service delivery capacity have always been valued alongside the more strategic activities prized by the senior officials in Dunleavy's bureau-shaping account. This is confirmed by attitudinal data compiled by the Personal Social Services Research Unit between 1990 and 1992. This research identified a considerable reluctance amongst senior social services officers to relinquish a direct service delivery role in community care areas. One social services director expressed this as preferring 'doing' to 'managing' (Wistow, et. al. 1994: 59).

Secondly, local government is considerably constrained in its spending decisions by central government. The influence of the '85% rule' in shaping local authority spending on community care has been noted in Sections One and Three. Any explanation of the changes that have taken place in the three case study authorities must incorporate the influence of central government in effecting those changes.

The following account of the changes that have been identified in Section Three, therefore focuses on a number of key factors:

- The constraints placed upon local authority spending after 1993 by central government;
- The difficulties experienced by senior local authority officers in running large-scale in-house services, under financial constraints;
- The preferences of senior bureaucrats in local government for policy work, alongside operational management work;
- The constraints placed upon these authorities' ability to contract out care services, stemming from the limited capacity of the social care market.

Central government's capacity to push local authorities towards increased contracting out of service delivery, through the conditions attached to the spending of the community care transitional grant, has already been demonstrated. The overall volume of central government support for local authority social services increased during the 1990's as a result of the introduction of the grant (Glennerster and Lewis 1996: 29-31). However, the way in which the grant was allocated (described in Section 1) resulted in widespread variations in the extent to which different local authorities benefited from this influx of new money. All three of the case study authorities had small numbers of private sector care homes in their areas prior to 1993, and all three had elderly populations well below the national average. Therefore all three fared relatively badly in terms of the amount of additional support they received from the community care transitional grant — they remained at the sharp end of central government's attempts to contain overall local government spending.

Within a cutback climate, all three authorities have been exposed to problems in the management and supply of community care services. Authority A has faced public criticism from its local health authority regarding alleged failures to find residential care places for elderly patients after the implementation of the community care reforms in 1993. More recently, it has been subjected to a number of high profile investigations of its in-house residential care services and legal actions surrounding other services, culminating in the publication of highly critical reports by both its own internal inspection unit and the Social Services Inspectorate. These incidents have resulted in adverse national press coverage for the authority's social services department and its senior officers and in one instance, public criticism from central government. Whilst Authority B has not experienced any such high profile service failures, it did suffer major financial problems in the late 1980s and early 1990s, requiring large cutbacks in social services expenditure. This was a key factor in triggering a yearlong strike by social services staff in 1991-1992. Meanwhile Authority C has been subjected to national press criticism of its services following a number of high profile fatalities of individuals in its care, during the period 1993-1997.

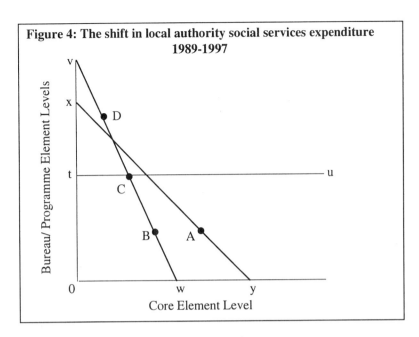

Figure 4: The shift in local authority social services expenditure 1989-1997

Bureau/ Programme Element Levels (y-axis)

Core Element Level (x-axis)

Under these conditions, there were strong incentives for senior officials within these authorities to distance themselves from the day-to-day running of in-house services. Although senior local government officials have traditionally sought to maintain or expand their capacity to deliver services, such activities become far less attractive in a cutback environment where opportunities for expansion are limited and services become prone to high-profile failure and external criticism from the press, regulatory bodies and central government. Therefore senior officials in all three authorities have contracted out a high volume of service delivery as a bureau-shaping strategy.

# References

Audit Commission (1986) *Making a Reality of Community Care*, London, HMSO.

Cope, S. (1997) 'The Bureau-Shaping Model and the Public Service' in *Massey, A.* (ed.) (1997) The Globalization and Marketization of Public Services, London, Macmillan.

Dowding, K. (1995) *The Civil Service*, London, Routledge.

Dunleavy, P. (1989) 'The Architecture of the British Central State', Public Administration, 67: 3&4.

Dunleavy, P. (1991) *Democracy, Bureaucracy and Public Choice*, Hertfordshire, Harvester-Wheatsheaf.

Dunleavy, P. & Hood, C. (1994) 'From Old Public Administration to New Public Management', Public Money and Management 14:3, pp.9-16.

Dunleavy, P. & Biggs, S. (1995) 'Local Government Organization in a 'Post-Bureaucratic' Age: A Bureau-Shaping Analysis', Paper to ECPR 1995 Annual Workshops, University of Bordeaux.

*Glennerster, H. & Lewis, J. (1996) Implementing* the New Community Care, Buckingham, Open University Press.

Griffiths, R. (1988) *Community Care: Agenda for Action*, London, HMSO.

Forder, J., Knapp, M. & Wistow, G. (1996) 'Competition in the Mixed Economy of Care', Journal of Social Policy, 25:2, pp.201-221.

Harrison, S. and Wistow, G. (1997) *A Tale of Two Reports: The Contribution to Health and Social Care Policy-Making of Sir Roy Griffiths 1982-92*, Unpublished Paper, Nuffield Institute, University of Leeds.

James, O. (1995) 'Explaining the Next Steps in the Department of Social Security: the Bureau-shaping Model of Central State Reorganisation', Political Studies, 43, pp.614-629.

Niskanen, W. (1994) *Bureaucracy and Public Economics, Gloucestershire*, Edward Elgar.

Sabatier, P. (1986) 'Top-Down and Bottom-Up Approaches to Implementation Research', Journal of Public Policy 6, pp.21-48.

Secretaries of State for Health, Social Security, Wales & Scotland (1989) *Caring for People*, Cmnd. 849, London, HMSO.

Secretary of State for Health (1990) *Caring for People: Policy Guidance*, London, HMSO.

Walsh, K. et. al. (1997) *Contracting for Change: Contracts in Health*, Social Care and other Local Government Services, Oxford, Oxford University Press.

Wistow, G., Knapp, M., Hardy, B. & Allen, C. (1994), *Social Care in a Mixed Economy*, Buckingham, Open University Press.

# 7 The Logic of 'Evidence-Based Medicine': Should it Appeal to Patients?

STEVE HARRISON

## Acknowledgement

The work reported in this paper was supported by the award to the author by the University of Manchester of a Hallsworth Research Fellowship in the Department of Government during 1997-98.

## Introduction

Evidence-based medicine (EBM) is the doctrine that professional clinical practice ought to be based upon sound biomedical research evidence about the effectiveness of each diagnostic or therapeutic procedure ('intervention' hereafter). This doctrine has been manifest in the formal policy for the NHS of both the last Conservative Government and the present Labour Government. In the former case, policy held that

> 'The overall purpose of the NHS is to secure, through the resources available, the greatest possible improvement in the physical and mental health of the people....In order to achieve this, we need to ensure that decisions about the provision and delivery of clinical services are driven increasingly by evidence of clinical and cost-effectiveness, coupled with the systematic assessment of actual health outcomes' (NHS Executive 1996a, p 6).

In the latter case, it is necessary to piece together a number of quotations from the white paper *The New NHS: Modern, Dependable* to obtain a parallel statement:

'We are proposing . . . to shift the focus onto quality of care . . . in its broadest sense: doing the right things, at the right time, for the right people, and doing them right . . . Nationally, there will be new evidence-based national service frameworks [which will] bring together the best evidence of clinical and cost-effectiveness . . .' (Secretary of State for Health 1997, pp11, 17, 18).

There are perhaps two main ways in which the policy can be described. One is in terms of its *institutions*, of which there are two types. First, there has existed since 1991 a national research and development (R and D) strategy for the NHS, involving the creation of national and regional directors of R and D, the establishment of national and local research budgets to be the object of competitive bidding, and reorganisation of the flow of research fund through NHS hospitals (Department of Health 1991; Task Force on R and D Funding 1994; for a general review, see Baker and Kirk 1996). The central objective of this strategy was to disaggregate the large proportion of health interventions stated never to have been the subject of proper evaluation into two categories: the effective and the ineffective. Second, a range of specialist institutions has been funded as the means of reviewing, collating and disseminating the findings of effectiveness research to the NHS; these include the Cochrane Centre at the University of Oxford; *Effective Health Care* Bulletins co-ordinated from the University of Leeds, the NHS Centre for Reviews and Dissemination at the University of York and the Outcomes Clearing House at the University of Leeds. (For a full list, see NHS Executive 1996a.) The post-1997 Labour Government is currently (January 1999) in the process of establishing a National Institute for Clinical Excellence 'to give a strong lead on clinical and cost-effectiveness' (Secretary of State for Health 1997 p18), as well as a Commission for Health Improvement with the responsibility of auditing the performance of hospitals in respect of EBM (NHS Executive 1998 pp51-8).

The second way in which the policy of EBM can be described is in terms of two of its key underlying assumptions. The first defines 'sound evidence', that is, that which may be relied upon to contribute to the classification of an intervention as effective or ineffective, as evidence derived from studies conducted in a certain way held to be 'scientific': from aggregations of randomised controlled trials. This approach is typified in the influential 'hierarchy of evidence' proposed by Canadian academics (Canadian Task Force 1979) but widely cited as an authoritative definition of the soundness of scientific research purporting to demonstrate the effectiveness of medical and similar interventions. A simplified version of this hierarchy is displayed in Table 1.

Table 1: The Hierarchy of Evidence

| Level of Validity of findings | Type of research |
| --- | --- |
| I | Strong evidence from at least one systematic review of multiple well-designed randomised controlled trials |
| II | Strong evidence from at least one properly designed randomised controlled trial of appropriate size |
| III | Evidence from well-designed non-randomised trials, single group pre-post, cohort, time series or matched case-controlled studies |
| IV | Evidence from well-designed non-experimental studies from more than one centre or research group |
| V | Opinions of respected authorities, based on clinical evidence, descriptive studies or reports of expert committees |

*Source:* adapted from Canadian Task Force (1979)

The principle which underpins this hierarchy is *validity*, that is the elimination from research findings of bias arising from any differences between patients treated by means of the intervention being researched and patients not so treated (that is, treated with other interventions or simply not treated). The pinnacle of the hierarchy is occupied by the randomised controlled trial (RCT) in which patients are conscientiously allocated randomly (and with informed consent) between the group who will receive the intervention under investigation and whatever group(s) with whom they will be compared: 'control' groups receiving perhaps placebos, or no treatment, and/or existing conventional treatment, as the case may be. Ideally, it is held, RCTs should be 'double blind', that is neither the treating clinician nor the patient should know which intervention they are receiving. This ideal cannot of course always be met; for instance it is hard to conceal whether or not surgery is occurring or ethically to perform a dummy operation. Special methods, such as 'meta-analysis' and systematic

97

reviews, have been developed in order to aggregate the results of several RCTs. Other research methods rank lower in the hierarchy, with other types of *controlled* study second to the RCT and uncontrolled methods a poor third; in practice, advocates of RCTs tend to regard uncontrolled methods as suitable only for hypothesis-building with a view to an eventual controlled study.

The second key assumption upon which EBM is based is that the most useful, though not necessarily exclusive, method for disseminating sound research evidence as defined above to practising clinicians is the 'clinical guideline' (NHS Executive 1996b); clinicians cannot be expected to read every research study relevant to their practice as it is published. The logic (though not always the overt form) of guidelines is essentially algorithmic, that is, it guides the user to courses of (diagnostic or therapeutic) action, dependent upon stated prior conditions: 'if....then' logic. The logic is also normative, that is it tells the clinician what *ought* to be done. In general, guidelines do not claim to determine clinical action completely, and degrees of discretion are left. (Note that not all guidelines are evidence-based.) A central role for the new National Institute for Clinical Excellence will be

'. . . drawing up new guidelines and ensuring they reach all parts of the health service' (Secretary of State for Health 1997, p18).

EBM, then, is firmly ensconced as formal policy. It seems a highly rational policy. It is very much a common-sense aspiration for a health care system such as the NHS; after all, who wants to be the object of ineffective interventions? Surely people do not want health care for its own sake but only for the improvement that it will bring to health. This argument, which seems to be widely held, has been neatly summarised by a distinguished health economist in the following formal terms:

'Patients seek care in order to be relieved of some actual or perceived, present or potential, 'disease'. The care itself is not directly of value; it is generally inconvenient, often painful or frightening. As a thought experiment, one could ask a representative patient (or oneself) whether he/she would prefer to have...a condition perceived as requiring care plus the best conceivable care for that condition, completely free of all...costs, or

would prefer simply not to have the condition . . . [C]are is not a good
usual sense, but a 'bad' or 'regrettable' made 'necessary' by the even
regrettable circumstances of 'dis-ease'. It follows that patients w
receive *effective* health care, i.e. care [in respect of which] ther_
reasonable expectation [of] a positive impact on their health!' (Evans 1991
pp118-9, emphasis original).

The logic of EBM thus seems unassailable; perhaps the new policy
should be welcomed unequivocally by patients and the public. Yet, despite
its neatness, this formulation is inadequate in four ways, two in respect of
what it says and two in respect of what it does not say. Each of these four
inadequacies is the subject of one of the following sections. The first
examines EBM's assumption that health care is not valued for its own sake.
The second explores the concept of a 'reasonable' expectation of a positive
treatment outcome. The third section addresses the question of what is to
count as sound evidence upon which to base clinical decisions. The fourth
addresses the acceptability of EBM as a criterion and mechanism for
decisions about NHS priorities. The conclusion is that, far from being
based on unassailable logic, EBM is a contested concept.

## Is Care of Value for its Own Sake?

It is clear that people sometimes do value care for its own sake, irrespective
of its effectiveness. Any GP has the story of a patient who demands a
prescription despite being assured that it will do no good, and the public
often value heroic but obviously vain rescue attempts, whether medical or
at sea or on the mountains. The term 'rescue principle' was employed by
the philosopher Ronald Dworkin to refer to the belief that the moral
imperative of medicine is to attempt to help those who are acutely ill or
whose lives are threatened (Dworkin 1994). The moral content of such
action is in the process (hence 'attempt') rather than in the outcome.
Although the application of such a principle clearly implies potentially
significant opportunity costs (since others may suffer whilst resources are
expended on hopeless cases) it is one which seems to receive wide support
in public policy generally, underpinning as it does such services as air/sea
rescue and mountain rescue. As Boyd *et al* (1979) pointed out nearly two
decades ago, it is a view widely held within medicine. Indeed, it is the
ostensible moral basis of medicine; as the BMA's *Handbook of Medical
Ethics* puts it:

'Within the [NHS] resources are finite and this may restrict the freedom of the doctor to advise his [sic] patient . . . [and thus] infringes the *ordinary* relationship between patient and doctor . . . The doctor has a general duty to advise on equitable allocation and efficient utilisation [but this] is subordinate to his professional duty to the individual who seeks his clinical advice' (British Medical Association 1980 p35, emphasis added).

Perhaps ironically, such a stance is not necessarily rendered illegitimate even by utilitarian principles. As Goodin and Wilenski (1984) have noted in their seminal analysis of the principles of public administration, there is no reason why the public who are paying for a service should not value process as much as, or more than, outcome.

## What is a 'Reasonable Expectation' and who says So?

The question of what is taken to be a positive outcome can be examined from two angles. First, the currency in which outcomes are expressed; Evans's formulation clearly entails the positiveness of outcome as perceived by the patient. But clinical research upon which evidence-based medicine is predicated does not usually employ such outcome concepts. Physiological outcome measures, and the thresholds in them deemed to be significant to researchers, may not relate to patient satisfaction. Thus, for instance, the outcome of treatment for benign prostatic hyperplasia may be measured in objective terms, such as improvement in urine flow, which bear no necessary relationship to patient perceptions of feeling better or coping better. Moreover, patients may feel better as a result of a placebo effect.

The second angle concerns probability. Of course decisions about intervention have to be made *prospectively* and there are few certainties, so that Evans is correct to base his formulation on expectations. However, the reasoning that such expectations could be a guide to the determination of consensual health care priorities rests entirely on the ability of the relevant social actors to agree upon what constitutes a 'reasonable' expectation of a positive outcome from treatment. It is easy to see that, in fact, such agreement is not always forthcoming, as was graphically demonstrated in the much-publicised case of Jaymee Bowen ('Child B') who was denied a second bone marrow transplant by her local health authority; NHS specialists differed amongst themselves and with a private consultant over the probable effectiveness of such treatment whilst her father evidently felt that any positive probability was acceptable. (For details of this case, see New 1996, and for an earlier case see Freemantle and Harrison 1993). The feeling of being cheated by reliance on evidence was expressed by a 62 year old Wakefield man who had been denied arterial surgery on the grounds that his continued smoking increased the risks of treatment and reduced the probability of benefit as follows:

'I have worked since I was fourteen up until recently and paid a hell of a lot in taxes to the government both in income taxes and on the forty cigarettes a day I smoked. Surely it is not too much for me to ask to have an operation that might ease my pain in my old age and make me live a little longer' (*Yorkshire Evening Post*, 26 August 1993 p1).

Moreover, public pressure groups in the health field may well articulate specific demands for interventions (the Multiple Sclerosis Society's demand for the drug Beta Interferon and the National Osteoporosis Society's demand for bone density measurement are examples), based on their own readings of the evidence and their own thresholds of reasonableness. The Internet, to which access is increasing, already carries a wide range of websites through which individuals and groups with a shared interest in a particular medical condition exchange information and opinion, a development which is likely to increase direct demand for particular technologies (Coiera 1996).

**What Counts as 'Sound Evidence' and who says So?**

In the passage quoted above, Evans does not discuss what is to be regarded as evidence of reasonable expectataion. The epistemological underpinnings of randomised controlled trials and meta-analyses which, as we have seen above, form the basis of the EBM movement are in fact not necessarily identical with the way working clinicians think about evidence of effectiveness. This has recently been examined in a small-scale, but important American study of clinicians (Tanenbaum 1994). In her study, Tanenbaum contrasts the traditional biomedical model of research, which is based in laboratory methods, with that entailed by RCTs. This contrast is summarised in Table 2.

## Table 2 Alternative Epistemologies in Medicine and Research

| *Naturalistic Epistemology* | *Positivist Epistemology* |
| --- | --- |
| Reveals cause-effect mechanisms (via aetiology, pathology etc); implied metaphor of the body as a machine. | Demonstrates statistical relationships from past experience; implied metaphor of the body as a 'black box'. |
| Provides knowledge of what logically *ought to be* effective, and why; 'logic of treatment' is important. | Provides knowledge of what is *likely* to work, irrespective of why. |
| Learning from experience. | Learning from external sources. |
| Based on deterministic models. | Based on probabilistic models. |
| Espoused by working clinicians | Espoused by epidemiologists and health services researchers. |

*Source*: adapted from Tanenbaum (1994)

The naturalistic model is traditionally taught to and espoused by clinicians and relies on the discovery of cause-effect mechanisms by the observation of the way in which disease processes develop over time and impact upon normal physiological processes. Treatment is therefore very much a *logical* process of intervening in the aetiology (natural history) of a disease so as to arrest, reverse or retard it. The model is *deterministic* (that is, it assumes that clinical events necessarily have causes which can be identified and, in principle, modified) and its dominant metaphor is that of the human body as a machine. The model is also *naturalistic* (that is, it entails a belief that phenomena should be studied in their natural context rather than in isolation) and largely assumes that learning takes place by personal experience. The positivist model is the foundation of epidemiology and the relatively new discipline of health services research. It consists primarily of the *inference* of cause-effect relationships from past statistical relationships between treatment and outcomes. It is therefore less concerned with disease processes than with establishing what interventions are *likely to be effective, irrespective of why*. The model is therefore *probabilistic* (that is, one where the cause-effect relationships are inherently uncertain) and *positivist* (that is, one where knowledge can best be obtained by careful study of individual variables). Since the approach implies a pooling of knowledge, learning must be largely acquired from sources external to the individual.

For the sake of contrast Table 2 presents the two epistemologies as ideal types, though in the real world it seems unlikely that many clinicians are not influenced by elements of both, and indeed there may well be clinicians (perhaps psychiatrists) who hold a more constructivist position. The point, however, is that *in the last analysis* it is the traditional model that predominates in medical decisionmaking. In contrast, as Table 1 above makes clear, the positivist model which underpins EBM places clinical observations at the bottom of the hierarchy of evidence. Whilst it is not necessarily the case that Tanenbaum's US findings are generalisable it is worth noting that they are consonant with the individualistic ethic of the practice of medicine and to the habit of doctors of being influenced by their own experience of single cases, a habit that is reflected by the frequent anecdotal filler articles (often alongside reports of RCTs) in the *British Medical Journal* with titles such as 'A Memorable Patient', 'A Patient With a Message' and 'A Patient Who Changed My Practice'. It is thus possible that clinical doctors are more likely to be influenced in their practice by their own and close colleagues' experience with similar types of patient, and by their own reasoning about treatment logic, than by the publication of meta-analyses of large numbers of cases.

**Whose Priorities? Public, Patients or Payers?**

The NHS is based on 'third party payment', the principle of which is that financial contributions are collected from population groups, irrespective of the immediate health care requirements of the individuals who compose them; such groups may represent a more-or-less complete national population, or narrower groups such as the members (voluntarily or compulsorily) of various insurance schemes. These contributions are collected by 'third party payers' such as government (as in the case of the NHS) or quasi-independent agencies or insurance companies, which employ the resources thus obtained to resource or reimburse health care providers (such as professionals and hospitals) for the care of individuals held to be sick. Such systems can be regarded in various, complementary, ways. They separate payment for care from its immediate need by the individual. They separate the financial contribution that the individual makes from the volume of care that s/he actually consumes (which is not the same as saying that there necessarily is no relationship between the amount required to be paid and the volume *predicted* to be used by an individual). They pool resources to smooth out the uncertainties of individuals' health states requiring more expenditure than the individual is able to make. What all third party payment systems risk is the inflation of demand over time. Whilst this is often conceptualised as being 'driven' by variables such as demographic shift (i.e. ageing populations), medical technological drift, and/or rising public expectations, they are not sufficient conditions, though they may appear as such in rhetoric. Demand increases are more appropriately theorised in terms two manifestations of the economic concept of 'moral hazard'.

*Consumer moral hazard* arises where some or all of the costs of care are met by the third party payers; it encourages a higher rate of use than would occur if full costs had to be met at the point of use (Pauly 1968), since the demander assumes that the cost of his or her usage will be spread over a large number of taxpayers, fund members or policy holders. However, if large numbers of people behave in this way, then total demand (for health care and hence for the resources to provide it) *will* rise. Consumer moral hazard in third party payment systems for health care is the consequence of divorcing payment for services from their use; it becomes easier for many people to obtain care than would otherwise be the case, but at the same time tempts them to increase their demands. Two points are important to note. First, although analyses often focus on the *price* of services, it seems probable that non-money costs of obtaining care can be significant. The user must take steps, such as telephoning for an appointment, rearranging a working day, travelling to the surgery or hospital, and perhaps sitting for some time in a crowded waiting area, in order to gain access. Costs can be higher. One may react adversely to the drug which is prescribed and the prospect of gastroendoscopy or sigmoidoscopy is not a pleasant one for most people. Second, and irrespective of cost, although people only demand services which they perceive to be good for themselves, such goodness is in the *perception* of the demander rather than reflecting some intrinsic feature.

*Supplier-induced demand* arises from information asymmetries; the consumer's lack of knowledge of a highly technical service coincides with a provider's interest in increasing provision and allows the latter to affect demand. Whilst patients do, of course, make generalised demands in the sense of arranging a visit to the doctor, it is typically (though not invariably) the physician or other clinical professional who translates such generalised demand into a specific demand for antibiotics, pathology tests, a specialist appointment, or a surgical operation. Such professional motivation may be material; if the clinician is remunerated on a fee-for-service basis, there are clear incentives to maximise supplier-induced demand unless the total fees are 'capped' in some way, and the same incentive may exist if the institution which employs the clinician is itself remunerated by the third party payer on the basis of its actual costs or any basis which is volume-sensitive. If this were a complete explanation of clinicians' motivation, a system such as the NHS in which clinicians were salaried or capitated would have the opposite effect of 'underprovision', since there would be no economic incentives to perform beyond the level necessary to retain one's job. However, this seems an unnecessarily narrow perspective on incentives; it seems plausible to argue that there may be ethical incentives to provider moral hazard; even if the hospital's budget is not volume-related and clinicians are remunerated by salary or capitation fees, one might still expect to see such demand increase as a result of the supplier's desire to behave ethically, that is to do the best possible for his or her patient

The consequent necessity is for third party payers to manage supply and demand ('ration') in the situation described, and for them to find a rationale and criteria for doing so that can be made to seem publicly acceptable. Certainly EBM provides a candidate for such a process, so that its political appeal is unsurprising. For two related reasons however, consumer moral hazard in health care is not avoided by simply observing that many health care interventions have not been evaluated by research which conforms to the hierarchy of evidence presented above. First, unless those who demand the services both know and care about this lack of research, their behaviour will be unchanged. Second, criteria other than effectiveness (which is the principle which underpins EBM) exist and have their advocates amongst public, patients and providers (Harrison and Hunter 1994). As noted above, the *rule of rescue* gives priority to persons in acute or life-threatening conditions, and tends to locate moral content in trying rather than in succeeding. *Deserts* are sometimes used as the basis of an argument for exclusion, often in the context of a health state which is considered to be self-inflicted (e.g. by smoking). And, as noted above, third party payment systems are underpinned by a preference for *equity*, that is to ameliorate the position of people who cannot afford the care from which they might benefit; *equity* and *equality* are concerned with the distribution

105

of services or of health status respectively. All these criteria are potential trade offs against effectiveness as implied in EBM.

## Concluding Remarks

Evidence-based medicine is a contested concept, as much a social and political artefact as a scientific or technical one (Harrison 1998). First, people may value the process of care as much, or more, than the outcome. Second, it is not uncommon to find disputes about what is the probability of an intervention's being effective, and about who is authorised to determine it. Third, not everyone agrees with the theory of knowledge which underpins EBM. Fourth, alternative criteria for rationing exist and have their supporters; it cannot simply be taken that the criterion of effectiveness which underpins EBM commands predominant support.

Such considerations are not abstruse academicisms; patients and members of the public (as well as health professionals) are capable of working out the consequences for themselves. Envisage a hypothetical patient denied a particular intervention as a result of his/her clinician following a guideline; it is easy to see that such a patient might thereby have been saved from enduring a painful, useless or harmful experience. But the patient might have been the statistical 'outlier' who would have responded positively to the intervention. We cannot know in respect of individual patients; what has happened has happened and can only be compared with a hypothesised counterfactual. Thus, even in its own terms, the potential benefits (including the reduction of opportunity costs) of EBM accrue to populations rather than to every patient within them. But there seems little reason to doubt that different patients have different thresholds of probability at which they believe intervention to be 'necessary' and indeed such thresholds may be different for different medical conditions. It may also be the case, though it is disputed, that clinicians have 'tacit knowledge' (Polanyi 1967) about the probable effectiveness of an intervention for a particular patient; they may know more than they can say. These considerations suggest that the rigorous application of evidence-based guidelines towards which public policy currently points cannot simplistically be claimed as the unassailably logical approach.

However, it is possible to envisage at least two ways in which a more open approach to EBM could be made to appeal to patients. First, medical researchers might do more to involve patients in the specification of appropriate outcome measures: to help to define what outcomes matter. Second, the publications and other outputs of EBM could become a vehicle for more rational and active discussion between clinicians and patients about the desirability of, and prospects arising from particular interventions. In an ideal world, this might be combined with an approach to clinical audit which focussed on clinicians learning from the results of their own and their colleagues' treatment decisions rather than upon narrow adherence to guidelines (Harrison 1996).

# References

Boyd K. M. (Ed) (1979), *The Ethics of Resource Allocation in Health Care*, University of Edinburgh Press, Edinburgh.

British Medical Association (1980), *The Handbook of Medical Ethics*, London.

Canadian Taskforce (1979), 'Taskforce Report: the Periodic Health Examination', *Canadian Medical Association Journal*, Vol.121, No.9, pp.1139-1254.

Coiera E. (1996), 'The Internet's Challenge to Health and Provision', *British Medical Journal*, Vol.312, pp.3-4.

Dworkin R. (1994), 'Will Clinton's Plan be Fair?' *New York Review of Books*, 13 January pp20-5.

Evans R. G. (1990), 'The Dog in the Night-Time: Medical Practice Variations and Health Policy' in T. F. Andersen and G. Mooney (Eds) *The Challenge of Medical Practice Variations*, Macmillan, Basingstoke.

Freemantle N. and Harrison S. (1993), 'Interleukin 2: the Public and Professional Face of Rationing in the NHS', *Critical Social Policy*, Vol.13, No.3, pp.94-117.

Goodin R. E. and Wilenski P. (1984), 'Beyond Efficiency: the Logical Underpinning of Administrative Efficiency', *Public Administration Review*, Vol 6, pp512-7.

Harrison S. (1996), 'Implementing the Results of Research and Development in Clinical and Managerial Practice' in M. Baker and S. Kirk (Eds) *Research and Development for the NHS: Evidence, Evaluation and Effectiveness*, Radcliffe Medical Press, Oxford.

Harrison S. (1998), 'The Politics of Evidence-Based Medicine' *Policy and Politics*, Vol 26 No1, pp 15-31.

Harrison S. and Hunter D. J. (1994), *Rationing Health Care*, Institute for Public Policy Research, London.

New B (1996), 'The Rationing Agenda in the NHS', *British Medical Journal*, 312, pp 1593-1601.

NHS Executive (1996a), *Promoting Clinical Effectiveness: a Framework for Action in and Through the NHS*, Department of Health, London.

NHS Executive (1996b), *Clinical Guidelines: Using Clinical Guidelines to Improve Patient Care Within the NHS*, Department of Health, London.

NHS Executive (1998), *A First Class Service: Quality in the New NHS*, Department of Health, London.

Pauly, M. V. (1968), 'The Economics of Moral Hazard', *American Economic Review*, 58: 531-57.

Polanyi M. (1967), *The Tacit Dimension*, Anchor, New York.

Secretary of State for Health (1997), *The New NHS: Modern, Dependable*, Cm 3807, Stationery Office, London.

# 8 Cervical Cancer Screening: Policy or Implementation Failure?

ALISON HANN

On the 4th of February 1999, in her speech to the House of Lords, Baroness Gould of Potternewton expressed what is probably the opinion of the majority of politicians. She remarked:

> Cervical cancer screening is essential for early detection. The cervical cancer screening programme offers a proven test.... My noble friend was so correct in her appeal to women to continue to attend screening for both breast and cervical cancer. Nevertheless, women throughout the country must now have reservations about the reliability of the system. Their confidence will be restored only when they see the success of the changes being made to improve the service and the elimination of the current unacceptable variations of provision in different parts of the country. (Hansard, 4/3/96)

There is almost universal political support for the *idea* of screening for cervical cancer. When questions are asked in the House, or when Ministers are driven to comment on the cervical cancer screening service, responses are always couched in terms of improving a service that is life saving and cost effective. What failings it has, are marginal, and are mostly the result of individual hospital trusts being lax in some way. Frank Dobson has been a staunch supporter of both the breast and cervical cancer screening programmes, and even after the scandal at the Canterbury and Kent hospital trust, he said:

> Overwhelmingly, the breast and cervical screening programmes in this country do an excellent job, and save women's lives. (DOH Press Release, 3/11/97)

Not only this, but the programme enjoys cross party support. Cervical cancer screening, it seems, is something that unites politicians of all parties.

109

This is evident from the construction of policy in this field. The Conservative Governments White Papers: *The Health of the Nation* (1992), and *Primary Care: Delivering the Future*, (1996), and Labour's Green Paper *Our Healthier Nation,* (1998), all set targets for the reduction in mortality from cervical cancer through national screening programme and few commentators, political or medical, question its usefulness.

Screening for cancer of the cervix has been routine in the UK since the mid sixties. It is clear to even the most niave observer of public policy that it has been dogged with problems and difficulties. Serious failures have regularly been reported in the popular press. Consequently there have been a whole series of working party reports, internal inquiries, policy reviews, overhauls and reorganisations. Particularly in the last decade. Yet the problems with the service have persisted. One recent high profile case concerned the Kent and Canterbury Hospital Trust where 82,000 women had to be recalled for rescreening, and involved a series of mistakes spanning nearly five years. This case led Baroness Jay to instigate an Independent Review of cervical screening services, headed by Sir William Wells, chairman of the NHS Executive at South Thames, who in his introductory remarks stated that:

'The aim of the review was to restore public confidence . . . and to ensure that lessons were learned for the future' (p5).

Both of these things are clearly crucial if a population based screening programme such as this one is going to succeed, and the purpose of this chapter is to examine the recent experiences of the cervical screening programme and to explore why it seems to experience very similar crises at regular intervals, and to explain some of the poitical and administrative factors involved. But, before we examine in detail the growth in the UK of the cervical cancer screening programme, some attention needs to be paid to the controversy surrounding the test itself, and to its usefulness as a diagnostic tool. This controversy has been raging for almost as long as the Pap smear test has been in existence, and is central when considering the validity of the national programme and also the problems that it has been experiencing.

There is no doubt that established carcinoma of the cervix is a serious and life threatening disease. But it is uncommon, particularly in young women. There is no hard and fast definition of 'common' but by comparison to breast cancer, cancer of the cervix is unusual, and a GP would not expect to sign a death certificate with this diagnosis more than once or twice in a professional lifetime. One of the major problems (clinically speaking) with screening for cervical cancer is the questionable significance of minor abnormalities (or low grade lesions). It is estimated that some 20% of women who are screened have lesions of this kind (McMeekin, 1998), and most of these would not progress to cancer if left alone. The benefit of screening is based upon the assumption that at least some of these lesions are precursors of invasive cancer, and that their identification and treatment will prevent serious disease. But in fact the natural history of these abnormalities is poorly understood. In one study for example Montz and co-workers (1992) found that 71% of patients had spontaneous regression to normal after a classification of this kind, while other researchers have reported from between 40% to 62% regression rates (Nash, 1987; Nasiel, 1986).

Population screening strategies should comply with a number of criteria: they should be cheap, acceptable, valid, reliable, repeatable, specific, sensitive and risk free. And each of these criteria should ideally be examined (and satisfied) if a national policy is to make any sense, medically, economically and politically.

Cost Estimates of the cost of a single smear vary from £15-35, and the test has to be repeated at regular intervals (the exact interval is still under debate). Analysis of the costs of the programme are complex because the determination of 'total' or 'full' costs is very elusive, but the latest estimate given by the National Audit Office is the programme costs 'around £130 million' per year. In addition, the Commission noted that there were 'wide variations in unit costs at screening laboratories and follow up clinics that were hard to explain'. While doctors are held increasingly accountable to function within health care budgets, cost effectiveness is rarely specifically addressed with respect to the cervical cancer screening programme, and in particular with regard to opportunity costs (the amount of alternative services that must be sacrificed to screen more patients or offer more effective screening services), and to the broad economic costs of 'overdiagnosis'. Screening has the potential for generating excessive spending when patients who will never develop cancer are repeatedly screened or treated. In a meta-analysis carried out by Fahey (1995) it was found that:

> Pap smear sensitivity may be closer to 20% or 30% than to the commonly held 80% or 90%. Therefore understanding the limitations of Pap smear surveillance strategies is essential in counselling patients and in providing

safe and cost effective screening. Although smears in themselves are relatively inexpensive, they can lead to further diagnostic work-up (e.g. colposcopy, biopsy) and patient anxiety. These costs . . . include variables that can be difficult to factor into any cost-effectiveness equation (p3) and in addition to this new technologies have the actual potential to increase total cost by increasing the identification of clinically insignificant lesions. Overdiagnosis clearly leads to 'overtreatment' and increased costs. In a study of more than 225,000 English women screened, 15,000 smears were found to be 'abnormal' and roughly 6000 of these women underwent colposcopy. Using data collected from an era prior to the initiation of widespread cervical cancer screening, 200 cases of cervical cancer would be anticipated from a similar population of 225,000 women.

The investigators suggested that widespread screening results in the excessive identification of 'at risk' patients, leading to unnecessary work-up of more than 95% of women (5,800 of 6000) many of whom would also receive treatment. Other commentators have also noted the tendency to overtreat and overdiagnose. Alwyn Smith (1998) discusses the number of women who are referred for colposcopy on the basis of marginally abnormal smear results. He says:

It is absurd to conduct a screening test in such a way that nearly 40 women are referred for an expensive and possibly hazardous procedure for every one who is at risk of developing serious disease. We need more common sense and a more discriminatory assessment of the results of screening tests (p1670).

## Acceptability

Because the test involves a vaginal examination with a speculum, it is by no means universally acceptable to women, especially when it is carried out by a male doctor. Attendance rates would suggest that this is particularly the case for some groups of women. The poor and those women over the age of 40 are less likely to attend than younger and better off women. There is also evidence to suggest that women from ethic minority groups, particularly those of the Moslem faith are much more likely to view the test as unacceptable due to cultural and religious mores.

112

## Repeatability and Reliability

Repeatability and reliability refer to a tests ability to produce consistent results, and the interpretation of slides has been problematic, especially where low grade lesions are concerned. Studies conducted by Richart (1993) and Raffle, (1995) both point out that subtle abnormalities are increasingly diagnosed as 'possibly dysplasic' as pathologists becoming concerned about being accused of 'missing' cancers err on the side of caution. In addition they found that tests that are repeated at short intervals are likely to yield inconsistent results.

## Specificity and Reliability

The validity of the Pap smear test is low for a variety of reasons. As mentioned earlier there are problems associated with the interpretation of the slides. One reason for this is that many slides are technically unsatisfactory. For a smear to be correctly analysed, the specimen must be adequately collected. In one study (Gay, 1985) it was reported that sampling errors by the clinician accounted for 62% of false negative smears. These errors included inadequate sampling of the transformation zone, poor collection and fixation of the specimen, and the inclusion of excessive blood, inflammatory or necrotic material. But leaving aside technical problems related to the slide itself, it has been estimated that approximately 20% of slides are falsely negative, while the rate of false positives is difficult to estimate due to the ambivalence of low grade abnormalities.

## Risk

The Pap smear test is generally thought of as being risk free, there is limited evidence to suggest that there is some risk of cross infection from speculum contamination (McCormick). In addition there is the morbidity associated with the diagnosis of low grade abnormalities and the psychological strain caused by the unnecessary follow up of such lesions including colposcopy and biopsy.

There are very few randomised controlled trials of screening for cervical cancer and little immediate prospect that any are likely to be carried out. The most influential study that has been done, was the one conducted in Canada that gave rise to the enthusiasm for cervical screening in the first place. The Canadian study achieved very high levels of population screening in British Columbia but not in the rest of the country. The reduction in mortality from carcinoma of the cervix was no greater than in the other provinces, and this pattern of falling mortality has been observed elsewhere, and seems to be independent of the screening for women for the disease. Recent trends in the UK show a virtually unchanged mortality rate despite more than 80 million smears, and some have argued that this reflects containment of a deteriorating problem. Raffle (1997) for example remarks;

> A fall in the number of deaths from cervical cancer occurred in each successive cohort this century. This trend predated screening (pp953-954).

In the UK the fact that the cervical cancer screening programme was based on somewhat flimsy evidence of benefit right from the start was (and still is) openly acknowledged. In an annual report published as recently as 1991, the National Co-ordinating Network admitted that:

> unfortunately cervical cancer (screening) was introduced before randomised controlled trials . . . furthermore it would now probably be impossible to obtain ethical approval for such a trial because of assumptions about the effectiveness of the screening test, in part because the women themselves believe in it so strongly in the effectiveness of cervical cancer screening it would be difficult to recruit controls, even if ethical approval for the trials could be obtained (p3).

But despite this recognition, enthusiasm for the programme grew unabated, with support, it seems from all quarters.

Unlike the breast cancer screening programme, the cervical cancer screening programme began, not as a fully fledged national programme, rather it 'just growed' as a piecemeal service offered, at first by individual Health Authorities throughout the sixties. By 1965, over 700,000 smears had been taken and by 1985, a decade later, this figure had risen to 3 million. But despite all this screening activity, there did not appear to be a commensurate decrease in the mortality rates, and the programme was being subjected to growing criticism, with one particularly swingeing attack being published in *The Lancet* in August 1985. The editorial pointed to a number of organisational inadequacies, that it claimed had led to large

114

numbers of women dying due to the inefficiency and bad organisation of the programme. In particular, the author noted problems with the call and recall systems, and the organisational chaos including the lack of clear lines of accountability and poor communication and co-operation between the various departments within the NHS that deal with the different stages of the processing of screening. With reference to the call and recall systems *The Lancet* editorial described a system which was 'untouched by computer'. The staff in Health Authority offices simply stacked duplicates of requisition forms — kept them for five years, and then posted them back to the woman concerned. No register was kept and it was not possible to monitor the frequency of elicited repeat examinations. Neither was there any way the system could link one smear with another. 'Positive' rates were calculated from numerators and denominators obtained from two different sources. The denominators were based on small samples and were estimated by measuring the thickness of heaps of papers with a ruler (pressed down to compensate for paper clips) and the numerators were provided by the laboratories.

Growing concern over the inefficiency of the screening programme was fuelled by worries over its ineffectiveness after a series of scandals were reported in the media concerning a number of women dying of cervical cancer after either having received false positive results, or because they had not been informed of a positive result. As a result of the these cases the Department of Health took an number of steps in 1986 and 1987 designed to promote clear national policy guidelines. The then Minister for health called for a computerised call and recall system. But his directive was largely ignored due to administrative confusion caused by the separation of FPC's from the Regional and District Health Authorities, the net result of which was that no one was left with overall responsibility for maintaining records.

In 1988 the Department of Health issued a major circular on cervical cancer screening and an inter-collegiate Working Party report was published, both of which made recommendations to improve the screening service which was still suffering from serious problems. These recommendations were:

1) Health Authorities must introduce a computerised call and recall system
2) A system of external quality control (EQA) must be ensured, and

115

3) A named individual with overall responsibility must be appointed.

But the publication of a policy document and recommendations does not necessarily result in an improvement in service. No additional resources were put into the management of the programme, and the requirement to nominate an individual to be responsible for the 'organisation and effectiveness of cervical cancer screening' was not accompanied by the provision of resources to enable that person to carry out the task. In addition, while it was recognised that there was inadequate training and monitoring of 'smear takers' which was leading to a high proportion of technically inadequate smears, the recommendation that 'a comprehensive education programme to train doctors and nurses in how to take smears' (DoH circular HC(88)1) was not accompanied by any allocation of resources either.

1991 saw the creation of the National Co-ordinating Network, who were charged by the Department of Health with the job of improving the screening programme. In their first annual report they concluded that:

1) A 'distressingly high' proportion of women found to have abnormal smears were not adequately investigated,
2) The majority of women who had participated, were not informed of the result of their test,
3) The quality of smears submitted for cytological appraisal was frequently unsatisfactory, and
4) Funding and resourcing for the screening programme had not had the priority that the size of the problem warranted.

Between 1991 and 1994 no less than 21 groups and committees had been appointed either by the Department of Health or by the National Co-ordinating Network to examine and monitor standards and practices, and to make recommendations for improvements. In addition, the National Audit Office identified a whole range of technical and administrative problems with the programme. As to the general quality of the programme, the National Audit Office commented:

The cervical cancer screening programme was introduced in the NHS in the 60's without the benefit of prior clinical trials, and there is even less consensus now within the medical profession on the best way of dealing with abnormalities found during the screening process. Although guidance exists, it is not universally accepted, and there are no quantified standards against which Authorities can compare their performance. Further guidance on interpreting smears and on the best way of dealing with abnormalities had been developed and is currently under discussion (p27).

But despite all the official activity, scandals continued to find their way into the media. In the first two months of 1994, 4,000 women had to be recalled for rescreening after a Health Authority admitted that it had 'forgotten them'. 362 women had to be recalled from a Birmingham practice when it was discovered that a nurse was using the wrong spatula and 500 women had to be recalled following 'uncertainty' over test results at a Norfolk hospital. A further series of scandals in 1995 over ineffective smear tests led to the publication of two Department of Health circulars: *Quality in the Cervical Cancer Screening Programme* and *Improvements to the Operation of the Cervical Cancer Screening Programme*. In these circulars FHAs were urged to learn how to 'use effectively' the computerised call and recall systems that they had had installed, and it was also recommended that extra effort should be made to ensure 'effective' collaboration. This included the dissemination of information between specialists, laboratories and practices. In the same year (1995) a Working Party set up by the Royal College of Pathologists, the British Society for Clinical Cytology and the NHSCSP published a joint report: *Achievable Benchmarks for Reporting and Criteria for Evaluating Cervical Cytopathology*. The working Party was primarily concerned with internal quality assessment (IQA). This involved the publication of guidelines for improving the accuracy of reading smear tests, which was essential if the 'Health of the Nations' targets were to be met. The working party's stated aims were:

1) To reinforce and to revise existing guidelines for reporting cervical smears and clarify areas of potential misunderstandings,
2) To propose standard ranges for reporting negative, inadequate and abnormal categories of cervical smears,
3) To identify pitfalls which may lead to false positives or false negatives, and to
4) Propose criteria and standards for evaluating performance and effectiveness of cervical cytopathology, and in addition this report emphasised the continuing importance of external quality assessment (EQA) and clinical audit.

117

What seems clear so far, is that the screening programme suffered from recurring problems in the same areas over and over again. Moreover, these problem areas i.e. call and recall, technical problems regarding both the taking and the interpretation of smears and the lack of co-operation and communication between involved professionals, although well recognised and documented seem to have presented intractable problems despite all the reports, committees and directives. But worse was yet to come. In February of 1996, yet another scandal was to make national headline news. Over 80,000 women were to be recalled for repeat tests after checks revealed 'errors' at a Kent hospital. The sheer size of this incident prompted the Secretary off State for Health to instigate an independent review headed by Sir William Wells. The Wells Report was published in October of 1997, and made a number of observations:

1) Although guidelines had been widely published via circulars and executive letters concerning the importance of EQA, it was not 'compulsory' that departments should take part in EQA exercises. In the case of the Kent and Canterbury Hospital Trust 'excessive workloads' was given as a reason for two of the three consultants in the hospital refusing to participate in the South East Thames Region Cytology EQA Scheme.

2) The Kent and Canterbury cytology laboratory never enrolled for the recommended external accreditation scheme. Trust managers seemed unconcerned by the lack of EQA and accreditation, even though junior members of the team had warned Trust managers a number of times, over a four year period, that the error rate was unacceptably high.

3) The high workload was exacerbated by staff shortages, which in turn were caused by quarrels between consultants and pathology laboratory technicians over who to appoint, and for which bench the new appointee would have IQA was carried out by a colleague who was not actually qualified, and when the inquiry team asked for the IQA report, it 'could not be located'.

4) With the advent of the internal market, responsibility for the various elements of the screening programme became even more fragmented and disorganised: 'lines of accountability for the already complex local screening programme have been

118

further fragmented by the separation of the purchaser and provider functions within the NHS' (p9).

5) With regard to the actual taking of the smear — although smear takers were 'invited' to undertake training and refresher courses, many did not, and it was not clear 'how comprehensive the training is' (p13).

6) There was clear evidence that there had been a catalogue of mistakes concerning the 'reading' of smears by the Kent and Canterbury Laboratory: 'Evidence available to the review team included several cases of serial misreporting of smears from the same women, which in some instances extended back into the 1980s. The nature of the errors suggested that they included major errors of interpretation' (p31).

Once the report was published, the political response was swift. Baroness Jay published a statement which said that 'women were let down by unacceptable errors' and that 'action will be taken to address the failures of the cervical cancer screening services . . . I am dismayed by the litany of management weaknesses, unheeded warnings and poor quality control systems detailed in the report'.

In December 1997, Sir Kenneth Calman (Chief Medical Officer) announced a 'far reaching action plan' which he claimed would 'strengthen' the cervical screening programme. The package of measures included an insistence that all laboratories carrying out cervical screening must apply for accreditation, and that all smear takers must receive 'adequate training'. Exactly how effective his action plan will be, remains to be seen. But the intransigence of individuals within the system to directives, action plans and educational drives remains, and is illustrated by two incidents in November 1997. In one case 738 women had to be recalled when it was discovered that a GP was found to have been collecting cervical smears using his finger, (which the doctor claimed was 'suitable for women from lower socio-economic groups') while in another incident Mr Monoghan, a consultant in gynaecological oncology was found to have been keeping his test results 'a secret', and reporting his own pathology results. In addition, the National Audit Office completed their investigation of the screening service in May 1998 and noted that there was still 'considerable scope for improvement'. Especially with respect to call and recall systems. What is clear, is that the problems being experienced by the programme in 1998 are not so very different from the ones that it faced in 1965. Even to the most cynical observer this seems extraordinary, and deserves some explanation. Can the difficulties experienced by the programme really be blamed on organisational or administrative failures alone?, or is there a more fundamental question to be asked concerning the implementation of a national programme of screening based on a medical test which had flimsy evidence of benefit? Especially when the inadequacies of the screening test were well recognised within the medical establishment.

The late Petr Skrabanek describes the use of population based cervical cancer screening as the triumph of wishful thinking over clinical evidence. And what is more he suggests that this 'wishful, but woefully unscientific thinking' has become institutionalised: 'The Royal College of General Practitioners have fervently embraced the cause because they believe the axiom that prevention is better than cure (which is by no means always the case). Furthermore, the mistaken assumptions concerning the benefit of screening have become so entrenched with the lay public that to suggest that the programme may be ineffective or mistaken in its precepts is to commit a kind of heresy' (1996). This point is also made by Suzanne Fletcher in her article *Whither Scientific Deliberation in Health Policy Recommendations* (1997). She reflects upon the way in which cancer screening policy was formulated in the USA, and pointed to the way that strong public opinion in favour of screening meant that despite clear medical evidence to the contrary, Congress reversed a previous ruling which found that in the light of medical evidence that universal screening of women, in this case for breast cancer, was 'not warranted'. She comments:

> The events surrounding the report by the NIH panel on breast cancer screening raises the fundamental question of how best to make clinical policy. Should scientific controversies be approached by examining the facts, deliberately and carefully, with the aid of unbiased, independent scientific experts representing multiple disciplines? or should these controversies be settled on the front page of The New York Times or as a lead story on ABC World News Tonight? (p1181).

In other words she is claiming that the careful consideration of scientific evidence becomes secondary to other, and more political interests. But 'wishful thinking' has other and more serious ramifications. Because the conventional wisdom of benefit is never seriously questioned, the cervical screening programme continues to expand, the costs are huge and the vested interests vast. As Skrabanek (1994) points out 'the fact is that screening is a swinging, lucrative business' (p35).

But has the programme been a failure?. This of course rather depends upon how 'failure' is defined, and by whom. Furthermore, as Wildavsky observes: 'whether certain policy episodes are to be judged as major failures strongly depends on who is doing the judging, and what yardsticks they use, when they do it, and on the basis of what information'. Bearing this in mind, the programme might be considered a success in two ways. Firstly, it has been a success in terms of its public acceptance and support, and secondly in terms of its political acceptance and support. What is crucial in securing both public and political support for a policy programme is not just its substance, but how it looks. Political judgements about the success or failure of a programme (or policy) are more often than not based on impressions about the effects and costs of the programme, especially in the case of technical areas where specialised knowledge is needed in order to understand the complexities of possible costs and benefits. Approval and support therefore may or may not be related to 'actual' or 'real' benefits that the programme may have produced. In this case then clearly the programme has been a success since its public and political support seem obvious.

Another way of looking at relative success or failure is to consider how much, if any, damage has been done. That is to say that on some level or other, the cervical cancer screening programme has done more harm than good. But this also turns out to be a complex issue. Some commentators, such as Skrabanek, have pointed out that hundreds of women every year are subjected to 'unnecessary' procedures such as biopsy or colposcopy, and that this is clearly damaging or harmful. But as was mentioned above, the relative success or failure of a programme may not be judged by the public on the basis of their 'real' benefits. Instead success may be judged on the basis of images or symbols. To some women perhaps, the procedures of biopsy and colposcopy may represent a kind of symbolic cleansing, for which they are grateful. They feel that they have been 'saved', 'purified' and of course 'cured'. Similarly, the professionals involved in the process feel that they have successfully treated a case of cervical cancer, and so could easily have saved the woman's life – furthermore the programme is one which 'everyone knows' is praiseworthy, saves lives and prevents disease.

Another problem associated with the label 'failure' is that it also suggests, that at some level someone is to blame. This leads to questions such as 'did the policy makers fail to see that there were problems with the

121

programme, and did they deliberately ignore it. Did they deliberately choose the wrong way of dealing with the perceived problem?' The answer to these questions is complex. Given the above discussion, it seems clear that the time scale needs to be considered. The programme, after all, spans a number of political administrations and has gained considerable political momentum, it would be difficult to apportion 'blame' to any single agency or individual. Rather, each administration has, to borrow a phrase, lurched from crisis to complacency with each successive scandal. Instigating inquiries, issuing guidelines and overhauling practice. Each dealing with an existing state of affairs, but never questioning the wisdom of having the programme in the first place. The answer then, to the question posed at the beginning of this chapter: (is it the cervical screening *policy* that is apparently failing, or is it a failure of *implementation)* is the time honoured 'that depends'. Problems have undoubtedly arisen due to faulty organisation, poor (or absent) funding, clinical incompetence and structural difficulties caused by such things as the internal market, and some of these things can be 'blamed' on the badly constructed policy, and some are clearly matters concerned with weak and sometimes haphazard implementation. But clearly, however one defines success or failure, it cannot be denied that the cervical cancer screening programme has not lived up to its promises. Some commentators, such as Skrabanek (1988) would argue that the cervical cancer screening programme can never live up to its promises, however well organised or well funded it may be because the test is flawed and the promises false.

# References

*Daily Telegraph,* (1997), 29 April.

Department of Health, (1997), *Review of cervical cancer screening services at Canterbury Hospitals NHS Trust.* London: DoH.

Department of Health, (1997), Press Release, 3 November.

Editorial (1998), 'The screening muddle', *The Lancet* 351, Number 9101, 14th February, pp 101-102.

Fahey, M., lrwig. L., Macaskill, P. (1995), *Meta analysis of Pap test accuracy, Am J Epidemioly* 336:1180.

Foster, P. (1996), *Women and the health care industry,* Milton Keynes: Open University Press.

Furedi, F. (1998), *Culture of Fear,* London: Cassell.

McMeekin, (1998), *Cervical cancer prevention: towards a cost effective Service,* Medscape Women's Health, hhtp://www.com..

McCormick, J. (1989), 'Cervical smears: a questionable practice', *Lancet* : II: 207-209.

Medscape Womens Health, (1998), hhtp://www.com.

Office For National Surveys (1998), *Cancer Incidence selected sites.*

Office For National Surveys (1998), Causes of Death in 1998. *Mortality Statistics, cause: England and Wales)* series DH2, no. 23.

*Hansard, 19* May, (1998), col. WA162.

Raffle, A., Alden, B., Mackenzie, E. (1985), 'Detection rates for abnormal cervical smears: what are we screening for?', *Lancet* 345: 1469-1473.

Raffle A. (1997), *Deaths from cervical cancer began falling before screening programmes were established, BMJ* 315: 953-954.

Sabatier, P. (1988), *An advocacy coalition framework of policy change and the role of policy oriented learning therein. Policy Sciences* 2, 129-169.

Shrader-Frechette, K. (1991), *Risk and Rationality: Philosophical Foundations forPopularist Reforms,* Berkeley: University of California Press.

Skrabanek, P. (1987), *Cervical cancer screening. Lancet* 1: 1432.

Skrabanek, P. (1994), *The Death of Humane Medicine and the Rise of Coercive Healthism,* Bury St Edmunds, Suffolk: The Social Affairs Unit.

Widavsky, A. (1972), *The art and craft of policy analysis,* London: Pluto. England and Wales. *ONS Monitor DH2 98/1.*

# 9 Some Are More Equal Than Others: Differing Levels of Representation in Primary Care Groups

KERRI SMITH and ROD SHEAFF

## Introduction

It is often argued that the NHS has undergone more fundamental transformation during the last decade than it has seen during its entire history (Robinson 1998, King's Fund 1998). This is especially true of its organisational structure. The focus on organisational direction through strongly defined general management gave way to an internal or quasi-market culture as a result of the reforms introduced by the NHS and Community Care Act of 1990. Thus began a paradigm shift producing tremendous organisation culture movement which changed the whole framework within which the NHS operated. The main features of this structural reorganisation included the new provider/purchaser split, the search for increased efficiency and effectiveness of services through introduced competition, and GP fundholding. It also became clear that there was an incremental change towards a primary care-led NHS.

In 1997 the Government also faced the first change of hands that it had seen in 18 years. While the Labour Party fulfilled its role as 'The Opposition', the move towards market values in the public sector was strongly and consistently denounced. Party rhetoric centred around arguments of the inappropriateness of the marketisation of a public service, inequality and two-tierism, increased fragmentation and an absence of any accountability structures. A central tenet of their election manifesto was the abolition of the internal market in the public sector. Once in office, however, the rhetoric shifted. The first NHS White Paper *The New NHS. Modern. Dependable.* (1997) outlined an emphasis on building on the successes of the last reforms, such as the purchaser/provider split, and the phasing out of those deemed unsuccessful or unpalatable like GP fundholding.

In this paper we will attempt to examine a central policy reform outlined in the White Paper: the establishment of Primary Care Groups (PCGs). In particular, we will address the issue of representation and partnership in PCGs. We begin by outlining the purpose and intended functions of PCGs paying special attention to the rhetoric surrounding their development and their ensuing governance structures. We specifically make the point that there is a discrepancy between the early policy rhetoric, and the subsequent guidance and implementation. This paper will focus on the disparity of power and influence that various stakeholders have wielded during the planning and development stages of the new Primary Care Groups and that the changes in rhetoric and guidance have allowed certain groups to dominate the implementation of PCGs, facilitating the 'capture' of the agenda. As the White Paper (1997) highlighted the roles of GPs and nurses as the 'driving force' that would carry the reforms forward special attention was paid to these groups. Our points will be illustrated by empirical evidence drawn from a programme of work carried out at the National Primary Care Research and Development Centre at the University of Manchester.

**The Form and Functions of PCGs**

*The New NHS: Modern. Dependable* presented an agenda for establishing Primary Care Groups (PCGs) across England. While Scotland was charged with setting up Local Health Care Committees (LHCCs) and Wales Local Health Groups (LHGs), there are significant differences between these and PCGs, and for the purpose of this paper only PCGs are considered. There will be approximately 480 PCGs in England alone, based on 'natural communities' of around 100,000 populations and coterminosity with agencies' existing boundaries. Where natural communities are deemed not to exist, these groups have in many cases developed out of existing primary care innovations such as Locality Commissioning Groups (LCGs), Total Purchasing Projects (TPPs), multi-funds, and GP fundholding. Indeed, central guidance has encouraged basing PCGs on existing innovation experiences. Although not officially 'live' until April 1st 1999, PCGs were in shadow form by November 1998 in order to develop organisational structures and gain experience and knowledge of the functions they would be expected to fulfil. As there is evidence pointing to a lack of uniformity in provision and performance in Primary Care (and experiences of innovations), PCGs have been given the choice (in negotiation with their Health Authority) of 4 stages of development, ranging from an advisory role to complete responsibility for commissioning Primary and Community Care and Trust status. The aim is that every Primary Care Group progresses, over time, to stage 4.

At stage 3 and 4 when PCGs attain Trust status, and to a lesser extent at stage 2, PCGs will have responsibility for commissioning services in their respective localities; monitoring performance and developing primary care, especially in terms of collaboration with other agencies such as the acute sector, community health, social services and local communities. It is in this role that PCGs will be expected to contribute to Health Authority Health Improvement Programmes (called HImPs at the moment, but also known as HIPs in earlier documentation which caused confusion with Local Authority Housing Improvement Plans).

PCGs are governed by a 'Board' (Table 1) which is multi-agency in nature. The Board is accountable to the Health Authority, through the Chair and Chief Executive, and its status is that of a sub-committee to the Health Authority. It must adopt Health Authority standing orders around corporate governance and probity.

Table 1: Composition of the PCG Board

| | |
|---|---|
| 4-7 | General Practitioners |
| 1-2 | Community or Practice Nurses |
| 1 | Social Services Representative |
| 1 | Health Authority Non-Executive |
| 1 | PCG Chief Executive |
| 1 | Lay Person |

**The Guidance: from Partnership to GP Capture**

PCGs were introduced as an effective way to put doctors, nurses and local communities at the forefront in managing local health care. The White Paper (1997) went on to say that an effective delivery of services depended on the ownership of decisions by a wider group of stakeholders. Joint governance, corporate action, inclusion of all those with a legitimate interest — all these have been heavily emphasised, flying the flag for partnership, openness and accountability (Smith and Dickson 1998). However, as we will demonstrate, the subtext of the central guidance is subtly different, and the reality of the implementation of the policy is markedly different.

As with any White Paper or policy decision, it is the subsequent circulars and guidance on implementation which will shape what actually happens. The White Paper sets the philosophy and tone, the guidance deals with the mechanics. After the White Paper (1997), a series of circulars from the Department of Health were issued to direct and facilitate the setting up of PCGs. The first of these circulars identified a range of criteria which health authorities were told they must follow as they finalised the configuration of PCGs:

'. . . proposals for the configuration of the groups should be bottom up, emerging from discussions between Health Authorities, GPs, nurses, other health care professionals, community and acute NHS Trusts, and social services. As Primary Care Groups are to be formed around natural geographical communities it is important that the views of local people are properly taken into account' (HSC 1998/065, p7).

This must have greatly pleased many nurses, in particular those who were disillusioned with the continuing erosion of the profession's contribution to health care planning and development. PCGs seemed to offer a more pluralist approach to primary care development and commissioning (Smith, Dickson and Sheaff 1999). Nurses would have places on the PCG Boards, be called upon to contribute to the drawing up of local Health Improvement Plans (HImPs), and there were hopes of helping to construct a new social model of primary care (Antrobus 1999). As Baroness Jay said (1997):

'Nurses will be key drivers for change in the new NHS, bringing their unique understanding of patients' needs to the new powerful Primary Care Groups . . . The NHS White Paper marks a turning point for nursing. By giving community nurses a formal place on Primary Care Group Boards, the White Paper signals a recognition of the massive contribution nurses can make to improving local health care . . . In the new NHS nurses' views will be heard and valued. Tokenism will not be accepted.' (Department of Health Press Release, 11/12/97).

However, a crucial turning point in the PCGs debate occurred when GP organisations such as the British Medical Association (BMA) and the General Medical Services Committee (GMSC) responded to the reforms by threatening a policy of non-co-operation unless their demands were met. The then Health Minister, Alan Milburn, began lengthy talks with GP organisations and pressure groups. During May and June of 1998, a series of correspondence passed between the head of the GMSC, John Chisolm, and Alan Milburn. Milburn was all too aware that PCGs would not work without the full co-operation of GPs and so the 'Milburn Letter' (see the May 30th issue of Pulse to see an example) eventually gave in to this pressure. Consequently, GPs won a number of concessions; such as the right to refer and prescribe regardless of financial restrictions, assurances that overspends would remain the responsibility of Health Authorities, and 'appropriate remuneration'.

GP demands relating to the composition of the Board were also met. Despite earlier guidance that said that the Board should not be dominated by one professional group, or small circle of individuals, HSC 1998/139 gave GPs the right to a protected majority of up to 7 places, and the Chair. This guidance (HSC 1998/139) stated that if GPs decided to have a GP Chair, then they could decide locally who that Chair should be without any recourse to other stakeholder groups. As this decision was often taken before the rest of the Board was in place, the other Board members were not consulted. GPs were also influential in terms of the configuration of PCGs. Before NHS regional offices approved the configurations, the Health Authorities were forced to detail the involvement and support of GPs and local medical committees (LMCs). These concessions retained medical dominance in primary health care to the cost of nurses. Nurse representation was not at the level they had expected: instead of partnership nurses got 1-2 places on the Board. However, it is also true that this is an improvement on their previous position of no voice at all.

There is only one member from the Local Authority Social Services Department (LASSD) on the PCG Board. This person may serve on more than one PCG, reducing the opportunity for each Board to have the input of operational LASSD staff with specific locality knowledge. There is also only one lay member per Board, and there is no requirement for that person to belong to any organised community, or specialist interest group.

The language used to describe the processes for filling these places was significant. GPs were to be 'elected', Social Services 'nominated', nurses 'determined' and lay members 'appointed'. Whereas GPs were selected by their peers, nurses had a two-tier selection process; an initial nomination process followed by selection by the Health Authority. The guidance on Board standing orders reinforced the dominance of GPs. Meetings of PCG Boards will only be deemed quorate *if one third of members (including the Chair) is present and where the majority of those present are GPs.* For a PCG Board with nine members (the minimum) 3 GPs could take decisions about local services.

## The Empirical Evidence

*The Project*

The work on which this paper is based is part of the programme of the National Primary Care Research and Development Centre (NPCRDC), based at the University of Manchester and supported by the Department of Health. The data were generated by an exploratory project conducted by the authors. The aim of the study was to explore the formation processes behind the new PCGs. As indicated by the nature of an exploratory project, initially a very wide focus was taken. The need for reflexivity called for a qualitative approach, and the tools used drew from this paradigm. Semi-structured interviews were constructed based on our existing knowledge of primary care organisations (NPCRDC has been involved in work on topics such as Total Purchasing, Primary Care Act Pilot Sites, GP fundholding and GP co-operatives, for example), the White Paper and ensuing central guidance. We also gained access to early planning meetings such as Steering Groups and various PCG-linked sub-committees.

We looked at 4 embryonic PCGs, an inner city site, an industrial town, a suburban site and a rural site, with varying experiences of primary care innovations. During the course of the exploration we spoke to most of the stakeholder groups, including Health Authorities, the Local Authority Social Services Department, Community Trusts, Community Health Councils, GPs and nurses. The timescale of the project was 6 months and coincided with the early planning processes in April 1998, to the end of October 1998 just prior to the PCGs going live in shadow form.

## Stakeholder Representation and Influence in the Implementation Process

In the period January to October 1998, Primary Care Groups did not exist, and as such were just a collection of different agencies, organisations and professional groups who were required to work together to establish new fully operational PCGs by April 1, 1999. The need to resolve PCG configuration by the July 1998 deadline was the first priority for Health Authority managers.

The national guidance was unequivocal on the need for open local debates about PCG size and boundaries which involved *all* the relevant stakeholders. However, a comprehensive, effective partnership operating across health and social care boundaries certainly did not materialise in any of the four study PCGs. It quickly became clear to us that some stakeholders had more impact than others, and the health authorities varied in their willingness to facilitate real debate.

Between February and June 1998, each of the four study health authorities released a consultation document setting out their own proposals for PCG configuration. These documents were circulated widely to local GPs, Community Trusts, LASSDs, local councils, MPs, Community Health Councils, and in the case of locality D, the public via libraries and voluntary groups. No effort was made to consult clinical nurses directly in any of the four localities and it was clear that Trusts had inadequate or non-existent mechanisms for representing the views of practice and community nurses.

*Health Authority*

Unsurprisingly, until February 1998 the implementation agenda of PCGs was largely driven by Executive Teams at the Health Authorities. These teams pushed the early agenda forward in isolation from other stakeholder groups. By April, the creation of PCGs had been rolled out in each of the four PCGs to include the establishment of Steering Groups which were multi-agency in nature. It became clear that there was a core of stakeholder groups who were deemed to have a legitimate interest in the PCGs and were consequently included in each of the Steering Groups. These included the Health Authority, the Local Authority Social Services Department, Community Trusts, GPs (sometimes in the form of LMC representation), Community Health Councils and in two instances, fundholding managers. In three of the Health Authorities studied, the multi-agency representation was restricted to high-level managers and directors from each stakeholder group. In PCG C anyone could attend if they were considered to have a legitimate interest, i.e. were members of identified stakeholder groups. Consequently, attendance at these meetings was often in excess of thirty. These Steering Groups monitored the implementation of all PCGs in their districts but were, for the most part, information-sharing fora rather than decision-making exercises. It is unclear to the authors, because of the limited nature of the exploratory study, what impact these Steering Groups have had on the implementation agendas of the Health Authorities.

By the summer of 1998, offshoot committees were established to take specific agendas forward, e.g. financial matters, IM&T, organisational development and human resource issues. Again these were based at the Health Authority (although multi-agency in nature) and were concerned with all PCGs in their given areas. Thus a complex and hierarchical managerial structure was very quickly established.

Under these committees came individual PCG project teams. These teams were either co-ordinated by Health Authority-appointed Project Managers or the existing Primary Care Development Managers (PCDMs). These Project Managers remained the official link between the Health Authority and the PCGs, and became responsible for developing the PCG agenda in each of the constituencies. They were also instrumental in getting the stakeholder groups into embryonic partnerships locally. Notably, GPs were clearly outnumbered on the Health Authority-based meetings, an outcome seen by some as an attempt to curb GP influence:

'To my mind this is becoming rather top heavy and its duplication, and it smells a bit of the Health Authority wanting to ensure that they've got proper . . . control, but I think GPs see it as potentially a way of reducing PCG autonomy . . .' (GP, PCG A)


It is worth emphasising that although much of the implementation agenda for PCGs was inclusive of most stakeholder groups, it never became clear to us to what extent the multi-agency views canvassed were actually incorporated into the Health Authorities pre-existing plans. The Chair and the majority of members on each of these groups and committees (except for the individual PCG Project Teams) were Health Authority representatives.

In each of the 4 PCGs studied as part of this project, both the Health Authority and the GPs saw their relationship with each other as the most important partnership to be developed and maintained if PCGs were to operate effectively. This relationship did not evolve from the early planning stages. At that stage it was about multi-agency partnership. However, there was a substantial shift in emphasis in the aftermath of the Chisolm letter which agreed to GP Groups demands for dominance, and so it necessitated a firmer alliance with GPs. Thus the Health Authority and the GPs formed a dominant coalition in PCG planning. The Health Authority felt that the control they had initially began to dissipate as the GPs gained more influence, as this first quote illustrates:

'I think the Chisolm letter really set the cat amongst the pigeons. It took everyone by surprise. The nurses, voluntary organisations and the Borough Council had been thinking in terms of equal partnership. A lot of work has gone in to reassuring all the stakeholders, except the GPs of course, they don't need reassuring. They know they have control now.' (Health Authority, PCG B).

As a result of GPs perceptions of the Health Authority 'running the show', it became evident that GPs had begun to meet separately to discuss the implications of PCGs. In turn, this provoked some tensions amongst the remaining stakeholder groups and organisations:

'In the [A] locality...the initial meetings were GPs only and they didn't want anyone else involved. So they didn't want nurses, practice managers, social services, any other associated professions muscling in on their discussions . . .' (Health Authority, PCG A).

'I have been to meetings early on in this process that have been GP only. When they actually invited me to speak (at first I was there to observe, not allowed to speak), I said "well what about the others?" They said, "we'll invite them when we need them." I said "but you need them now to start shaping the groups, you need them in right from the start and not later on".' (Community Health Council, PCG B).

Many of the other stakeholder groups have had little confidence in the ability of GPs to undertake their new dominant role, pointing particularly to the difference between their rapid worlds of 'see, diagnose, treat, send them out the door', and the strategic approach that they would have to learn as leads in the new PCGs. This is somewhat unfair, however, and underestimates the learning that GPs underwent with fundholding, total purchasing and locality commissioning. It also misrepresents the clinical work of GPs when approximately half of all consultations are follow-ups, or chromic disease management, for example. The stakeholder groups asked, however, also felt that GPs have not appreciated that the flip side of power is responsibility and accountability. The Health Authorities were not so concerned:

> 'There's not much that any PCG can do without the Health Authority's blessing. And if someone from the Health Authority wasn't out there with the practices nothing would happen, to be honest. They wouldn't organise themselves. No. They'd still be reading the White Paper [laughs]' (Health Authority, PCG C).

This view did not gel with the views expressed by many of the stakeholders that GPs are waiting to snatch control of the PCGs. GPs insist, on the other hand, that PCGs could not operate effectively without the GPs input and support:

> 'If GPs don't agree with the HImP at the end of the day it won't get implemented. The vast majority of the HImP will be delivered within primary and secondary care and without the active co-operation of primary care upon whom secondary care are often beholden, then its not going to work . . .' (GP, PCG A).

There were also concerns amongst other stakeholder groups that GPs do not form a cohesive group, so their ability to work together in such a dominant role is under question:

'I think there were lots of fears around GP ability to work together with each other because their nurses' experience is that at practice level they don't agree with each other between partners. Now we're not just talking about the odd practice here, I think that there is an overwhelming feeling from everybody that their experience of working in practice is that if there's three or more [GPs] they don't get on with each other. So how does that augur for the future when we've got to have practices not getting on with each other within a PCG area? (Community Trust, PCG C).

The general feeling amongst other stakeholder appeared to be that the problem with GP representation is that if you ask GPs for an opinion you tend to get a whole range of replies because GPs still act individually and will need time to develop a corporate or collective view.

There were fears that fundholding has caused too negative an influence on GP relationships and there were descriptions of bad blood between fundholders and non-fundholders, exacerbating the condition of an already fragmented group. Apparently, there were also fears that fundholding affected GPs relationships with other professional groups:

'Fundholding drastically affects PCG development for the other professions, because I think that the culture here is that doctors rule OK...I do think that fundholding very early on, what it did was completely squashed any professional networks...the level of clinical network has almost exclusively been down to doctors networking with each other and consultants to the exclusion of the other professions'. (Community Trust, PCG A).

Again this shows a contradiction in stakeholder views around whether GPs are a strongly organised profession waiting for the opportunity to seize exclusive control, or a collection of individuals who will never be able to collaborate with each other. Views fall into two camps; either PCGs would fail because GPs would assume full control for their own profession to the exclusion of all other groups, or PCGs would fail because GPs cannot work with each other.

While there is evidence to suggest that GPs who have been members of a strong LCG collaborate with each other more effectively, the downside of this may be that a more cohesive GP faction will dominate a PCG Board even more successfully, to the exclusion of all other groups.

GPs have experienced particular difficulties with the new clinical governance agenda. Consequently, discussions around clinical governance were still as such unformed: this compounded by the fact that definitions are vague and that there does not seem to be a shared understanding of the term, or to whom clinicians should be clinically accountable - their profession, the public or the Health Authority?

'You can't be clinically accountable to anybody unless all the clinicians and all the managers or organisations have some joint understanding of what that is'. (Community Trust rep, PCG A)

'What is clinical governance, exactly? How will it work, do you think?' (GP, PCG C).

For nurses and Community Trust managers, clinical governance was about accountability to patients. In contrast, GPs saw clinical governance as an issue about the accountability of GPs to their peers on the (GP dominated) PCG Boards. Both the Health Authorities and the GPs stressed that if clinical governance was going to work, GPs would need to feel a sense of ownership over the process. This was a sensitive issue, with some GPs feeling a certain amount of 'natural suspicion' that Health Authorities would use clinical governance as an attempt to control practice.

GPs stressed the importance of developing supportive, rather than punitive, mechanisms for achieving clinical governance. It was recognised that the issue of how to deal with clinicians who were 'not up to scratch' was a potential minefield'. Exactly how clinical governance could be implemented had not yet been discussed in any great detail, either by the Health Authorities or by GPs. It is expected that this will change rapidly once the clinical governance leads have had time to create their roles more effectively.

135

The lack of formal or informal communication channels between health authority managers and clinical nurses helps to explain why the latter were largely excluded from the boundaries debate. Most practice and community nurses had no real history of strategic working together — let alone with the health authority — as a result, it took several months for lead clinical nurse representatives to be identified. Nurses did not exactly hit the ground running:

'There's a lot of dreadful resentment and I think it got PCGs off on the wrong foot really...the fact that nurses were excluded initially and I think that there was a lot of misinformation as to why we were excluded, was this what was going to happen? And were we going to be excluded? And would it carry on with very little change from fund holding, but with new labels on the doors?' (Nurse, PCG C).

Within nursing, the development of PCGs was met with particular ambivalence, some welcoming the public health focus, others cynical about the GP dominance and aggrieved at their own lack of involvement in the development process. Nurses' role as partners and major stakeholders in the process were downplayed in each of the 4 PCGs we studied. There was very little evidence to suggest that nurses were really consulted, never mind included in the decision-making process. The nurse input was co-ordinated by Health Authority leads or Community Trust managers, to the nurses disadvantage, as this quote shows, they've not exactly been taken seriously as partners:

'Some of the nurses in this area wrote a letter to Mr Milburn arguing that there should be 4 GPs and 4 nurses (2 community and 2 practice nurses). They weren't just being sarcastic either. They genuinely felt that they should write this letter, which just indicates how far from reality they really are. It may just be me being unkind but I think they had ideas above their station [laughs]' (Community Trust, PCG B).

'In terms of the social model of care, and in terms of developing links with communities and other organisations, they [nurses] are much better placed than GPs. Community nurses and health visitors in particular have to work with so many agencies throughout every day. I keep saying to GPs "don't ignore these skills, use them". But there are an awful lot of community nurses who aren't very good, I mean they are good at being nurses, but not at seeing the wider world. And the Health Visitor association can be a bit of a dinosaur of an organisation...not a positive organisation at all'. (Community Trust, PCG C).

While nurses appeared to be losing their ground, GPs grew more confident of their ability to influence the formation of PCGs. They *were* 'primary care':

'To begin with some other professionals thought they would equal with the GPs [Like Who?] Pharmacists, dentists, nurses...And they were of the view that if GPs are there we have as much right — well you don't, you know, this is a primary care-led NHS.' (Health Authority, PCG A).

*LASSD*

The involvement of the Local Authority Social Services Department was variable in our PCGs. Despite a number of recent documentation, such as the White Paper (1997), the Green Paper 'Our Healthier Nation' (1997) and Partnership in Action (1998), which outline a system of partnership and integrated care emphasising the need for effective joint working, there was very little input from LASSDs in 3 of the PCGs. The reasons for this ranged from disinterest on their behalf, to a lack of effort from the Health Authority to involve them. For the most part, LASSDs were invited to discussions, and mostly attended, but had very little to do with strategic planning. It is difficult to predict what impact this will have on the implementation of the Health Improvement Plans in those localities with minimum LASSD input. It is generally believed that factors affecting the lack of LASSD involvement have been the focus on their own internal reorganisation, the traditionally poor relationships that they have with Health Authorities and their very different agendas. However, it was also evident that they feel that they have rather poor relationships with GPs, and feel that the cultural differences between them may prove to be difficult to overcome:

> 'One of the things that has been commented on by the people attending the PCG meetings that involve GPs is the constant talking about money. We are not used to that, we get a salary and do what needs to be done. GPs say "I can't work for nothing" and I'm thinking "I've worked 'till midnight every night this week and on the weekend, don't talk to me about working for nothing". I don't think that we can underestimate the different cultures at work. We don't bill for our time, but a GP won't leave his practice unless he gets some cash for it. I'd like to know what they don't get extra cash for, what do they do exactly for their basic money?' (LASSD, PCG C).

## The Public

The NHS Executive's summer guidance called for greater user and public involvement in the NHS, to ensure that there is a strong public voice in decision-making, and that PCGs can play a key role in communicating with local people and ensuring public involvement in decision-making about local services. By this stage there had been a total absence of lay consultation in the planning process, aside from Community Health Council attendance at some meetings. Patients had no part in discussions. Health Authorities generally felt that it will be the responsibility of the PCG Boards to ensure that a partnership with the community it serves is established. It had not been a priority so far, however, as this first quote illustrates.

> 'How do we get this lay representation? And what does it mean? I have to be honest, I haven't really given it a great deal of thought, because at the moment we are sorting the structure out'. (Health Authority, PCG A).

It is also interesting to note that this stakeholder, in common with others actually, did not feel that the lay public has any role in determining the structure of the PCG.

The involvement of the wider community may prove to be impeded, however, by the pervading belief on the ground that lay involvement is not effective. In terms of time and the types of people who want to participate. Some talked about the difficulty in finding someone without an axe to grind. There were also some strange definitions of lay participation on behalf of some of the GPs, as the second quote shows:

'I think community involvement will be a two-way process, the community will inform us but we could be a bit more open with them, tell them how they can improve the quality of services. Perhaps by attending their appointments, or setting up patient groups that won't take too much of the GP's time'. (GP, PCG C).

The Community Health Council in PCG C did attempt to hold public meetings but the attendance was very poor, with some attendees actually thinking that the meeting was about primary schools. The Community Health Council was also concerned about their roles in the process, they were worried that they were being used as a *substitute for* community participation.

Table 2: Hierarchy of Influence

Health Authority
|
GPs
|
LASSD/Trust
|
Nurses
|
Community Health Council
|
The Community/Service Users

Table 2 outlines the hierarchical nature of the structure at work in the decision-making process during the planning stages of the PCG. It shows at what level each of the stakeholders have had an input for each of the 4 PCGs. This model is an incorporation of the 4 PCGs and as such is something of a generalisation. For example, level 3 shows that the LASSDs and Trusts were on the same footing, whereas in fact for 3 PCGs the LASSD occupied this level with the Trust below it, and in the 4th it was vice versa. Whichever was dominant however, the other still occupied a significantly more dominant role than the nurses.

An example of how this model works can be seen in the PCG size and configuration debates that took place between February and June 1998. By February 1998, 3 of the Health Authorities included in this study had devised a list of criteria by which to determine the size and boundaries of the PCGs. The 4th PCG did not begin this process until early June. These criteria included natural or artificial phenomena (such as rivers and roads) which represented existing boundaries around natural communities, population, local government wards, and existing GP organisations such as Locality Commissioning Groups and multifunds.

Considering these criteria, the Health Authorities issued consultation documents outlining possible configurations for the PCGs. In all cases the documentation was issued to GPs, LASSDs, MPs, Councillors, CHCs and local Trusts. Nurses were not included separately from the Trust and only one area attempted to solicit the views of the local community, by posting the consultation document in libraries, practices and with community groups.

Overall the term 'consultation document' could be considered something of a misnomer. The average length of consultation was one month, and there appears to be little evidence to suggest that stakeholder groups had much impact on the Health Authorities' decision-making. This is certainly true of PCGs B and C. PCG A incorporated the needs of the LASSD, while the GPs had the upper hand in PCG D.

Coterminosity with other agency boundaries was not of paramount importance in the decision-making process, with the exception of PCG A (although it could be said that this was allowed because it did not impinge on the Health Authority's preferences). The magic number of a population of around 100,000 also does not appear to have been particularly important either, ranging as it does between just under 100,000 to just under 160, 000.

In each of the sites, the resolution of the configuration debate inevitably left many groups unhappy, feeling excluded or ignored. This was true of all groups except the Health Authority and the LASSD in PCG A; the Health Authority and the Trust in PCG B; everyone except the Health Authority in PCG C; and the Health Authority and GPs in PCG D. On this analysis, the Health Authority appeared to be the only 'winners' across the board. In all sites there is evidence to suggest that the GPs' arguments were based on maintaining parochialism and separateness. The Trusts and LASSD have been concerned about PCG boundaries crossing their own (necessitating their own internal reorganisation). Nurses' or lay people preferences have remained invisible in the debate.

## Election versus Selection

As already said, the national guidance paved the way for inequalities in the Board selection process. This was seen by many as an illustration of the differences in status of the stakeholder groups, and consequently their representation. While few fully understood the roles and functions of the PCGs and their Boards, all were interested in who would be on it. There was a substantial amount of evidence pointing to tensions between different groups about the dominance of GPs, and the relative inequality for other groups. The GPs got a protected majority and the Chair, whereas the nurses (probably the only group who have genuine experience of cross-agency collaboration) were left with a maximum of just 2 places.

All four PCGs elected the full 7 GP places, and nominated a GP Chair. This caused some tension in one of the PCGs that we tracked. At one stage, there was a document in circulation that contained a letter written by a practice in PCG C to the Chief Executive at the Health Authority. The letter stated that the decision to elect a Chair before the rest of the Board was in place was undemocratic and contravened the spirit of partnership. They accused their colleagues of 'stitching it up between themselves'. The Health Authority initially agreed, unfortunately the guidance supports such an action. The Health Authority can only refuse if they make fully explicit their reasons for doing so. The controversial Chair consulted the BMA and a solicitor who both back the move, arguing that if the Health Authority interfered they would be acting unlawfully.

Many nurses were disgruntled by the disparity in the selection process, they felt that if GPs were appointed by their peers, then so should they be. If nurses had to be interviewed, then so should GPs. In PCG B the nurse member is not even an operational-level nurse, but head of Community Nursing at the Trust. It was a Trust nomination and was decided in isolation from any other stakeholder groups. In the other three sites, however, nurse members were selected according to a two-tier template. Initially the nurses declared their interest by nominating themselves with support from other colleagues. An application form was assessed by the Health Authority against a list of competencies deemed necessary for the post. There was a short-listing process, and then interviews at the Health Authority where candidates outlined their skills for the post and proposed strategies to maximise the nursing input on the PCG Board.

There were, however, many perceived barriers to nurses nominating themselves. There was in particular a general perception that the list of competencies issued as part of the job-description was huge, and that only Community Trust Locality Managers already possessed the necessary skills:

'Nurses got the idea that it was for management only, like the [Community Trust] locality managers. They were discouraged by the emphasis of management experience on the competencies list. At a very early meeting, the Community Trust made a great show of saying how glad they were that the locality manger had nominated herself, the message being that that was the sort of person who was eligible'. (Nurse, PCG C).

It was often not explained to nursing groups that the Health Authorities' intention was that the skill list included many that the candidate could be 'reasonably expected' to gain while in post. GPs were not expected to conform to any list of competencies before their election to the Board.

Striking little thought was given to the appointment of the lay member until the last moment, and in all cases the post was advertised and recruited by the Health Authority, without recourse to external expertise, such as the Community Health Council for example. However, as the recruitment process did not begin until we had left the field, we did not observe it.

**Discussions and Conclusions**

The development of PCGs was essentially a Health Authority-led strategy. GPs have been in possession of some strong influence, but it really has been a top-down concept with some room for negotiation around the margins. While this is understandable, and probably necessary, the consequences of such a process could be a complete lack of ownership and loyalty to the PCG within the various stakeholder groups. Decisions taken in isolation may lead to confusion and disagreement about purpose and progress at Board level. This is clearly facilitated by the large number of different agendas that different groups will attempt to address.

It is enormously difficult for an organisation like a Health Authority, which is centralist and controlling to let go. It makes sense that such organisations attract those with a managerial focus, those who perhaps are not particularly interested in working for a community project or for GPs. Many at Health Authorities have backgrounds in the secondary sector, and the concern is that they do not have a tradition of working with GPs.

There are also concerns that the Health Authority is not providing the necessary levers to help people make the culture change. In light of these viewpoints, it was perhaps naive to expect Health Authorities to promote and facilitate the creation of PCGs. Not only will responsibility have been devolved, in some cases, to something of an unknown quantity, but PCGs will change the size and function of Health Authorities. Jobs will be lost by the very people who are operational in the development of primary care. How will the implementation of primary care strategies be affected, when implemented by those who were essentially and consciously preparing for their own funeral?

It can be seen that GPs and nurses reacted differently to the policy proposals. Partly this may be explained by the existence of organised, self-interested professional networks which enable GPs to mobilise quickly. The fundamental structural differences in power between GPs and nurses ensured that GPs would have more influence in the debate. However, note that GPs had absolute confidence in their 'right' to be at the forefront of PCG development. GPs have been established longer (since 1858) than nurses in their roles as professionals, so they were able to capture the dominant role in health care. They have longer training, more legitimated status and more autonomy from supervision than nurses. These factors combine to ensure that not only are GPs more confident negotiators — they are also far more likely than nurses to engage in negotiations in the first place. As others have pointed out, nursing has a long history of subordination to the medical profession (e.g. Freidson 1970, Stacey 1988, Walby and Greenwell 1994). The hierarchical nature of the health services ensured that at the critical moment of policy inception nurses were much less confident of their ability to influence PCG direction.

One of the main factors differentiating GP and nurse power can be illustrated by the negotiations of John Chisolm and Alan Milburn. The Government knew that it was crucial that GPs were on board, otherwise the reforms did not stand a chance of survival. Essentially this ensured that GPs could threaten not to 'play' in order to get their demands met. What would have happened if nurses had refused to play? While we cannot be absolutely sure, it would be fair to say that they would have been told that they have no choice. The structural inequalities linked with their employee status means that any rebellion in that vein would have been met with less seriousness than that of the GP groups. Nurses just did not have the same power base from which to issue ultimatums.

The status of the lay member on the Board is particularly problematic. Those stakeholders who are members of professional bodies are selected by their peers and colleagues and so have formalised reference groups who give them legitimacy and support. By contrast the solitary lay person is appointed by the health authority and expected to represent 'the public' — a constituency so large and heterogeneous as to be meaningless for practical purposes. We would argue that the notion that a single lay person can represent a natural community of 100,000 is flawed, and that the position of the lay member as the solitary voice of the people is unenviable on a PCG Board dominated by health and management professionals.

One of the most difficult issues the PCG will face is how to reconcile such very different cultures, especially that of General Practice and LASSDs, but it is also true that PCGs will depend on the successful collaboration of independent practices. While GPs have had experience of joint working within LCGs and TPPs, for example, they have never been required to work together in such large numbers before. It must also be remembered that GPs have had no choice in who they work with. In TPPs and to some extent in LCGs (by not joining) GPs had a choice. PCG configurations were largely decided by the Health Authorities. Fundholders and non-fundholders will have to work together, reconciling themselves to sometimes very different ideological backgrounds. There appear to be very few incentives for this to occur. To complicate matters even more, GPs have very little experience of sharing a management role with nurses. It must be ensured that nurses are furnished with effective negotiation skills to give them the best possible chance of success. Thus it is clear that the successful reconciliation of the differing cultures and agendas on the Board is going to be one of the most demanding challenges the PCGs have to face, but is also the crucial key to effectiveness.

We are not suggesting that PCGs are doomed to a future of non-co-operation and lop-sided domination. This study was conducted while PCGs were still in the planning stages. Although there is a risk that the planning process lays the foundation for future direction, there is still hope. The Government appears to remain committed to the partnership ideal (See Department of Health Press Release 'Partnership is at the Centre of the New health Bill' 1999 for latest example before going to press). Partnership is still a statutory duty. Government needs to see that all stakeholder groups are committed to joint-working initiatives and collaboration. There is still time to shift the balance.

The authors would like to acknowledge the valuable comments that both Professor David Wilkin and Professor Martin Roland made on an earlier draft of this paper.

# 10   Health Scares: Media Hype and Policymaking

HELEN DOYLE

## Introduction

The aim of this paper is to try to draw together previously unconnected arguments about health scares and their effects on policy. The argument draws on the appropriate bodies of literature and interview evidence from my PhD research. I have not used specific examples of reports or headlines in this paper, although obviously these will appear as a body of evidence in the thesis.

I will firstly discuss 'health scares', what they are and how and why they make the news so regularly. This will take into account issues such as sources of stories and the pressures on journalists and newspapers to get a good 'scoop'. I will then move on to discuss the hype which characterises the health scare story using two examples; firstly Necrotising Fasciitis is briefly assessed, the portrayal of this condition in the national press highlights how the media can 'create' a panic from virtually nothing, or at least from something which was always there; secondly, I will use the example of HIV/Aids to show media effect on government handling of the issue, from influencing initial policy action through to aiding policy implementation.   In the final section of the paper I move on to look more generally at media effect, by drawing on interview evidence and in utilising Hall's framework of policy paradigms.

I hope to show in this paper that the *way* in which the media present certain types of health issues as 'health scares', has an effect on policymaking (and in fact the policy process) around this issue. I argue that this is particularly significant in the case of health scares, because the 'policy paradigm' within which the state understand and handle such issues, is not a coherent one. The state are therefore more vulnerable to outside pressures such as the media.

It is important to highlight early on in the paper something which other people working in this area have recognised and elucidated;

147

The media, of course, rarely, if ever, act alone in influencing public policy. Politicians, industry, public interest groups, lobbyists, lawyers and professional associations also influence decisions. Nor do the media influence policy in a way that is quantifiable. As a result, analyses such as the ones offered in this volume, are qualitative and represent a series of judgements based on an apparent preponderance of evidence from various sources. (Klaidman 1991 p47).

I would argue Klaidman raises central issues here about studying the media and its effects, which should be made clear at the outset. It is clear that studying policy and policymaking is an extremely difficult enterprise as the process is so complex and often problematic in terms of accessing information. In trying to bring the media explicitly into an analysis of policymaking, these problems are compounded due to the largely invisible and immeasurable nature of media effect both on the public and on policymakers. What I am striving to do, both in this paper and in the thesis, is to use quite well-defined case study areas to investigate media presentation (newspaper evidence) and their consequent effects on health policy (interview evidence and official information). Hopefully, this paper will shed some light on some of the pertinent issues relating to the media and health policy; I have used health scares to try and achieve this aim. It is important to highlight that for reasons of time and accessibility, my thesis does not include analysis of the broadcast media. (References to 'the media' throughout this paper are used where other commentators have used the term generically; otherwise from my own analysis I will refer specifically to newspapers).

**What are health scares?**

In the context of this paper health scares are defined as the presentation of public health risks by national newspapers. These health risks have some unique features in that they usually present a universal threat to the population's health. The risks, associated with the issue, which are often very small, are then magnified or 'hyped' by the media and become a health scare. One of the characteristics of the health scare is that the risk to the population is not presented in terms of probability, i.e. the chances of people actually 'getting it' (which can often be minimal). Media health scares seem to have a number of characteristics:

- They present a universal threat
- The threat is largely invisible
- The patterns of the disease seem unpredictable
- The condition is presented as new or that there has been a recent increase in cases
- The pathogen results in a horrible illness and sometimes death
- The condition is unusual or bizarre
- There may be some blame attached (often to official actors and institutions)

Other features and characteristics of the typical health scare are discussed below.

## Explaining the rise in coverage

There is a general perception that there has been a rise in the coverage of health scares by the media over recent years (further research would be required to actually prove whether or not this is the case). In the context of my thesis I intend to undertake an historical analysis, comparing news coverage in *The Times* in the 1940s and the 1990s. Combs and Slovic, writing in 1979, perhaps noticed the beginning of this change in their work on newspaper coverage of death; they argued that accidents and homicide were more often reported in newspapers than disease except where a disease threatened to become epidemic (Combs and Slovic 1979). It seems that this has been one of the crucial factors in health coverage of this sort; many more issues are presented as having the potential to reach epidemic proportions.

It is useful at this stage to briefly provide a framework with which to understand why there appears to have been this proliferation in media coverage. Beck's work on the 'risk society' can help us to do this; in a sense this work responds to the uncertainty in advanced societies in relation to social and economic conditions. He argues that the risky nature of contemporary societies is inevitable largely due to our dependence on public institutions where family and kinship systems have been eroded. Risks are now no longer hierarchical but universal and this is especially the case with environmental and public health risks. The risk society is a society 'of abundance' which is held together by a common appreciation, and fear, of risk, uncertainty and hazard (Beck 1992). Thus the media devotes such attention to health scares because they fit with the risk society.

## Making the News

One of the initial questions to ask is how do health scares find their place in the news media? Establishing this provides a starting point for beginning to understand why there have been so many column inches devoted to health scares and what the effects of this coverage might be.

There are a number of factors which can affect a story's chances of getting into print and these are discussed briefly in this section (Galtung and Ruge 1969). Negrine cites a former editor of The Guardian and his listing of factors which are likely to influence news selection.

- Social, political, economic and human significance of events
- Drama — excitement and action
- Surprise — unexpected and fresh
- Personalities
- Sex — scandals
- Numbers — numbers affected. (Negrine 1989 p141)

My own research has been able to uncover how people actually working in various sectors (media, government, trade unions, pressure groups, think-tanks and consumer groups) explain the elements which constitute a good health story.

> It sounds a bit like stating the obvious but it does help if its new...it does have to be something that is new or novel or different . . . something that will help a lot of people — but the converse is also true, very rare diseases fascinate people . . . the rarity value makes that news. [Interview with health correspondent A] .

> There are unwritten rules guiding what makes a good health story and defining the constituents is very difficult. But for me the main elements are that it provokes public reaction, it's new, it's unusual, who says what — if it's those in authority it makes a better story, what is said — is it bizarre or extraordinary, and if it's bad news. Better stories make the reader think it

will affect them directly — you have to try and relate events to the individual [Interview with health correspondent B].

These examples provide some sort of conceptualisation of what makes a good health story. It is clear how close the degree of fit is with many of the typical health scares we have seen over the last few years. This then provides us with an indication of the reason why health scares seem so pervading — they fit very closely with media professionals (and other relevant actors) conceptions of a good story.

There are other influences, even if a story is 'good', in terms of whether it will reach the pages of a newspaper and therefore the public. These influences pertain to the actors involved in the news making process — from sources to journalists and through to editors.

Clearly, the science and medical journalist has to search for news offering headlines that are interesting not only to the potential reader, which is the over-riding objective of any journalist, but also to their own section colleagues and even more so to the person in charge of the decision to publish the story and position it in the newspaper. Thus, the news of killer bacteria, exterminating viruses, and miraculous therapies tends to have greater appeal because such stories compete with murders, rapes, ecological catastrophes and declarations from famous people...(De Semir 1996 p1163).

There is then a process of constant competition for space and coverage. In many cases health correspondents find that the 'health scare' story fits the conception of a good story and is thus more likely to appear in the news pages.

The 'source' of stories and the ability with which they are able to sell their point of view to health correspondents is also a factor here. It is commonly perceived that the state or the government play an integral role in management of news. It is not possible to say whether or not this is the case in other policy arenas, but certainly in the case of health news, and specifically health scares, the state do not appear to be managing to sell their line very effectively. It can be argued that the Department of Health [DH], in terms of scare stories, appear to be cast in a very reactive role. This can be seen from interview evidence.

They [DH Press Office] are chaotic, I mean they are a shambles. They are under a lot of pressure, they do get an enormous amount of calls — they know they're going to get attacked by journalists but half the time they don't even try very hard I don't think. [Interview with health correspondent C].

Its an uphill struggle, I liken it to pushing a snowball up a hill in the middle of summer. Its very difficult, very difficult! [Interview with member of staff from NHSE communications unit].

In many cases these stories burst upon the scene and government simply has to react to them and try to lessen the blow. Sometimes, the force of the coverage is so great that certain other responses may follow (this is discussed below). It is clearly important to the theoretical development of the paper that the restrictions of the state to manage health scare stories is established. Clearly, in many cases such stories pertain to information which the government may rather conceal than publicise.

It seems that various other organisations and sources are more effective; they are able to sell their stories which can, in some cases, implicate government and force their reaction. Many health stories are generated from a wide variety of organisations which can be termed health pressure groups. This point was made by a health correspondent:

The BMA are an active source of stories, they have a very slick press-media operation. ...So as long as it is presented in terms of how it affects the public then yes we do listen to special pleadings from all sorts of people. The big research charities...again very adept at putting out their material. So there are research bodies, medical scientists, Royal Colleges, pressure groups and patient groups, who are increasingly adept at harnessing us for getting their points of view across. [Interview with health correspondent A].

In the case of health scares in particular, journalists may often obtain their information from medical journals such as the BMJ or The Lancet. This is perhaps due to the fact that journalists themselves have no independent set of criteria by which to evaluate the truth of news stories, so they tend to value the status and authority of medicine and science; 'So, when apparently reputable and high status research gives new and

152

controversial findings, it is difficult for journalists to ignore' (Miller and Reilly 1994 p19).

## Media Distortion — Don't Believe The Hype!

Where science and scientific journals are sources of stories they provide a good example of how issues can become distorted. Newspapers and scientific journals have very different aims; for researchers, findings are tentative and unsupported until they are certified by peers to fit into the existing framework of knowledge. However, for journalists, established ideas may be old news and they may be more attracted to non-routine events or new research findings (Nelkin 1996). There are other factors too,

> Media constraints of time, brevity and simplicity preclude the careful documentation, nuanced positions, and precautionary qualifications that scientists feel are necessary to present their work . . . Furthermore, readability in the eyes of a journalist may be over-simplification to a scientist. Many accusations of inaccuracy can be traced to reporters' efforts to present complex material in a readable and appealing way (Nelkin 1996 p1601).

It has been argued that this cultural gap between science and journalism is particularly evident and sharply brought into focus in communication around risk and uncertainty (Peters 1995). Raymond argues that continued technical debates around risks and health give reporters few guidelines as to how to direct their news coverage, but the increasing nature of the problem means it can be impossible for journalists to wait for all the 'facts' before writing a story (Raymond 1985).

Some commentators go further in criticising journalists and newspapers more generally for their distortion and misuse of scientific papers,

> Few journalists in Britain understand the rudiments of critical appraisal, and even if they do, the battery farms that constitute modern newspapers don't give them time to use them (Smith 1996 p983).

153

Newspapers seek to entertain as well as to educate; it is not difficult to see how this might lead to some distortion, meaning that certain issues become hyped. The fact that they are businesses, plus the other factors we have looked at, can go some way to explaining how scare stories come to be represented.

News values, novelty and the economic logic of media organisations clearly have an important impact on the emergence and coverage of public issues such as food safety...(Miller and Reilly 1994 p14).

This point was also revealed in my interviews:

We're a business; we are there to make money. To be cynical we are almost a branch of showbiz, we have to entertain, have to at least interest people so they keep shelling out their Xp each day. [Interview with health correspondent A].

This health correspondent works for a broadsheet newspaper where it is sometimes assumed that a more responsible reporting of issues occurs. It is not possible to discuss the issue of the difference between tabloid and broadsheet reporting and the influences of each here; suffice it to say that it is evident from this statement that many of the same factors influence broadsheet style reporting and they have been seen to have been as influential in the creation and sustainability of many a media hype.

**The Scare Story**

The various reasons for the distortion of scare-like stories have been outlined — it is now possible to move on to look at how health scares are actually presented in the print media. This will be achieved by drawing on some of the literature, using some interview evidence and focusing on some examples of health scares which have appeared recently in the national press.

The discourses employed in scare stories are often remarkably similar; there is widespread use of metaphors, analogies and sub-texts which serve to link topics to wider socio-political discourses. A very common way of intensifying hysteria and hype is the use of the quantification rhetoric; the use of numerical expressions of the problem with associated verbs to indicate changes in numbers such as 'increase', 'multiply' and so on (Fowler 1991, Browne, Chapman and Lupton 1996). There also seems to be a trend in the narrative of the health scare: there is a contradiction in that the issue is personalised right down to individual sufferers while at the same time rhetoric's are used which imply epidemic proportions.

The language used to describe risk in terms of health scares is thus crucial. Selective use of labels, metaphors and images can point the finger of blame and imply responsibility for action. Language therefore carries implications for the formulation of policy (Douglas 1992, Nelkin 1985).

There are many examples of health or health/food scares in the media such as HIV and Aids, Salmonella and Listeria, Necrotising Fasciitis, Ebola virus, the Plague, Ecoli, Meningitis and BSE/CJD. I am going to look at two such scares in slightly more detail in this paper.

## Necrotising Fasciitis or 'Killer Bug Ate My Face'

This condition was discovered in 1994 following an essay in the BMJ which actually discussed that relatively few people were developing the condition, whereas it had at one time been a considerable problem for surgeons. Reports began to appear in several national papers of deaths from a horrible form of infection and the numbers of these reports started to grow over the course of a week. There were a small number of doctors who were often quoted and there was the inevitable personalisation with people who had had the condition appearing in articles (Radford 1996).

It does seem that media intentions were far from honourable in this case,

> Flesh eating killer bugs — again we caused a huge and needless show over that, it was just freak show journalism, the government was forced to respond. I don't think we are entirely an unalloyed force for good [Interview with health correspondent D].

Perhaps unsurprisingly, DH officials did not disagree with this sentiment,

Necrotising fasciitis — now that horribly fast gangrene, though it has been with us for a long time and at a fairly consistent level in terms of its appearance in the population and the way it affects, the media treatment of it meant it became something that the public were living in fear of contracting. There you could say that the flesh eating killer bug was almost a creation of the media [Interview with DH press officer].

This scare lasted an average amount of time for this type of story — just a few days of prominent and unrelenting national news coverage. The length of time a story runs for, seems extremely important in terms of the effects on the government and policy — this is discussed further below. However, medical officers and DH officials had to respond to this panic (even though it ran for a relatively short period the coverage was intense); they were reported as saying there was no evidence of a rise in the number of cases (Radford 1996). It seems it is the cumulative effect of these relatively short, yet hype ridden and panic laden scares which is influencing the DH press office to consider protective if not preventative action.

We have started to generate a lot of comment, a lot of discussions about how public health scares should be handled themselves. We're quite interested in actually calling in certain figures in the print and broadcast media and saying do you want to have a chat and kick it around and maybe establish ground rules . . . The lesson is before these things hit you, to try and get out and think beyond it and change the way it is, this is otherwise a horrible reactive job which you're never going to win [Interview with DH press officer].

In these cases there seems to be minimal effect on policy *per se*, at least in terms of around that particular issue. However, in a wider and more general sense they do force government officials, MPs and Ministers to react and respond and there may be very many more widespread policy effects in the long term.

There have been some health scares which have run for a considerably longer period of time and where the effects on policy are a little more palpable. The three main examples here are HIV/Aids, salmonella and BSE. I will look at one of these areas in more detail here, although they will all be studied in some detail within the thesis.

It is particularly useful to chart the coverage of Aids and HIV as a health scare story; clearly it is not the only disease to have received wide media attention but it did have a particularly high profile and it has been argued that it was the 'first media disease' (Berridge 1996, Berridge 1991). It seems that HIV and Aids had a particular character which meant the media had a higher than usual degree of interest in it as an issue. It was mysterious; there was a great deal of uncertainty around both HIV and Aids; Aids itself had varied manifestations and is an extremely distressing disease; and finally (something pretty much unique to Aids) there were a number of stigmatising factors which appealed to the tendency of the media to stereotype (Day and Klein 1990). It is clear that certainly the first three factors are common to many recent health scares, particularly BSE and CJD.

The media played a considerable role in policymaking around Aids so it provides a useful model which can be applied to other arenas. Aids was, and to some extent still is, a policy issue which raises the question of how government reacts when it does not know what the precise scale or future development of the problem is; when the definition of the problem shifts over time; and when all the signals indicate that no-one knows what to do (Day and Klein 1990). It is clear that these are issues which face government in many health scares and thus are worth discussing in this context.

Berridge provides a chronology of the way the media covered the Aids issue. In the early 1980s, it was presented as the 'gay plague' which fitted well within the established newspaper tradition of sexual sensationalism. From mid 1983, the focus of reporting shifted and included the possibility of the spread of the virus to the heterosexual population. However, the narratives around the gay plague and victim blaming were still very much in evidence. 1985 saw the peak of press attention as there were fears of epidemics and other routes of transmission. There was a decline in the intensity of the reporting after 1987 — there was a normalisation of Aids coverage, in that it was covered more routinely and less as a health scare (Berridge 1991).

Berridge argues that there are three ways in which the media has had an impact on the policy process around HIV and Aids. Firstly, the media constructed the issue for the gay community and mobilised the community to act and lobby; secondly, the policy community around Aids used the media to achieve general policy aims; and thirdly, the media had particular impact in that the type and magnitude of its coverage stimulated high level political reaction to the disease (Berridge 1991). The period of high-level government reaction in 1986 where Aids became a political priority at the highest level with the establishment of a Cabinet committee, came not long after a spate of panic-laden articles about the disease. Also at this time there were a number of parliamentary debates, an increase in the research budget, large extra grants for the NHS and the launch of a major public education campaign.

Day and Klein argue that there were a number of factors which persuaded government to respond to Aids at this time. Firstly, there was growing evidence to suggest that Aids might threaten the whole population. Secondly '...there was the increasing attention given to Aids in the media, both sensational and serious' (Day and Klein 1990 p347). Thirdly, Norman Fowler (Secretary of State for Social Services) visited the US at that time and saw the extent of the problem there and returned vowing to do more in the UK. Finally, the increase in the number of cases raised concerns about how the NHS would cope. Day and Klein argue that the government were as concerned about the social and political reaction to Aids as well as about the epidemic itself. This indicates the significance of the media in scares such as this — governments need to be seen to be doing something to minimise any adverse reactions or threats to their governance.

It is clear that the pressures for government action were widespread at this time and it is consequently difficult to isolate media effect, however this is not something which I am aiming to do in my research — it would be impossible. It is clear though, that many groups used the media to voice their views and calls for action and so in this way alone it appears the media contributed to policy development around Aids.

The 'policy community' nevertheless stirred up concern over Aids through the media, and this growing media focus on Aids does appear to have helped to structure the response of central government. (Berridge 1991 p183).

Interview evidence indicates that the media may have played an even more integral role in the policymaking process around Aids:

We started off the Aids strategy in about 1985/1986 and before we did anything we had a huge range of talks with various influential groups in society and that included the churches, major opinion formers, the press, the TV, the broadcasters...(interview with DH official A).

It seems they were involved in the debate before action was taken plus the same interviewee also revealed that without media support of the government education programme, the implementation of policy around Aids would have been impossible:

Their was no doubt that without their, co-operation is too strong a word, but the sympathetic view that the press took of what we were trying to do, we couldn't have done it as well as we did (Interview with DH official A).

Policy around Aids shifted in the 1990s from being a very discreet area of policy to being much more integrated into the general provision of NHS sexual health services. This DH official argued that there had to be a move towards this when it seemed that the predicted epidemic was not going to happen — again he saw the media as playing a central role in this policy shift:

It's [Aids policy] much more now embedded in other sexual health programmes, NHS treatments and care and LA social services care and that's good, I mean that is a helpful development and one we'd have had to move to anyway and it was partly driven by the media and partly by the media interest galvanising all sorts of other people (Interview with DH official A).

It appears that the media played a vital role, both in the initial spurring on of the government to act on Aids and seemingly right the way through the policy process. It provides a good example of a public health scare which was covered intensely and over a long period of time by the media and where this coverage had obvious effects on policy.

## What are the effects of media health scares on policy?

In reiterating the arguments about what makes a good story, pressures on journalists, their sources, the tensions between science and the media and the various ways in which distortion occurs — it is apparent that all of these factors can influence the way a health scare story appears in the media. The way such issues are reported — the sensationalism, drama and panic narratives are significant in terms of influences on reactions and responses — i.e. it becomes something more than the actual issue.

The precise way in which media presentation of scares influences policy is difficult to unravel — one argument is that it causes widespread panic amongst the general public which has to be appeased. Media presentation of health scares means that much of the information which people are exposed to about risks is distorted and can cause people to overestimate their likelihood of exposure (Slovic, Fischoff and Lichtenstein 1982) thus creating panic. Media presentation relates closely to many of the heuristic biases discussed by Tversky and Kahneman (1982) in relation to assessing probabilities of risk. This then compounds the public's and decision-makers' judgements about risk and can lead to effects on policymaking.

Another point is that media coverage of health scares may not significantly affect public opinion but because it is occurring in the public arena it has the potential to do so and therefore must be addressed, or seen to be addressed. Other arguments relate to other groups and actors which can hear about relevant issues from the media and then use the media as a strategy to publicise their aims and hopefully influence policy.

Interview evidence highlights what the people involved believe:

> . . . it does seem that it is the welter of publicity and the ground swell of public opinion that actually does get things done. If we'd not written a word about it, I wonder whether it would have happened just the same. I can't believe that would be the case because the political process wouldn't have been engaged [Interview with health correspondent E].

> It [the media] must affect policy — ministers are political animals, ministers are affected by what happens in the press. If it weren't that important, we wouldn't have a ruddy great information division [Interview with DH official B].

Interviewees commented on whether issues were on the government's agenda anyway, or whether the media actually put them there.

> I'm sure the media has the power to change policy, particularly if it was pushing on an open door although it might not know the door was open. I suspect there are issues where in fact there is already concern and then the media gets hold of it and then there is the generation of public concern and so actually the two things come together (Interview with senior DH official).

> You can certainly point to successful newspaper campaigns where either something wasn't on the agenda or where something was on the agenda, but not so far up the batting order, where a good strong media campaign actually achieved results (Interview with DH official C).

Hall's work on social learning with regard to economic policymaking provides a framework for understanding the effect the media can have on policy. He argues that policymakers work within 'policy paradigms', which are frameworks of ideas and standards in relation to the policy area. In terms of policymaking there are three levels of change which can occur; first and second level policymaking can be seen as normal policymaking, in that the changes which adjust policy do not challenge the overall terms of the policy paradigm (relates to incremental and satisficing models). Third-order change is marked by '...radical changes in the overarching terms of policy discourse', i.e. there is a paradigm shift (Hall 1993 p279). This can be seen to have occurred in relation to HIV and Aids where the policy reaction from the government was new and unique.

Hall argues that the shift from Keynesian to monetary economics can be seen as a paradigm shift and he analyses how this shift occurred. He says that a feature in the shift was, '...an extraordinary intensification in the debate about economic issues in the media' and '...the already high volume of economic commentary in the press grew larger and even more sophisticated' (Hall 1993 p286). Hall goes on to argue that,

It was not civil servants or policy experts engaged by the government, but politicians and the media who played the pre-eminent role in this process of policy change (Hall 1993 p287).

He argues, therefore, that the process of policy change was not state initiated nor did it occur solely within the confines of the state; external pressures were vital. This analysis brings other agencies centrally into the analysis of policymaking, and enables the role of the media to be included — it is a very useful model to apply to the role of the media in terms of policymaking around public health scares.

One further point which Hall makes and which can help illuminate the importance of the role of the media in policymaking around health scares, is that the state appears more vulnerable to outside interests at some times more than others. Hall relates this back to his conception of policy paradigms in arguing that the state is in a stronger position when armed with a coherent policy paradigm (Hall 1993). In the case of health scares, the policy paradigm appears to be weak or non-existent. As we have noted, health scares are unique because the size of the problem can be unclear, the definition of the problem is not static and there is often confusion amongst experts. In such cases there is not a strong paradigm within which to deal with the problem; judgements and decisions may often be made in situations of uncertainty (Tversky and Kahneman 1982), and so the state may be more vulnerable to media pressure and effect.

Interestingly, interview evidence has shown that DH officials and press officers are searching for strategies with which they can handle health scares; this could be construed as a sign that they are searching for a new paradigm within which to contain public health scares.

## Conclusion

The media do not create the public health issue but they do construct or create the health scare around the issue. The media 'discover' the issue from one of many potential sources, and can 'accelerate its development and magnify its impact' (Kingdon 1984). The significance of the media lies in its ability to give prominence, through widespread coverage, to an issue. The media reinforces and may influence public opinion around an issue. Due to the power the media has to affect and speak for the public, the state often has to respond to media coverage in order to comply with their democratic remit.

The significance of health scares is related to the distortion of issues around the issue. The media presents the concept of risk using a rhetoric of panic which has the potential to lead to widespread panic in the population. In this sense the power of the media to symbolise people's fears around disease, dying and death are significant. This presentation can lead to panic in government as they have to respond to the crisis. As argued above, there is often little the government can do in the case of public health scares, in terms of actually isolating and eliminating the pathogen, but there are other strategies and policy responses which they may be expected to adopt.

The effects of the media on policy are influenced by the policy paradigm within which the state are structuring policy around a particular issue. If, as in the case of health scares, the policy paradigm is not sufficiently robust enough to deal with the new issues arising, then the state becomes vulnerable to pressures such as the media and the media effect on policymaking can be understood and analysed more fully.

# References

Beck, U. (1992), *Risk Society: Towards a New Modernity,* Sage, London.

Berridge, V. (1991), 'Aids, the Media and Health Policy', *Health Education Journal,* 50,4, pp179-85.

Berridge, V. (1996), *Aids in the UK,* Oxford University Press, Oxford.

Browne, J., Chapman, S. and Lupton, D. (1996), *Infinitesimal Risk as Public Health Crisis: News Media Coverage of a Doctor-Patient HIV Contact Tracing Investigation,* In: *Social Science and Medicine,* 43,12, pp1685-95.

Combs, B. and Slovic, P. (1979), *Newspaper Coverage of Causes of Death,* In: *Journalism Quarterly,* 56, pp837-43.

Day, P. and Klein, R. (1990), 'Interpreting the Unexpected: the Case of Aids Policy Making in Britain', *Journal of Public Policy,* 9, pp337-53.

De Semir, V. (1996), 'What is Newsworthy?', *The Lancet,* 347, pp1163-66.

Douglas, M. (1992), *Risk and Blame: Essays in Cultural Theory,* Routledge, London.

Fowler, R. (1991), *Language in the News: Discourse and Ideology in the Press,* Routledge, London.

Galtung, J., and Ruge, M. (1969), *The Structure of Foreign News,* In: Tunstall, J. (Ed.) *Media Sociology,* Constable, London.

Hall, P. A. (1993), 'Policy Paradigms, Social Learning and the State', *Comparative Politics,* April 1993, pp275-96.

Kingdon, J. W. (1984), *Agendas, Alternatives and Public Policies,* Little, Brown and Company, Boston.

Klaidman, S. (1991), *Health in the Headlines,* Oxford University Press, New York.

Miller, D. and Reilly, J. (1994), *Food Scares in the Media,* Glasgow University Media Group, Glasgow.

Negrine, R. (1989), *Politics and the Mass Media in Britain,* Routledge, London.

Nelkin, D. (1985), *Introduction: Analyzing Risk,* pp11-23, In Nelkin, D. (Ed.) *The Language of Risk,* Sage, Beverly Hills.

Nelkin, D. (1996), 'An Uneasy Relationship: the Tensions Between Medicine and the Media', *The Lancet,* 347, pp1600-3.

Peters, H. P. (1995), 'The Interaction of Journalists and Scientific Experts: Co-operation and Conflict Between Two Professional Cultures', *Media Culture and Society,* 17, pp31-48.

Radford, T. (1996), 'Influence and the Power of the Media', *The Lancet,* 347, pp1533-35.

Raymond, C. A. (1985), *Risk in the Press: Conflicting Journalistic Ideologies,* pp97-135, In: Nelkin, D. (Ed.) *The Language of Risk,* Sage, Beverly Hills.

Slovic, P., Fischoff, B. and Lichtenstein, S. (1982), *Facts versus Fears: Understanding Perceived Risk,* pp463-93, In: Kahneman, D., Slovic, P. and Tversky, A. (Eds.) *Judgement Under Uncertainty: Heuristics and Biases,* Cambridge University Press, New York.

Smith, R. (1996), 'Three Rules to Cut the Hype', *British Medical Journal,* 312, p983.

Tversky, A. and Kahneman, D. (1982), pp3-23, In: Kahneman, D., Slovic, P. and Tversky, A. (Eds.) J *Judgement Under Uncertainty: Heuristics and Biases Judgement Under Uncertainty: Heuristics and Biases,* Cambridge University Press, New York.

# 11 Understanding the New Public Health: Towards a Policy Analysis

ROB BAGGOTT

Over the last few decades industrialised nations have placed a renewed emphasis upon strategies to promote health and prevent illness, in line with the New Public Health (NPH) philosophy (see Ashton and Seymour, 1988; Goraya and Scambler, 1998). However, many of the core ideas of the NPH are not entirely new: the importance of health promotion, disease prevention, healthy lifestyles and environments was acknowledged by the earliest civilisations. Furthermore, what most observers identify as the distinctive nature of NPH — a combination of individual and collective action on a range of fronts to deal with the underlying causes of illness — also has a long history (see Rosen, 1993).

It is therefore more accurate to state that there has been a revival, a rediscovery or a re-emphasis of public health principles. In the 1970s industrialised countries began to develop national strategies aimed at preventing some of the main causes of illness and death such as heart disease, cancer and accidents (Lalonde, 1975; US Department of Health and Human Services, 1980). The World Health Organisation (WHO), particularly through its European regional office, began to encourage member states to embrace the public health agenda. This process began with the declaration of the objective of Health for All by the Year 2000 at the Alma-Ata Conference on primary health care of 1977 (WHO, 1978), and reiterated since in documents such as the Ottawa Charter on Health Promotion (WHO, 1986), the WHO Regional Office targets for Health for All (1985; 1993) and specific WHO-sponsored activities such as the Healthy Cities initiative (Davies and Kelly, 1993).

Although the UK failed to adopt an explicit public health strategy until the 1990s, faltering steps in this direction had been taken earlier. In 1976 the DHSS produced a consultative document on prevention and health (DHSS, 1976) followed by a White Paper (Cmnd. 7047, 1977). Although these documents did much to stimulate debate, they hardly constituted a strategy. In any case during the following decade the prospects of a comprehensive pubic health strategy were undermined by the Thatcher government's overt hostility to interventions which it associated with the 'Nanny State'. Nevertheless, public health remained firmly on the political agenda during this period, largely in view of a series of food and health issues, such as salmonella, listeria and BSE/CJD, fears about infectious diseases such as HIV, meningitis and legionnaires' disease, and the government's own preference for high profile campaigns on drug abuse, heart disease, smoking and AIDS. Meanwhile the socio-economic policies pursued by the Thatcher administrations, which were linked with widening health inequalities, continued to highlight a range of public health problems associated with deprivation and unemployment.

Following Thatcher's departure, the Major government formulated a health strategy, first in the form of a consultative document in 1991, followed by the Health of the Nation White Paper in 1992, which set out a range of health targets and how these might be attained (Cm. 1523, 1991; Cm. 1986, 1992). Subsequently, the Blair Government has continued this approach, with some modifications: notably a more explicit acknowledgement of health inequalities and the socio-economic roots of ill health (Cm. 3852, 1998).

Given the importance attached to the NPH as a guiding philosophy, we clearly need to reach a greater understanding of its emergence, development and application in the UK. We need to know how and why and in what way it became acceptable to policy-makers. We also need to examine the extent to which it has actually influenced UK strategies and policies and in particular why certain policy aims and instruments have been adopted, while others have been rejected. At the same time we need to adopt a more critical approach to the New Public Health than that normally offered by health policy analysts when assessing the political implications of pursuing its principles. This chapter attempts to explore these issues with a view to setting a future research agenda for policy studies in this field. It does so first of all by examining the ideological context, followed by an analysis of institutional factors, and finally by exploring the social and cultural setting.

**Ideologies and the New Public Health**

One way to understand the support for NPH is as the product of a dominant ideological consensus. Certainly there seems to have been broad agreement among governing elites on the need for a greater emphasis on public health and prevention. For example Freeman (1992, p.40) noted that the rhetorical power of prevention policies is felt across the political spectrum. Furedi (1997, p.42) made a similar point with regard to perceptions of risk, stating that 'the entire political spectrum — left to right, conservative to liberal — shares a common consciousness of risk'. Lupton and Peterson (1996, p11) also observed that the basic tenets of the new public health were in accordance with the impulse of social movements such as environmentalism as well as neo-liberalism. But are NPH principles really consistent with contemporary political ideologies such as socialism, neo-liberalism and the Green ideology.

As Allsop has argued (1990), the maintenance of good health and the prevention of illness should be central to a socialist strategy. Indeed NPH appears to be highly consistent with several socialist principles. First, public health implies a key role for the state in protecting citizens' health (Doyal, 1979) and provides arguments for state intervention, collective action and public service provision. Moreover, as Beauchamp (1988) has argued the protection of public health depends in part on preventing the market sphere from invading or dominating other spheres and that therefore public health becomes a central task of government. Or as Dicey (1912, quoted in Weale, 1983, p.806) put it 'a collectivist never holds a stronger position than when he advocates the enforcement of the best ascertained laws of health'. Indeed it was no coincidence that the growth of the state in the Victorian and Edwardian period was closely associated with concern about public health (Fraser, 1973).

Secondly, public health intervention resonates with Marxist notions of oppression and power. Capitalist exploitation and the class structure are viewed by those on the left as major forces of ill health that are only partially ameliorated by the provision of health care services. As Navarro (1978) puts it, people are fooled into thinking that what is politically and collectively caused can be individually and therapeutically cured. From this perspective, collective action to deal with the sources of ill health is far more effective than the provision of treatment for individuals.

Thirdly, and related to this, the emphasis of NPH on 'Health for All' embraces concepts of equity — that all people have a right not only to good health care services but to good health in all its aspects, irrespective of class, race or gender. Moreover, the full-blooded version of the Health for All philosophy bears the hallmark of the democratic socialist, with its emphasis on participation.

Although the philosophical links between socialism and public health are not in doubt, the relevance of socialism to the re-emergence of public health can be challenged, given that the Labour Party was out of office from 1979 to 1997. Socialist principles were less influential over policy in the 1980s and 1990s than in previous decades, though it would be wrong to argue that they had no influence at all. Indeed socialist ideas remained entrenched in several ways: through the accumulation of years of legislation, the continued existence state agencies, the persistence of policy networks (see Marsh and Rhodes 1992), and public opinion, which despite almost two decades of neo-liberal government remained firmly attached to the welfare state. Hence, the desire of government to roll back the state was limited to some extent by the inertia of a post-war collectivist state based on very different principles.

Furthermore socialist principles were reflected to some extent in Green Political thought, which was influential during the 1980s and 1990s (Ryle, 1988). The emphasis of the latter on sustainable growth, the prevention of social and environmental problems, and the need to restrain the polluting activities of large corporations, endorsed the kind of public health interventionist philosophy supported by a socialist perspective. However, Green political thinkers go further in emphasising the role that individuals and groups can play in adopting and promoting lifestyles conducive to a healthier and more sustainable environment (Porritt and Winner 1989; Dobson, 1990). They also favour smaller-scale and decentralised solutions to problems, while the traditional socialist position has tended to argue for large-scale state intervention.

Green ideas exerted considerable influence over the political agenda of the late 1980s and 1990s. Although the holistic and radical nature of 'Deep Green' ideology had little impact on government policy, environmental concerns did force a response from government in a variety of policy areas. Notably the demands for intervention, particularly on issues such as health-related pollution and food safety (Hall, 1990; Lawson, 1996). Although this was acknowledged by some writers — who argued that a greening of public health was taking place (Draper, 1991; Petrioni, 1991), the exact relationship between public health and environmental politics was not clearly articulated.

Surprisingly perhaps, neo-liberal ideology has also supported aspects of the NPH, in spite of the natural hostility of the right to the so-called 'Nanny State'. Though opposed to moves that gave the state greater powers to regulate corporations and individuals, neo-liberals endorsed measures to prevent illness largely on the grounds that they promised two things: the curbing of state expenditures on health care (Lewis, 1992; Webster, 1997);

and an increase in personal responsibility (and a corresponding reduction in state responsibility) for health (see Freeman, 1992).

In fact neither of these outcomes can be guaranteed. Prevention of illness is not necessarily a cheap option and can involve considerable additional costs such as those associated with screening large numbers of people for illness or caring for a population that survives to an older age (see Cairns, 1995). Similarly, there is no guarantee that the encouragement of individual responsibility will reduce the demands on the state to intervene to protect health. Indeed, if anything, recent experience of food and environmental scares has shown that greater public awareness about health risks generates further pressures for state regulation.

In summary, the NPH principles have been sufficiently broad to arouse support from a range of different political perspectives. This meant that the revival of public health occurred in a broadly favourable ideological climate, particularly with respect to the high profile of environmental issues on the political agenda, the dominance of new right ideas in UK central government, and the persistence of socialist ideas in society, within government agencies and in policy networks. Specific prevention issues and policies, however, have not received the same universal endorsement. Hence the neo-liberal emphasis on policies promoting personal responsibility have been seen by socialists and to a lesser extent by Greens as 'victim blaming', while policies supported by the socialists and Greens to regulate and curb health-damaging activities of large corporations have been opposed by the right. A political-ideological account therefore not only explains the rise of NPH, but also suggests why certain policies have been adopted and others rejected. However, a second approach, focusing on political institutions and the policy process, provides a more detailed explanation of policy selection.

**Institutions and the Policy Process**

The emergence of NPH can be explained in terms of the interaction of political actors and institutions within the policy process. The NPH was promoted in a number of policy arenas. From the 1970s, as mentioned earlier, the World Health Organisation became more proactive on health promotion, through its Health for All strategy which set out specific health targets (see Skrabanek, 1994). As other countries began to adopt health strategies, a form of peer pressure was exerted on the UK to follow suit. The growing interest of the European Community in public health issues during the late 1980s added to this pressure to conform.

169

Howard Leichter's (1990) comparative study of public health policies in the USA and UK confirms that similar pressures — in particular, concerns about the costs of health care — were behind the emergence of NPH in both countries. However, he also noted differences in approach taken by each nation. For example, the preference of UK policy makers for informal voluntary agreements with commercial interests such as the tobacco industry contrasted with the Americans' formal regulatory regime, though Leichter appreciated that increasingly powerful forces — such as transnational communications — increased the likelihood of policy convergence. He also analysed policy diffusion between the two countries — both from the UK to the USA (seat belt legislation) and in the other direction (AIDS policy) — noting that the flow of ideas was mainly in one direction, from the USA to the UK, an observation with which Skrabanek (1994) agreed. Yet, as Leichter acknowledged, the goal of policy learning is not always to emulate, but to avoid making the same mistakes and hence the diffusion of ideas and experiences in some situations could produce differences rather than similarities in policy outputs.

As well as being influenced by experience from overseas, and supranational institutions such as WHO and the European Commission, the NPH in the UK developed as a result of internal pressures. During the 1980s some local authorities, concerned about the social causes of illness such as poverty and deprivation, began to introduce their own health strategies. This in turn led to demands for a national strategy to guide and support these local initiatives. These calls were echoed by some NHS professionals and managers who realised that the efficiency and effectiveness of health services were often shaped by social factors outside their control. Furthermore, on specific issues — such as smoking, nutrition and alcohol for example — lobby groups began to press for a stronger national policy (see Baggott, 1990; Taylor, 1984; Cannon 1987). However, their efforts were countered by organised interests opposed to further government intervention, including commercial lobbies and libertarian groups (some of which received financial support from the industries concerned).

The media played an important role in the development of the NPH by highlighting health risks and dangers, particularly relating to food safety issues such as Salmonella, BSE/CJD and Listeria (Baggott, 1998; Doig, 1980), as well as HIV/AIDS (Berridge, 1996; Day and Klein 1989) and Alcohol abuse (Baggott, 1990). Although some sections of the tabloid press adopted a rather fatalistic approach to these new and newly perceived threats to public health, the balance of media coverage served to raise public awareness and to promote a policy response from government.

These external forces interacted with internal pressures within government. From the 1970s, the Treasury and the Department of Health and Social Security (and subsequently the Department of Health) sought to emphasise the importance of prevention and public health. In the 1980s, following an official inquiry, stimulated by a series of high profile failures, the Thatcher government set out plans to reform the public health function (Cm. 289, 1989). It also introduced new prevention policies in areas such as alcohol misuse and food safety around this time, largely as a response to media coverage of these issues. Nevertheless, it remained opposed to the adoption of a national health strategy, which, as mentioned earlier, was not adopted in England until Thatcher was replaced as Prime Minister by John Major. However, other parts of the UK, had already taken steps to establish strategies before Thatcher's resignation.

Within government, specialist advisors — such as doctors and scientists — played a key role in policy development on public health issues, including AIDS for example (Klein and Day, 1989; Berridge, 1996). The health strategy was also strongly influenced by scientific (and especially. medical) advice, as reflected in its emphasis on quantifiable risk factors and targets (see Radical Statistics Health Group, 1991). This provides a further illustration of Fischer's (1990) point that as politics becomes a more technologically oriented task, the expertise of technocrats becomes a key resource in governance. Another general observation — that such experts give legitimacy to government decisions (Barker and Peters, 1993) — is also reflected in the field of public health, notably on issues such BSE/CJD (Baggott, 1998) and smoking and health (Collingridge and Reeve, 1986).

But over and above their legitimation role, technical experts have contributed directly to policy development. Their work has often set the agenda and the terms of the political debate. Even when government selects its advisors carefully and excludes certain scientific views (Collingridge and Reeve, 1986), it is difficult to suppress alternative perspectives. In the BSE case for example, the media gave plenty of coverage to the views of scientists excluded from the advisory process, such as Professor Richard Lacey.

It is also evident that experts can have an impact on policies outside their immediate sphere of interest. This occurs when principles they devise spread to other policy fields. For example, some concepts devised in the environmental field have been increasingly applied to health and social policy issues in recent years. An example is the 'precautionary principle' which shifts the burden of proof on to those allegedly causing the problem in question and involves a more comprehensive assessment of costs and benefits of activities likely to be harmful to the environment (O'Riordan and Cameron, 1994).

## Social and Cultural Models

Technical experts, such as doctors, health scientists and other health professionals have undoubtedly played a key role in the development of specific policy initiatives in the field of public health. But their role has gone beyond that legitimising or advising on policy. Experts, and the concepts they employ, have a much broader social and cultural significance which enables them to exert enormous influence on the parameters of political debate, political agendas and ultimately, policy outcomes.

In recent years a number of writers have explored the socio-cultural role of technical experts and expertise in relation to public health and, more specifically, to the definition and identification of risk in contemporary societies. These authors focus on similar themes: the role of experts in shaping the public perception of risk; the reasons why we appear to be more aware of certain risks than others; and the role of risk and 'risk expertise' in promoting forms of regulation. However, as we shall see, these contributions differ in several important respects.

There are many different views on the role of technical experts in relation to public health and to perceptions of risk in general. But these appear to fall into two main camps. First, there is view associated with Giddens (1991) and Beck (1992) — see also Lash et al. (1996) — that we live in a 'risk society', where political conflict is increasingly defined by high-consequence risks linked to industrialisation and globalisation. In such a society, there is a declining faith in scientific expertise as individuals become ever more aware of and anxious about the hazards of everyday life. Scientific calculations of risk lose credibility as they appear inconsistent with individuals' own perceptions, partly shaped by direct experience and partly indirectly, through the media. In addition, declining consensus among technical experts is perceived as undermining their credibility. As conventional science loses its dominant position in relation to other interpretations and explanations of risk, it is transformed by the opening up of critical debates about scientific purpose and ethos. At the same time, the individual begins to make sense of the array of hazards presented and makes choices accordingly.

Others have challenged the notion of the reflexive, autonomous individual. Writers such as Castel, Armstrong, Petersen, and Lupton focus particularly on social and cultural processes through which risks become identified. Others, such as Furedi, Wynne, Douglas and Wildavsky, and Skrabanek also adopt a 'social constructionist' approach but take a different line in certain aspects of their analysis, notably with respect to their examination of processes underlying the perception of risk and the role of technical experts.

Castel (1991) explicitly applied Foucault's work on governmentality to prevention strategies in health and social policy. He argued that there had been a shift in emphasis over the past century from 'dangerousness' to 'risk', which altered the focus of policy, away from dealing with individuals manifesting signs and symptoms of impending illness, abnormality or social deviance, towards an approach that sought to anticipate such problems. Meanwhile in relation to health, Skrabanek (1994) coined the term 'anticipatory medicine' as an approach which created 'a new mode of surveillance' involving the scrutiny of risk factors in the population as a whole and it these factors, rather than prima facie evidence, provide the basis for intervention.

Castel has drawn out the wider political ramifications of this, which include the erosion of professional power by administrators, who increasingly control flows of information and resources. Moreover, Castel (p. 281) noted that 'these new formulae for administering populations fall within the emerging framework of a plan of governability appropriate to the needs of advanced industrial societies', for example, allowing the state to deal with certain demands made upon it. This is underlined by Freeman's (1992) point that prevention policies and processes of risk identification serve as defensive and perhaps even symbolic strategies in the management of health and social problems.

Armstrong (1993) and Petersen and Lupton (see Petersen, 1997; Lupton, 1995; Petersen and Lupton, 1996) adopt a similar approach, but focus more sharply on public health issues. Armstrong examined the way in which four different regimes of public health have delineated a series of spaces in which individual identity has been located. These regimes are quarantine, sanitary science, personal hygiene and new public health, each of which are identified as dominant in a particular historical period. Each regime is seen as having power systems linked to it. Quarantine for example is a simple line of inclusion and exclusion; sanitary science regulates the movement between spaces, while personal hygiene is more of a psychosocial space regarding attitudes and behaviours. Armstrong argues that the NPH is distinctive from previous regulatory approaches in the way in which it generalises danger, increases the scope for surveillance and attempts to gear many aspects of behaviour to health objectives.

According to Petersen and Lupton, 'the new public health can be seen as but the most recent of a series of regimes of power and knowledge that are oriented to the regulation and surveillance of individual bodies and the social body as a whole' (Petersen and Lupton, 1996, p.3). Like Armstrong and Castel they argue that the NPH is comprehensive in its scope for intervention providing opportunities for the state to engage in moral regulation aimed at making subjects more self-regulating and productive in order serve society's broader interests. However, while accepting Castel's point about the growing power of administrators, Petersen and Lupton argue that preventive strategies also enhance the power of professionals (and in particular doctors and epidemiologists) as the scope for expert surveillance, assessment, and intervention is extended. Epidemiology, for example, is held to perform several crucial regulatory roles in relation to the discovery of disease, the evaluation of intervention, the identification of priorities and risk factors.

Petersen and Lupton are particularly interested in the ways in which public health science — and in particular epidemiology — is socially constructed. They argue that epidemiology constructs patterns of causation through particular expectations and processes of investigation, not to mention the selective use of evidence (Petersen and Lupton, 1996, p.33). Risk, too, is identified as a social construct, concepts of risk being seen as dominated by dubious epidemiological concepts. Notably, this contradicts the Beck/Giddens approach, which argues that heightened risks are revealed rather than constructed and that experts' monopoly of rationality is broken as people lose faith in conventional science.

Others have also pitched into this debate. Furedi (1997) leans towards the Beck/Giddens approach by acknowledging declining levels of trust in certain traditional forms of technical expertise, particularly those associated with innovation. However, he also observes that new forms of expertise are assisting the social construction of particular environmental, social and public health risks: purveyors of the precautionary principle and those with a vested interest in identifying risks and potential victims. These include professionals such as advisors, consultants, facilitators and counsellors. In his view, these developments have produced a net increase in the overall demand for expertise. Furedi also directly attacks the Beck/Giddens standpoint for conceiving risks as universal when in his view they are contingent on individuals' relative power and influence.

Like Petersen and Lupton, Furedi identifies the crucial role of experts in constructing the NPH, and is similarly critical of the quality of their knowledge base, challenging the basis on which epidemiological models of causation stand. He notes the tendency of professions involved with the NPH to exaggerate risks and manipulate information, while prioritising certain health risks that are not necessarily the greatest hazards facing individuals and society. Furedi shares Petersen and Lupton's concern about the moral regulation implicit in the NPH, but goes further in some respects in delineating what he sees as the debilitating and damaging impact of this philosophy upon innovation, experimentation and human intellectual activity. Finally, Furedi argues that the breakdown of trust, which writers like Beck and Giddens identify as the cause of a heightened awareness of risk, is rather a symptom of it. He identifies a culture of fear, inspired by professionals with a vested interest in identifying risks and victims, in the context of an increasingly individualised society, as a key factor in the decline of trust in traditional forms of expertise and institutions.

Wynne (1996), takes a similar line to Furedi, Petersen and Lupton in highlighting the role of experts in the social production of risk. He shares their criticism of the Beck/Giddens approach to risk and the faith they place in reformed science and the reflexive individual (see also Adams, 1995, who is similarly critical of 'realist' accounts of risk and the potential contribution of science to understand and help solve problems involving uncertainty). In addition, themes covered by these other writers, including the imprecision of scientific expertise and the imposition by experts of prescriptive models on lay people, are found in Wynne's work. However, Wynne is distinctive in two main ways. First, in his critique of expertise, he highlights the role of institutions dominated by experts as a means of promoting scientific ideas, models and arguments. Secondly, he is critical of the declining trust in experts' thesis, arguing that unqualified public trust in technical experts has never prevailed and that there has always been a level of suspicion about their activities. Notably, there is little empirical evidence to support the declining trust thesis. Although public opinion polls do indicate a lack of trust in modern science, there are important cross-national differences. Furthermore, there is no previous data with which to compare these results and it is therefore impossible to establish whether or not public trust has in fact declined (see Topf, 1993).

Wildavsky (1988; 1991) (see also Douglas and Wildavsky, 1983) challenges the claims about the risks of modern society, and challenges the evidence of scientists. He believes that science is dominated by hierarchies in such a way that risks are exaggerated and that the benefits of technology are not fully appreciated. Ironically though, as Adams (1995) has noted, Wildavsky like Beck places faith in reformed science to clear up misunderstandings and uncertainties. In other words, both adopt a rationalist approach, yet arrive at different conclusions about the reality of the risks involved.

Other writers provide a bridge between social constructionist approaches to public health and libertarian perspectives, traditionally opposed to interference from the state.

Skrabanek (1994) labelled the NPH as a form of 'healthism', where the pursuit of health becomes part of state ideology. Such an approach, he believed was dangerous, granting authority to the state and the medical profession for unwarranted intervention in personal matters. He noted that fascist regimes, such as Nazi Germany, were explicitly healthist and adopted campaigns against alcohol and tobacco (see also Proctor, 1988). While recognising the differences between fascist and democratic states, Skrabanek nevertheless believed important similarities regarding healthism could be identified. For example, the emphasis of the NPH on individual responsibility for health as personal duty, the interference in personal habits by the state and the use of propaganda to change individual lifestyles was for him as much a feature of 'friendly healthism' as the more overtly sinister forms found in fascist regimes.

According to Skrabanek, the NPH is driven by a thirst for power and control by the medical profession and other health professionals. Like Illich (1975) he perceives a medicalisation process, with the profession seeking to apply its expertise in ever increasing areas of life. Recognising that health promotion is big business, he also identifies a commercial interest behind the drive to promote changes in lifestyle, though it should be recognised that the drive for healthy living has had unambiguously adverse implications for some commercial interests, notably the tobacco industry.

Skrabanek attacks the knowledge base of the NPH. Like Petersen, Lupton and Furedi he identifies the shortcomings of epidemiology and the way in which associations and risks are treated as facts and not challenged. He illustrates his argument with examples of how in the past medical 'risks' associated with activities such as 'solitary vice' (masturbation), female cycling and even playing the piano have been exaggerated by healthists. Similar points are made by Le Fanu (1994) who observes that some associations — such as the link between high fat intake and coronary heart disease — are treated as facts despite evidence that confounds such a simple and direct relationship (see also Atrens, 1994), and by Lee (1994)

176

who urges caution in interpreting low level risks reported by epidemiologists.

Skrabanek is particularly concerned about the libertarian implications of the NPH. Such concerns are not new in the field of public health, as reflected by the often-quoted comment by *The Times* regarding the state's efforts to prevent outbreaks of infectious disease in the mid-Victorian period:

> The British nation abhors absolute power ...We prefer to take our chance with cholera and the rest than be bullied into health (Longmate, 1966, p.188).

The libertarian standpoint does provide an important counterweight to what some see as an uncritical acceptance of the merits of the NPH and its methods (see also Appleyard, 1994; Berger, 1991; Booker and North, 1994). However, libertarians do tend to emphasise the concept of negative freedom — the freedom to pursue one's own life without interference, providing that one does not harm others (Mill, 1974; Berlin 1969). Yet supporters of the NPH would argue that health is not exclusively an individual concern. One's health not only affects immediate family and social networks but — given the implications for health care costs and the possibility of transmitting disease from one person to another — is of concern to the wider community. Secondly, powerful interests in society — professional and commercial — restrict individual choice in many ways, for example by polluting the atmosphere and promoting consumer products that may be harmful to health.

Notions of positive liberty (Green 1911; Berlin, 1969) — which emphasise the importance of individuals being masters of their own fate and free from circumstances that reduce choice can also be used to justify a policy of non-intervention in habits and lifestyles. However, given that commercial interests and social circumstances also have an impact on choices, a case can be made for state intervention on the grounds that liberty in a positive sense may be reinforced by protecting people from these constraints, this providing some justification for restricting practices such as tobacco advertising in the interests of public health. This is clearly the position taken by Beauchamp (1988) for example, who argues that advances in public health and prevention have the potential to expand liberties.

177

This leads on to a final point about the social and cultural interpretations of the NPH: their tendency to downplay the significance of commercial and governmental interests in opposing particular public health strategies. We noted earlier that a number of industries profit from products and practices that have been associated with health risks. Government agencies too may have an interest in opposing certain interventions. The BSE crisis is a case in point, where potentially disastrous practices were allowed to continue despite concerns about public health (Baggott, 1998). Is it simply not enough to argue that risks are being exaggerated? In some cases they may well be, and unnecessary interventions and infringements of liberty may occur as a result. In others, however, political expediency may dictate that risks of the same or even greater magnitude are ignored.

Finally, we must mention in this context Weale's (1983) discussion of the liberal paternalist viewpoint. This combines a respect for liberty with an interest in public action to improve the health status of the population. It expresses a preference for economic incentives and softer forms of coercion rather than prohibition and direct regulation, and hence is perceived as less authoritarian (though the outcome in terms of reducing certain activities believed to be harmful to health may be similar). However, stronger measures are acceptable from this point of view if there is clear evidence (a) that the harm to health is occurring and (b) that such measures will prevent such harm. Both these points underline the importance of a sound evidence base for public health interventions.

## Conclusions

Although this is very much a work in progress, it is possible to draw some initial conclusions while setting and set an agenda for future research in this field. First, we have seen that despite the broad political consensus about NPH, which partly explains its emergence, there are important dissenting voices which have inhibited policy development to some extent. These include not only libertarians and commercial interests, who have been explicitly vociferous in opposing specific policies, but academics who in analysing the social and cultural implications of the NPH have expressed grave reservations about the project as a whole, largely on the grounds that it introduces moral regulation and authority structures based on exaggeration of risk and misplaced belief in new forms of expertise. On the other hand these accounts tend to downplay — perhaps without adequate consideration — the role of commercial interests and government agencies in ignoring certain risks and rejecting policy options that could improve public health. More detailed case studies — of issues such as food policy, environmental health and cancer screening for example — are certainly needed to shed light on the processes of risk assessment, policy advice and legitimisation.

Secondly, though there is broad agreement on why NPH has came to the fore, debate exists on the relative importance of the media, politicians and civil servants, technical experts, governing institutions, commercial interests, pressure groups and political ideologies. Further research must focus on the precise role of these factors in the generation, development and inhibition of public health strategies. This will require a more in-depth analysis of the recent history of public health policy-making than has hitherto been undertaken. In addition case studies of particular public health issues such as those mentioned above will make an important contribution here as they have the potential to reveal similarities and differences in patterns of influence in different policy areas, enabling us to draw more specific conclusions about politics and policy-making in the field of public health.

# References

Adams, J. (1995), *Risk,* University College London Press.

Allsop, J. (1990), 'Does Socialism Necessarily Mean the Public Provision of Health Care?' in Carrier, J., and Kendall, I. *Socialism and the NHS: Fabian Essays in Health Care,* Avebury, London.

Appleyard, B. (1994), *The Independent,* 21 September, px.

Armstrong, D. (1993), 'Public Health Spaces and the Fabrication of Identity', *Sociology,* 27(3), 393-410.

Ashton, J. and Seymour, D. (1988), *The New Public Health,* Open University Press, Milton Keynes.

Atrens, D. (1994), 'The Questionable Wisdom of a Low Fat Diet and Cholesterol Reduction', *Social Science and Medicine,* 39(3), 433-47.

Baggott, R. (1990), *Alcohol, Politics and Social Policy,* Avebury, London.

Baggott, R. (1998), 'The BSE Crisis' in Gray, P., t'Hart, P., and Peters, G. *Policy Disasters in Western Europe,* Routledge, London.

Barker, A. and Peters, B.G. (1993), 'Science Policy and Government' in Barker, A. and Peters, B.G. *The Politics of Expert Advice,* Edinburgh University Press, Edinborough, 1-16.

Beauchamp, D. (1988), *The Health of the Republic. Epidemics, Medicine and the Challenge to Democracy.,* Temple University Press, Philadelphia.

Beck, U. (1992), *The Risk Society,* Sage, London.

Berger, P. (ed.) (1991), *Health, Lifestyle and the Environment; Counteracting the Panic,* Social Affairs Unit, London.

Berlin, I. (1969), 'Two Concepts of Liberty' in *Four Essays on Liberty,* Oxford University Press, Oxford.

Berridge, V. (1996), *AIDS in the UK: The Making of Policy 1981-1994,* Oxford University Press, Oxford.

Booker, C. and North, R. (1994), *The Mad Officials,* Constable, London.

Cairns, J. (1995), 'The Costs of Prevention' *British Medical Journal,* 311, 9 December, 1520.

Cannon, G. (1987), *The Politics of Food,* Century Hutchinson, London.

Castel, R. (1991), 'From Dangerousness to Risk' in Burchell, G., Gordon, G., and Miller, P. *The Foucault Effect: Studies in Governmentality,* Harvester Wheatsheaf, Hemel Hempstead.

Cmnd. 7047 (1977), *Prevention and Health,* HMSO, London.

Cm. 289 (1989), *Public Health in England,* HMSO, London.

Cm. 1523 (1991), *The Health of the Nation: A Consultative Document for Health for England,* HMSO, London.

Cm. 1986 (1992), *The Health of the Nation: A Strategy for Health in England,* HMSO, London.

Cm. 3852 (1998), *Our Healthier Nation,* The Stationery Office, London.

Collingridge, D. and Reeve, C. (1986), *Science Speaks to Power,* Pinter, London.

Davies, J. and Kelly, M. (1993), *Healthy Cities: Research and Practice,* Routledge, London.

Day, P. and Klein, R. (1989), 'Interpreting the Unexpected: the Case of AIDS Policy Making in Britain', *Journal of Public Policy,* 9(3), 337-53.

DHSS (1976), *Prevention and Health: Everybody's Business,* DHSS, London.

Dicey, A. (1914), *Law and Public Opinion in Britain*, Macmillan, London (2nd edition).

Dobson, A. (1990), *Green Political Thought: An Introduction*, Unwin Hyman, London.

Doig, A. (1990), 'Routine, Crisis and Muddle: Mishandling the Egg Crisis', *Teaching Public Administration*, 10(1), 15-26.

Douglas, M. and Wildavsky, A. (1983), *Risk and Culture*, UCLA Press, Los Angeles.

Doyal, L. (1979), *The Political Economy of Health*, Pluto, London.

Draper, P. (ed.) (1991), *Health Through Public Policy. The Greening of Public Health*, Green Print, London.

Fischer, F. (1990), *Technocracy and the Politics of Expertise*, Sage, London.

Fraser, D. (1973), *The Evolution of the British Welfare State. A History of Social Policy since the Industrial Revolution*, Macmillan, London.

Freeman, R. (1992) 'The Idea of Prevention: a Critical Overview' in Scott, S., Williams, G., Platt, S., and Thomas, H. (Eds.) *Private Risks and Public Dangers*, Avebury, Aldershot, 34-56.

Furedi, F. (1997), *Culture of Fear*, Cassel, London.

Giddens, A. (1991), *Modernity and Self-Identity: Self and Society in the Late Modern Age*, Polity, Cambridge.

Goraya, A. and Scambler, G. (1998) 'From Old to New Public Health: Role Tensions and Contradictions', *Critical Public Health* 8(2), p.141-51.

Green, T. H. (1911) 'Lecture on Liberal Legislation and Freedom of Contract' in *Works*, vol. 3, Longmans Green, London.

Grubb, M., Koch, M., Munson, A., Sullivan, F., and Thomson, K. *The Earth Summit Agreements: A Guide and Assessment*, Earthscan, London.

Hall, R. H. (1990), *Health and the Global Environment*, Polity, Oxford.

Illich, I. (1975), *Limits to Medicine*, Penguin, Harmondsworth.

Lalonde, M. (1975), *A New Perspective on the Health of Canadians*, Information Canada, Ottawa.

Lash, M., Szerzinsky, S., Wynne, B. (Eds.) (1996), *Risk, Environment and Modernity*, Sage, London.

Lawson, R. (1997), *Bills of Health*, Radcliffe Medical Press, Oxford.

Le Fanu, J. (1994) 'Prevention. Wishful Thinking or Hard Science?' *Preventionitis*, Social Affairs Unit, London, 23-35.

Lee, P. (1994), 'The Need for Caution in Interpreting Low Level Risks reported by Epidemiologists' in Le Fanu, J. *Preventionitis*, Social Affairs Unit, London, 36-45.

Leichter, H. (1990), *Free to be Foolish. Politics and Health Promotion in the United States and Great Britain*, Princeton University Press, Oxford.

Lewis, J. (1986), *What Price Community Medicine?* Wheatsheaf, Brighton.

Lewis, J. (1992), 'Providers, Consumers, the State and the Delivery of Health Care Services in Twentieth Century Britain' in Wear, A. (ed.) *Medicine and Society: Historical Essays*, Cambridge University Press, Cambridge, 317-45.

Longmate, N. (1966), *King Cholera: The Biography of a Disease*, Hamish Hamilton, London.

Lupton, D. (1995), *The Imperative of Health. Public Health and the Regulated Body*, Sage, London.

Mill, J. S. (1974), *On Liberty*, Penguin, Harmondsworth.

Petersen, A. (1997), 'Risk, Governance and the New Public Health' in Petersen, A. and Bunton, R. Foucault, *Health and Medicine*, Routledge, London, 189-206.

Petersen, A. and Lupton, D. (1996), *The New Public Health: Discourses, Knowledge and Strategies*, Sage, London.

Navarro, V. (1978), *Class, Struggle, The State and Medicine*, Robertson, Oxford.

O'Riordan, T. and Cameron, J. (1994), *Interpreting the Precautionary Principle*, Earthscan, London.

Pietroni, P. (1991), *The Greening of Medicine*, Gollancz, London.

Porritt, J. and Winner, D. *The Coming of the Greens*, Fontana, London.

Proctor, R. (1988), *Racial Hygiene; Medicine under the Nazis*, Harvard University Press, Cambridge (MA).

Radical Statistics Health Group (1991), 'Missing — A Strategy for the Health of the Nation' *British Medical Journal*, 303, 299-302.

Rhodes, R. and Marsh, D. (Ed) *Policy Networks in British Government*, Clarendon, Oxford.

Rosen, H. (1993), *A History of Public Health*, John Hopkins, New York.

Ryle, M. (1988), *Ecology and Socialism*, Rodins, London.

Skrabanek, P. (1994), *The Death of Humane Medicine*, Social Affairs Unit, London.

Taylor, P. (1984) *The Smoke Ring: Tobacco, Money, and Multi-National Politics*, Bodley Head, London.

Topf, R. (1993), 'Science, Public Policy and the Authoritativeness of the Governmental Process' in Barker, A. and Peters, B. G. *The Politics of Expert Advice*, Edinburgh University Press, Edinburgh, 1-16.

US Department of Health and Human Services (1980) *Promoting Health/Preventing Disease. Objectives for the*, Government Printing Office, Nation Washington DC.

Weale, A. (1983), 'Invisible Hand or Fatherly Hand? Problems of Paternalism in the New Perspective on Health', *Journal of Health Politics, Policy and Law*, 7(4), Winter 1983, p.704-807.

Webster, C. (1996), *Government and Health Care Vol. II: The NHS, 1958-79*, HMSO, London.

WHO (1978), *Alma Ata 1977: Primary Health Care Geneva*, WHO/UNICEF.

WHO (1985), *Targets for Health for All: Targets in Support of the European Regional Strategy for Health for All*, WHO Regional Office for Europe, Copenhagen.

WHO (1986), *Ottawa Charter for Health Promotion. An International Conference on Health Promotion*, WHO, Copenhagen.

WHO (1993), *Health for All Targets: The Health Policy for Europe*, WHO Regional Office for Europe, Copenhagen.

Wildavsky, A. (1988), *Searching for Safety*, Transition, Oxford.

Wildavsky, A. (1991), 'If Claims of Harm from Technology are False, Mostly False or Unproven, What Does this Tell Us About Science' in P. Berger (Ed) *Health, Lifestyle and Environment Counteracting the Panic*, Social Affairs Unit, London. Chapter 10.

Wynne, B. (1996), 'May the Sheep Safely Graze?' Lash, S., Szerszynski, B., Wynne, B. *Risk, Environment and Modernity*, Sage, London, p.44-83.

182

# 12 Out of the Church and into Kwik Fit: The Nursing Profession and the Secularisation of Health Care

CHRIS NOTTINGHAM and FIONA O'NEILL

Nursing has scarcely been out of the headlines in recent months. The difficulties in recruiting trained staff to fill vacant posts and the high profile campaign for a substantial increase in pay have underlined the importance and sensitivity of nursing as a political issue. Commentators both inside and outside the profession agree that the present 'crisis' goes beyond the immediate problem of securing an acceptable pay rise, but there is less agreement about how the difficulties should be defined and still less on how they might be solved. This paper argues that the current crisis does indeed go deeper than recruitment or pay and that an effective solution will involve the nursing profession in an uncomfortable questioning of the most basic principles by which it defines itself and projects itself to others

Many nurses hoped that the election of a Labour government meant that they would be working in a more favourable political climate. This was understandable if only for the fact that Conservative initiatives, both in substance and style, had usually left nurses feeling marginalised. The Griffiths reforms began the process by denying nurses a secure place in the new management structure. Griffiths, in the words of one leader classified nursing as 'monumentally unimportant' (Clay, 1987,p.57). Health Service reforms continued to fundamentally alter the working environment but nurses had few chances to influence their formulation or implementation. In contrast, the incoming government's white paper The New NHS: Modern, Dependable, appeared to offer opportunities for nurses to become involved in a wide range of activities at both a strategic and a service level and was generally welcomed within the profession as containing a long overdue recognition of the importance of nursing in the health care system. Tony Blair's announcement of a new grade of consultant nurse, the so called 'supernurse', linked with the statement that nurses should have the chance of promotion without passing over into management, received a more

183

cautious welcome but most could at least welcome its symbolic significance.

However, twenty months into the new government there are tensions between ministers and nursing leaders and the prospect of more On the strength of promises in the white paper nurses had hoped that their representation on the management teams of the new primary care groups (PCGs) would enable them to take a substantial part in determining how and where money was spent locally on NHS services. As a result of a deal struck between John Chisholm chair of the BMAs GP committee and the Secretary of State it seems GPs will be guaranteed an effective and permanent voting preponderance within PCGs and the ability of both nurses and community representatives to exert influence will be, to say the least, far less than was originally hoped or promised. Many of the details remain to be sorted out but it seems likely that GPs will successfully assert their assumed right of 'ownership' over primary care and will be very much in the driving seat when the reforms take effect from April 1999, leaving nurses with little more than a token role (Smith & Dickson 1998).

There is also the vexed issue of nurse education. While representatives of the profession have attempted to keep the focus on poor pay and working conditions as the root cause of recruitment and retention problems, the government has announced its intention to review the Project 2000 (P2000) reform of nurse education amidst waves of criticism that it has become too academic and remote from day to day service requirements. (The Times, 16 Jan 1999). It is difficult to overstate the importance of this issue for the leaders of the profession. P2000 was the culmination of many years of campaigning by nursing leaders to sever the link between service provision and training. The closure of hospital based training schools and the granting of supernumerary status to student nurses who had previously been employees of the teaching hospitals, were elements of a long-cherished professionalising strategy which aimed to improve the status, influence and responsibilities of nurses within the health care system. As an all graduate profession nursing was to re-establish itself as a theoretically informed and research based activity in its own right, independent from but equal to medicine (Salter, 1998 pp 129-155).

Educational reforms are only one of the forces that have driven change in nursing in recent years. Of equal importance have been technological developments, changes within medicine, such as the reduction in junior doctors' hours which have resulted in nurses being allowed to perform functions previously reserved for doctors, and the organisational reforms which have fundamentally altered the working environment of nurses at all levels of the NHS. Perhaps most notably there has been an expansion in the number of nurses working in new roles; Nurse Practitioners now for instance provide a range of services within both acute and primary care settings and their work is seen to more closely approach the ideal of the independent professional (Vaughan, 1998).

Clearly there are both threats and opportunities for nursing within the new NHS and this is an appropriate moment to consider how well the profession is equipped to advance its interests. Nursing history is often presented as one of thwarted aspiration, of nurses denied the opportunity of advancing their profession by the more powerful medical profession, and all in the context of the structural inequalities which constrain a predominantly female work force. If such an approach has inclined anyone to fatalism and passivity in the past there can be little doubt that it is highly inappropriate now. Nurses, whatever their view of the constraints surrounding them, clearly need to be active and assertive if they are to meet the challenges posed by the turbulent and dynamic health policy environment. The question of the capacity of the profession to operate effectively in the developing situation is pressing and crucial. In reality the task of developing a strategy equal to the challenges of a modern health care system may involve the profession in a far more fundamental questioning of its current outlook than is commonly recognised. The assumption that the problems which nurses faced under the Conservatives would ease under a Labour government was based not so much on an overestimation of the good will of the new ministers but on an exaggerated assessment of their freedom of action. A change of government seems likely to prove of less fundamental importance to notions of nurses' professional role and function than the radical changes in the delivery of health care which have been underway for some time. Demographic pressures, new technologies and the demands of an ever less deferential public continue to grow and the Labour government, no less concerned with rising public expenditure than its predecessors, will adjust the rhetoric but will be unable to reduce the pressure for efficiency savings and accountability in healthcare providers. Given the tightness of the political margins, the government, any government, in such circumstances and in so potentially dangerous an area as healthcare will be much too busy looking after itself to spare much thought for others.

In examining the capacity of nursing leaders to respond to current pressures we use Rudolf Klein's model of conflicting ideals of health care; the church and the garage. The church metaphor is used to emphasise the view which sees the health care system as the embodiment of certain moral values. Klein argues that for at least the first three decades of the NHS policy makers, planners and professionals shared a 'church' view of the goals of the NHS. Professions within healthcare were seen as a vocations and their members expected to behave in appropriate fashion. Patients were required to show deference and gratitude. The NHS was seen in Bevan's words as a way to 'universalise the best'; the power of medical science could be harnessed and used to promote not only the health of the population but a sense of fundamental social unity:

The universality of a health care system is not just a means of ensuring access for all but a celebration of the common humanity of all citizens...Similarly, the stress on providing services free of charge is not just a way of ensuring access for all but a declaration of faith that medical care is somehow 'special' and must be distinguished from goods sold in the marketplace. (Klein, 1993, p.138)

The garage represents a more instrumental approach to the health care system. The relationship between professional and patient has become a transaction for the 'repair and maintenance of bodies' (Klein, 1993,p136), no different in essence from familiar commercial encounters. It represents a secular approach and reflects a number of cultural and political trends of the past two decades: consumerism and the rhetoric of choice, the emphasis on efficiency, effectiveness, opportunity cost and the quality of services, and the more general willingness of both the public and politicians to question the activities of professionals and demand service delivery on a more open, less paternalistic basis. Such pressures have encouraged the emergence of policy goals which are at odds with the ideals of the church, but perhaps the most important change is economic rather than cultural; the realisation that the founding principles of the NHS are not necessarily compatible with the provision of health care in a cost efficient way in an age which is individualistic, non-deferential and secular.

During recent difficulties there have been a number of instances where nurses have associated themselves with the 'church' view and exempted themselves from contemporary debates about health care and the changing role of the professional. The campaign mounted by the tabloid newspapers to pay 'our' nurses more may be welcome but it also smacks of stereotypical images of nurses as passive 'angels' incapable of fighting their own battles. Indeed the persistence of the angels metaphor in an age which is not noted for reverence for the caring professions illustrates the fact that even if nursing is often misunderstood it is still seen as 'special'. A recent publication, 'Come Back Miss Nightingale', argues that nurses' special status is being eroded. From what might be described as an ultra

186

ecclesiastical point of view, the authors lament the passing of vocational values and plead for matrons, traditional uniforms and the lost art of bedside nursing. The P2000 university courses are attacked as mistakenly elevating science above the old nursing values of 'love and charity'(Warren and Harris, 1998). Many nurses have been annoyed by this study but to an outsider it might appear as no more than a caricature of ideas already in circulation within the profession. This notion that nursing is a unique and special vocation, a 'calling' rather then a trade that has to be learnt, an amalgam of essentially moral values such as 'duty' 'service' and above all 'caring', has been a central and persistent theme. Melanie Phillips in an article entitled 'how the college girls destroyed nursing' argues that nursing has been invaded by the 'nihilistic, post-modern gibberish' imported from the social sciences, with the result that 'caring, kindness, compassion and dedication' have been driven out (Philips, 1999 p. 13). Similarly those now calling for the reversal of P2000 and a 'back to basics' approach to nurse training routinely allude to the 'vocational commitment' that is argued to be the essence of the caring nurse. Others make reference to the 'natural nurses' who have been put off entering nursing by an inappropriate emphasis on academic skills (Lawson 1996). However in one of the most influential books for the profession in recent years, Celia Davies, a core supporter of P2000, calls for nurses to regroup around the 'feminine' values of caring and reject the 'masculine' doctrines of the medical profession (Davies, 1995).

Thus while many nurses will reject 'back to basics' there is, at the heart of their more general discussions, a doctrine which is fundamentally similar. It is this approach which we suggest presents particular difficulties in the present climate. For instance it would seem to severely restrict the contribution that nurses can make to the current debate over health care rationing. The nursing view which has stressed that health care can only be provided or denied according to 'need' is, in the terms now accepted as realistic among policy makers, merely to avoid the issue. For the serious players need is merely a term politicians play around when in difficulties. Similarly it should be some cause for concern that such attitudes reinforce the notion of 'management' as a low status occupation merely providing the resources that professionals demand. There is an obvious link with the 'back to basics' argument that student nurses should have concentrated on acquiring bedside skills rather than being required to take management courses. The ideal of the 'hands on' nurse is upheld and training in strategic thinking required for effective participation in management decisions is seen as superfluous. In the longer term nursing influence will decline if management decisions are seen as a regrettable necessity and not recognised as being as vital for the provision of good care as direct contact with a patient. Some studies have argued for more effective management training and highlighted the need for nurses to assimilate the demands of the corporate culture into all their activities and decisions (Dix, 1996 and Edmonstone 1998) and there has been an expansion in post graduate courses for nurses which often include management training. But while many nurses do spend considerable time and effort achieving further qualifications courses have been criticised for being insular and not providing a rigorous enough preparation for the demands of managerial roles. The emphasis on how nursing is different and based on more 'feminine' values such as empathy and co-operation may make for soothing reflection but is unlikely to help nurses who are impatient to play an active role in the highly politicised environment of the NHS. Similarly it is has to be questioned if being caring is a sufficient qualification for today's nurses who, even if they are not working in a management role, are still likely to find themselves in a highly complex environment which makes more extensive demands then the direct physical care of patients (Allen, 1997).

Lessons could be learnt from studies which have looked at how nurses have approached management positions in the past. Inadequate preparation for management roles was recognised as a key factor in the difficulties encountered by senior nurses working within the consensus management teams which were established by the 1966 Salmon reforms. Nurse mangers had a generally poor reputation by the time of the Griffiths Review, and the resulting ambivalence towards nursing is thought to have contributed to the subsequent dilution of nurse representation in the new culture of general management (Strong and Robinson 1990). There is a danger that the new managerial roles for nurses in the PCGs will be another case of nurses losing an opportunity through lack of preparation and ability. Inward-looking definitions of the profession and its purposes are also likely to restrict the ability of nurses to function effectively in the political processes through which current issues will be mediated.

While there is a need for the Nursing profession to overhaul its strategy it must be acknowledged that it will be no easy task and it cannot be undertaken without risk. It is even difficult to develop a dispassionate view of the outlook that needs to be changed. Nursing is peculiarly, perhaps uniquely, resistant to techniques of analysis which produce easy returns in other places. Nurses' self presentation has often involved an element of pathos; a view that while others threatened, bartered and accumulated, they, because of some quality integral to their calling, could do no more than patiently wait for their dedication and service to be recognised and rewarded. It is also important to recognise that strategy is not something which can be changed at will. Effective strategies are rarely pure invention but more commonly involve a selection from a fixed menu. They involve choice, but choice within certain confines. Similarly it must also be noted, that while strategies have their instrumental elements the attitudes of those who are involved with their development are seldom purely instrumental. Those advancing a particular line become, to a greater or lesser degree, emotionally and intellectually engaged with their creations. It should also be remembered that changes of strategy will also involve political problems. Both within the organisation and without changes of strategy must inevitably have some effect on the perceived plausibility of leaders. The present level of discontent with Project 2000 is already opening up some of the divisions which have long been a feature of the very large and diverse occupation that is nursing. The way that such divisions are handled promises to provide a particular challenge for a profession which has always tried to smooth over the cracks and 'speak with one voice'.

Much of the literature on nurses, reflecting the church mentality, fails to engage with politically contentious issues. In particular two trends in nursing literature have gone a long way to reinforce such indifference. Firstly, the unrepentant whiggism of much of nursing history and secondly the tendency to discuss nursing almost exclusively in terms of what differentiates it from other groups. Anne Summers has illustrated how nursing history since the creation of the modern profession has been dominated by the notion of an essentially linear and logical progress which has seen the gradual unfolding of the 'proper' view of nursing. Rational purpose has been elevated, contingency and muddle ignored. Those advocating heterogeneous views have been dealt with as misguided or malign. However any survey of the reform of nursing in the last half of the nineteenth century reveals a complex and contradictory set of values where dedication to rationalisation, modernisation and sanitation was mixed up with missionary fervour, 'the reconciliation of social class divisions' and the 'glorification of the separate and largely domestic, sphere of female action' (Summers, 1989, p.31). While Florence Nightingale insisted that nursing should be properly remunerated she also asserted 'it is God's work more than ours': 'Modernisation' in nursing depended less on advances in medical technique and scientific knowledge than on a sense of 'spiritual vocation and noblesse oblige'. (Summers, 1989, p37.) Nursing was inevitably imbued with a notion of its own isolation and a suspicion of the public sphere.

The tendency for nursing to pursue a separatist and isolationist strategy was much in evidence in the philosophical and ideological changes known as the 'new nursing'. Closely associated with the expansion of university based nursing departments in the 1980s and the influence of a relatively small number of nurse academics, the 'new nursing' challenged the task oriented hierarchical model of working which had previously dominated the organisation of nursing work and substituted an individualised system of care, stressing the therapeutic encounter between the qualified nurse and her patient and the need to adopt a holistic view of the latter. But initiatives designed to maximise this way of working have run into difficulties in a hospital system increasingly geared to a rapid throughput of patients and a staffing structure which makes individualised care difficult to administer. Similarly if nurses see themselves simply as patient's advocates they risk exclusion from health care debates. By concentrating on the immediate patient they transfer to others the responsibility for thinking in terms of the potential patient and hence, the strategic allocation of resources.

The influence of a particular brand of feminism has also reinforced the separatist tendency in nursing. Associated with the work of 'difference feminists' such as Carol Gilligan, there has been widespread support for a view that nursing, as a female dominated profession, embodies a number of characteristics and attributes which are most likely to be held by women. Difference feminists most often downplay the impact of biological factors in determining gender based characteristics and instead focus on differences in the socialisation of male and female children which are reinforced by cultural norms about 'appropriate' roles and behaviour. Females are seen as more nurturing, caring and co-operative; males as more competitive, hierarchical and aggressive. What is crucial to difference feminists is the elevation of female characteristics, which are seen to have been suppressed and undervalued in a male dominated society. In many ways female characteristics are not just different they are also better, and public life would be vastly improved if there was a re-orientation away from male values towards female ones. Celia Davies draws on the work of difference feminists to make a case that nurses should build a 'new professionalism' which incorporates feminine characteristics and also exalts caring as the core of nursing. She argues that 'within a Western cultural heritage femininity-with its stress on dealing with dependency, acknowledging emotions and intimacy and nurturing others-comes to represent qualities that are feared and denied in masculinity' (Davies, 1995, p.183). Rejecting the masculine values inherent within the old professionalism would, Davies suggests, not only enable nurses to solve some of their own dilemmas but would also make space for nurses to bring an alternative and much needed feminine view to the policy making table. Davies' work fitted in neatly with the philosophy of the 'new nursing' which also emphasised the centrality of caring and has been welcomed and applauded by many leading nurses. Pippa Gough, for example, speaking in her capacity as the Director of Policy Development for the UKCC, nursing's regulatory body, explicitly linked the 'new professionalism' to the Council's development activities (Gough, 1996).

The appeals of such a view to a profession feeling a certain insecurity are not difficult to appreciate, yet such an approach does not seem to suggest any effective external strategy, particularly not one robust or flexible enough to enable nurses to make progress in the present situation. The problem is as much conceptual as practical. Carole Pateman has been a most effective advocate of the view that the notion of the public sphere as developed in the Western political tradition had been a male one and women have been confined to the private sphere as firmly in theory as in practice. She too looks towards a feminisation of the theory and practice of politics yet she, like her contemporaries in the nursing debate, fails to suggest how this might come about (Pateman, 1989). Politics while not immune to idealist argument is in the end a practical, continuous business. To withdraw to the moral high ground is, in most circumstances, to do no more than leave the initiative with someone else. An engagement with political processes does usually involve some sacrifice of moral coherence, but to refuse to use terms that the other actors employ is to fail to engage, and to fail to engage at a time of major change is a dangerous expedient. A practical and topical illustration is of how the 'new nursing' demand that nursing care should ideally be only given by nurses with a statutory qualification, tied the profession to an unrealistic ambition that is now coming home to roost. The number of non-registered nursing staff working in the NHS has increased with the creation of a new category of health care support worker, the health care assistant, to compensate for the reduced service commitment of student nurses after the implementation of P2000. These non-nurses who nevertheless perform basic nursing activities such as bathing patients, and can also be found engaging in more 'advanced' nursing duties such as dressing procedures and recording patient observations, can now be said to constitute a neglected element of the nursing workforce (Thornley, 1998). Although the creation of the support worker was accepted by the nursing leadership as one of the conditions for government acceptance of P2000, critics allege that nursing has done little to ensure that the development of this stratum of health care workers, who have access to the NVQ system of accreditation, be brought within its own sphere of influence. Shortages of qualified nursing staff have helped to increase the profile of health care assistants who, because they are cheaper, offer management an attractive and more readily available alternative (Salter, 1997). This loss of territory may well prove to be permanent not only in the light of continued shortages but also as part of a possible future with a more stratified nursing workforce, with a lower proportion of registered nurses supervising a higher proportion of support workers (Salter, 1997, p145). Such a vision is deeply unacceptable to that section of the profession who have been most engaged with the promotion of nursing as an academic discipline and who have vigorously supported the ideal of a fully graduate profession in spite of the evident political, economic and practical barriers to the achievement of such a goal.

One further point to consider is that the pursuit of a separatist agenda and attempts to define nursing by what differentia es it from other occupations has left nursing exposed and without the support of more powerful actors within the health policy arena. The attempt to clearly differentiate nursing from medicine often rested on overblown stereotypes of the limitations and shortcomings of the medical profession. As one doctor asserts: 'the accusation that [doctors] were only interested in diseases and not in people seemed wrong and offensive' (Rivett, 1997, 345).

However the greatest single barrier to change is the particular function which the Church approach has assumed in the development of the identity of the profession. The literature on professions is daunting but key variables in determining the status of an occupation may be identified as collective access to an exclusive body of knowledge, the degree of autonomy and independence members enjoy in their day to day functions, their ability to control entry to the profession and to distribute functions within it, their capacity to regulate of the profession, and the extent to which the practitioner enjoys a privileged and exclusive relationship with the client. To run through such a list with nursing in mind suggests two things; firstly that many of the current issues in health care politics seem designed to exert a major impact on nurses' professional status and secondly, that nurses might most usefully be classified as insecure professionals in that they could be defined in terms of a permanent uncertainty over and dissatisfaction with their status. This has led, as with other groups of insecure professionals, to a requirement for constant ideological self-projection. Where secure groups can opt for quiet effectiveness within power structures, insecure professionals have been characterised by the constant need to define and defend themselves in terms of broad social purpose. For the past fifty years British nurses have defined themselves and projected a favourable view of their profession on the basis of their claim to embody the values of the NHS; they have been the Service's firmest and most visible communicants. For much of its existence the NHS enshrined the view that health care bore little similarity to other services; that it was possible to deliver health care according to need alone and that the effective operation of the service did not require difficult political or economic decisions. Doctors drew more benefit from the Service than they were often prepared to acknowledge but for nurses it provided much more. Not only did it offer employment with professional dignity but it provided a context of ideological and spiritual purpose which satisfied the need for internal definition and external projection.

Although, as argued above, the ideological residue of this strategy has made it difficult for the nursing profession to rise to the challenges of the development of a health politics appropriate to a secular, individualistic and post deferential age, it would be foolish to imagine that the old position could be abandoned without pain. The transition from church to garage here, as elsewhere, involves a certain cost. The old strategy, after all, did deliver in certain respects. While the self evident usefulness of teachers and social workers did little to protect them from a severe loss of status in the great public sector conflicts of the 1970s and 80s, nurses emerged, if not unscathed, then with their status essentially intact. The image of the picket-line nurse never overwhelmed the other images with which nurses were popularly associated. It still remains the case that while public opinion views the social work profession in the light of the actions of its worst practitioners, it still sees nurses' misdemeanours as exceptional. Equally, it is hard to think, in the murky resentments of late twentieth century Britain, of any other profession for whom a substantial pay rise would attract such broad support. Yet while the existing strategy has proved a means of articulating a grievance and securing the occasional reward, it has been far less effective in permanently advancing a set of interests: it may have guaranteed an honoured place, but few within the profession have argued that this was a satisfactory place.

Prediction is a dangerous game but it is difficult to envisage any wholesale reversal of P2000. Comparisons are often problematic but it would surely not suit anyone to have university educated occupational therapists or radiographers working alongside college educated registered nurses. Moreover the nurse without research skills and the confidence to use them is as inappropriate to the modern healthcare process as the traditional uniforms so dear to some anti modernists. P2000 has it problems but the challenge is to develop it in ways which will help its products engage more effectively in the new organisational politics of health care. Perhaps there is a need to ensure that nurses are brought more into contact with the more robust aspects of social and management sciences; certainly the benefits of university education will be diminished if nursing courses turn in on themselves in terms of ideology, syllabus or organisation. There is, however no possibility of retreat to the old ground for it no longer exists.

The Church had many attractions and regret over its decline is understandable but the foundations are now being eroded in a way which is beyond the capacity of any group of politicians or professionals to halt. For nurses there is no alternative which can offer the same easy sense of unity and purpose and it is counter productive to pretend that there is. Active engagement with the new politics of health care will be uncomfortable in terms of both the internal and external relationships of the profession. Yet while 'Kwik-Fit' points to a future which is far less secure and dignified, nurses have more to gain by anticipating change than by waiting for the Church to collapse around them.

# References

Allen, D. (1997), 'Nursing Knowledge and Practice', *Journal of Health Service Research and Policy*, 2, pp.190-193.

Clay, T. (1987), *Nursing Power and Politics*, Heinemann, London.

Davies, C. (1995), *Gender and the Professional Predicament in Nursing*, Open University, Buckingham.

Dix, A. (1996), 'Tales by the Nurses Grim', *Health Service Journal*, 106, pp.38-39

Edmonstone, J. (1998), 'A Career in Management', *Nursing Management*, 4, pp.21-22.

Gough, P. (1996), 'The UKCC's Role in Policy Development and Implementation', Conference Paper, *Nursing Policy and the New NHS*, 26-27 Feb, Health Services Management Centre, University of Birmingham.

Klein, R. (1993), 'The Goals of Health Policy: Church or Garage?' in A. Harrison (ed.), *Health Care UK*, 1992/93, Kings Fund Institute, London.

Lawson, N. (1996), 'Is it the End for Nurses?' *The Times*, 26 December.

Pateman, C. (1989), *The Disorder of Women: Democracy, Feminism and Political Theory*, Cambridge University Press, Cambridge.

Phillips, M. (1999), 'How the College Girls Destroyed Nursing', *Sunday Times*, 10 January.

Rivett, G. (1998), *From Cradle to Grave, Fifty Years of the NHS*, Kings Fund, London.

Salter, B. (1998), *The Politics of Change in the Health Service*, Macmillan, London.

Smith and Dickson (1998), 'Silent Majority', *Health Service Journal*, Vol.108 No. 5635.

Summers, A. (1989), Ministering Angels, History Today, February edition. *Management*, Open University Press, Milton Keynes.

Thornley, C. (1998), *Neglected Nurses, Hidden Work*, Unison, London.

Vaughan, B. (1998), New Roles for Nurses, *King's Fund Newsletter*, 21, p.3.

Warren, J. and Harris, B. (1998), 'Extinguishing the Lamp', in D. Anderson (ed.) *Come Back Miss Nightingale, Trends in Professions Today*, The Social Affairs Unit.